The Cinema, or
The Imaginary Man

The Cinema, or
The Imaginary Man

Edgar Morin

Translated by Lorraine Mortimer

University of Minnesota Press
Minneapolis • London

This book was originally published in French as *Le cinéma ou l'homme imaginaire. Essai d'anthropologie* (Paris: Les Éditions de Minuit, 1956). This translation is based on a second edition of the text, *Le cinéma ou l'homme imaginaire. Essai d'anthropologie sociologique* (Paris: Les Éditions de Minuit, 1978).

An earlier version of the translator's introduction was previously published as "We Are the Dance: Cinema, Death, and the Imaginary in the Thought of Edgar Morin," *Thesis Eleven* 64 (2001): 77–95. Reprinted by permission of Sage Publications Ltd. Copyright 2001 Sage Publications Ltd.

Published by the University of Minnesota Press
111 Third Avenue South, Suite 290
Minneapolis, MN 55401-2520
http://www.upress.umn.edu

Library of Congress Cataloging-in-Publication Data

Morin, Edgar.
 [Cinéma, ou, L'homme imaginaire. English]
 The cinema, or The imaginary man / Edgar Morin ; translated by Lorraine Mortimer.
  p. cm.
 Includes bibliographical references and index.
 ISBN 0-8166-4037-8 (hc : alk. paper)—ISBN 0-8166-4038-6 (pb : alk. paper)
 1. Motion pictures. 2. Motion pictures—Psychological aspects. I. Title: Cinema. II. Title: Imaginary man. III. Title.
 PN1995.M613 2005
 791.43—dc22
                                                            2004028081

Printed in the United States of America on acid-free paper

The University of Minnesota is an equal-opportunity educator and employer.

12 11 10 09 08 07 06 05   10 9 8 7 6 5 4 3 2 1

Film art . . . aspires to be an object worthy of your meditations: it calls for a chapter in those great traditions where everything is talked about, except film.

—Béla Balázs

Contents

Translator's Acknowledgments

Many people have helped this translation come to life. I would like to thank Barrett Hodsdon for first drawing my attention to the original French text, Johann Arnason for exposing me to more of Morin's oeuvre, and students in the departments of cinema studies and sociology and anthropology at La Trobe University, Melbourne, who have found Morin's work both useful and inspiring. I was fortunate to be able to refer to the Spanish translation of the book by Ramón Gil Novales, published in 1972. Dana Polan generously passed on drafts of his own translation of three chapters of the book, completed when he was a graduate student. Chantal Babin worked with me on translation difficulties throughout, and Fuyuki Kurasawa worked on early chapters, helped mold my conviction that Morin's work should be better known in the English-speaking world, and then found me a publisher. It would be hard to ask for more! In the end, of course, all decisions regarding translation are my own, and any errors come back to me.

Glenda Ballantyne compiled the index. Library staff at La Trobe University, Eva Fisch in particular, provided ongoing, indispensable research support. I also want to thank Alain Masson, Faye Ginsburg, David MacDougall, Wendy Haslem, Simon McLean, Gabrielle Murray, Wayne Lynch,

Cass (especially for the tables) and Declan Mortimer Eipper, and Chris Eipper, among others too numerous to mention.

Mention must be made of Edgar Morin himself, who was supportive of the project from start to finish. I have benefited greatly from engagement with his work—indeed, I have needed it to be there. So it is a pleasure to be able to present this translation as a gesture of appreciation.

Translator's Introduction

The partitions and distinctions within the human sciences prevent us from grasping the profound continuity between magic, sentiment, and reason, although this contradictory unity is the Gordian knot of all anthropology. . . .

. . . Magic and sentiment are also means of knowing. And our rational concepts are themselves still imbued with magic, as Mauss observed.

—Edgar Morin, *Le cinéma ou l'homme imaginaire: Essai d'anthropologie sociologique*, 1985

In the desert of film theory in the 1970s and 1980s, to come across Edgar Morin's *The Cinema, or The Imaginary Man* was to be surprised by a plenitude.[1] After May 1968, a politicization of a discipline had begun. Film studies sought legitimacy in the academy and a "scientific" status. The old impressionistic, "romantic" criticism had to go, and, inspired by Louis Althusser's brand of Marxism, film scholars advocated a kind of surgical practice, one that tended to cut out the heart, soul, even the guts of the film experience to get to the cancer of Ideology. With Dr. Lacan assisting, they began to treat the radically debiologized subject/spectator as an effect of the film text, all (unconscious) mind, stripped of flesh, poetry, skepticism, and imagination. In the attempt to examine and expose the ways that ideologies that enslave us are in the very air we breathe, many theorists practiced what Morin has described as "ideological immunology," barring enemy ideas as though they were viruses, refusing to recognize common ground with an opponent for fear of contamination or recuperation—fearing complicity because they did not know how to be complex.[2]

In his intellectual autobiography, *Mes démons*, Morin tells us about an incident at a gathering of French intellectuals around 1960, when he declared his love of westerns and an indignant Lucien Goldmann leapt to the platform to explain that the western was "the worst of capitalist mystifications destined to anaesthetize the revolutionary consciousness of the working class."[3] Goldmann, as Morin remembers it, was greeted with thunderous applause. After the appearance of Morin's book on mass culture, *L'esprit du temps*, in 1962, Pierre Bourdieu, says the author, tore the book to pieces for its "two major mystifications": Morin had claimed that Charlie Chaplin and Edith Piaf were enjoyed across classes and ages and, in Chaplin's case, across societies, and he was guilty of concealing the fact that mass culture was "an instrument of alienation at the service of capitalism to divert the proletariat from its revolutionary mission."[4]

In *The Cinema, or The Imaginary Man*, Morin had seen Charlie Chaplin as the exemplary test of the universalities involved in cinema:

> Chaplin is the first creator of all time who wagered on universality—on the child. His films . . . have been welcomed and accepted . . . by adults, blacks, whites, the literate, and the illiterate. The nomads of Iran, the children of China join Élie Faure and Louis Delluc in a participation and an understanding that is, if not the same, at least common.[5]

If not the same, at least common—a way of thinking in which different audiences, different groupings, are seen to have a separateness *and* a relation to one another. Those in high society and those excluded from society could love the cinema equally.

Although he did not use the label at that time, Morin was already considering cinema as a *complex* phenomenon and was struggling against the "paradigm of disjunction/reduction/ simplification which leads us to shatter and mutilate the complexity of phenomena."[6] It mattered that the participant investigator Morin and his object of investigation, film, were not respected by intellectuals who wanted to revolutionize the world in the 1960s, just as it mattered that a Marxist avant-garde in the 1970s and 1980s often accorded little respect to spectators and their films, deforming both to fit their theories. But more is at stake here than film and film viewing. Mutilating thought is not inoffensive. In the end, the willingness to reduce and mutilate, to refuse complexity, can cost lives. Complexity is an intellectual practice, a world-view, a politics, and an ethic. In *Introduction à la pensée com-plexe*, Morin stated his credo, reiterated in various forms in various of his works and informing them all: he believes that the less mutilating a thought is, the less it will mutilate humans. Simplifying visions have brought about devastation not only in the intellectual world but in life: "Much of the suffering that millions of people are subjected to results from the effects of fragmented and one-dimensional thought."[7]

Beginning with his study on Germany and its people in the aftermath of the war in *L'an zéro de l'Allemagne*, Morin's oeuvre, always radically democratic in complexion, has en-tailed an ongoing dialogue between the "humanities" and the "sciences."[8] He has written on contemporary life, pop-ular culture, fundamental anthropology, ecology, scientific method, and politics.[9] A young member of the French Resistance, Morin had been a war-formed Communist. His *Autocritique* in 1959 traced the milestones along the road to his break with communism, his "timid cultural resistance," his own and other anti-Stalinist dissidents' growing inabil-ity to continue with the Party, feeling what Solzhenitsyn would later formulate as an imperative: "Do not participate in lies."[10] Abiding by such an imperative meant refusing Manichaean thinking and politics, organizing against the Algerian war, but intellectually and morally refusing unconditional support for the Front de libération nationale. Not participating in lies meant refusing (existentially comforting) political absolutisms that offer relief from contradiction and complexity. (In relation to Algeria, refusing support for the FLN in its use of terrorist tactics meant being denounced as a traitor and collaborator by many on the French Left.[11] So did refusing the "reenchantments" offered by Maoism, Vietcongism, and "Althusseran neodogmatism."[12] This was not just a French affair. Where the French academic Left went, much of the Western Left followed.)

Morin's refusal to reduce and mutilate, aspiring to truth and totality while recognizing that totality is impossible and uncertainty our lot (what he calls his "mission impossible"[13]), takes place in a context, is played out against a backdrop, that is dramatic in itself. For all our incertitude, there is one certainty humans can count on—death. Resistance to the cruelty of the world is the most profound and primordial of resistances. As in Camus, a keen appreciation of the materiality of existence, of the concrete and the sensuous, sits with the ever-present consciousness of our unearned death penalty. In *Mes démons*, when Morin describes what his family taught him, it is the aromas, tastes, and textures of the Mediterranean that figure strongly. During his immersion in the popular culture of Paris's Ménilmontant, where he became addicted to the cinema, his father's songs were a part of everyday life. One popular song in particular, "El Reliquario," came to resonate, he recalls, with "infinite love and irremediable death."[14] His mother died when he was nine years old, and he learned that all that was dearest to him was fragile, perishable, and would ultimately vanish. Years later, part of his confronting theoretical and existential complexity was to throw off the "explicative armory" of classical science that offered some protection against this fact. It meant abandoning the ideology of Christianity and Western humanism that man is above nature, and it meant recognizing the omnipresence of contradiction, the normality of chance, and the fact that "all that is solid melts into air."[15] We are not on firm ground at the center of the world, but on a "flying carpet" in a marginal galaxy.[16]

This notion of man, doomed to die and lost in space, is already expressed toward the end of Morin's second book, *L'homme et la mort*, published in 1951.[17] What is ahead of us is

> immense cosmic death, that of a world with its millions and millions of stars, its nebulae that speed by one another at dozens of thousands of kilometers per second, its suns that extinguish themselves, explode, disintegrate; a world that expands like a bubble, universally, toward a death into which everything vanishes.[18]

It is as though Morin evokes here what will appear in filmic metaphor a few years later with James Dean in *Rebel without a Cause* (1955), with his character's moment in the planetarium—the immensity and the inexorability of the universe, the protagonist so small, solitary, and vulnerable but full of life. Morin ends *L'homme et la mort* with the final lines of Percy Shelley's *Prometheus Unbound*. In the context of the mass culture of the 1950s it was Dean, "the Shelley of mass culture," who embodied "the myth of total life."[19] His rage to live (*La fureur de vivre* was the French title for *Rebel*) involved the "anthropological revolt" Morin admired and felt.

It was in writing *L'homme et la mort* that Morin created his transdisciplinary culture that would inform *The Cinema, or The Imaginary Man*. To write the earlier book, he needed to elaborate an "anthropo-social" conception of two neglected aspects of anthropology that the problem of death threw into relief: the biological reality of the human being, mortal like all other living beings, and the human reality of myth and the imaginary, which posited a life beyond death.

He used the word *anthropology* in the German rather than the Anglo-Saxon sense. Unlike disciplines that carved up into sections the understanding of a phenomenon, anthropology considered history, psychology, sociology, economics, and so on as components or dimensions of a global phenomenon. Each phenomenon had to be considered "in its fundamental unity (here man) and in its no less fundamental diversity (men of different character, different environments, different societies, different civilizations, different epochs, etc.)."[20]

It was Marx's *Economic and Philosophical Manuscripts* that got Morin interested in anthropology in this sense, in the idea of natural and cultural, generic man. There being no wall between nature and culture, the sciences of man and nature had to embrace each other. It was from Marx that he was convinced of the limited utility of the various disciplines and the need to seize on anthropo-social problems in their multidimensionality. Marxism was thus an opening rather than a closure for him. Whereas official Marxisms were exclusive and excluding, Morin declares that his own was integrative and ensured that in a book like *L'homme et la mort* he was not turned away from any school of thought.[21]

Morin speaks of a "science" of man to insist on the necessity of empirical verification.[22] Striving for thought that is as little mutilating and as rational as possible, he wants "to respect the exigencies of investigation and verification proper to scientific knowledge and the exigencies of reflection proposed by philosophical knowledge."[23] Order, clarity, distinction, and precision are a part of complex thought, but complex thought calls into question hyperspecializations that mistake the parceled up, neatly packaged theories and models of the real for the real itself, mistaking disciplinary boundaries for boundaries in reality, blinding us to the complexity of the real and often rationalizing the irrational.

In tune with Frankfurt school thinkers Horkheimer,

Adorno, and Marcuse, Morin does not jettison the category of reason but insists on the necessity of reason questioning itself, knowing that reason can carry within itself its own worst enemy, rationalization.[24] True rationality "recognizes irrationality and dialogues with the unrationalizable"; true rationality "is profoundly tolerant in regard to mysteries." "False rationality," on the other hand, has always treated as "primitive," "infantile," or "prelogical" populations displaying a complexity of thought, not only in relation to the technical but in the knowledge of nature and in myths.[25] As he emphasized in *Pour sortir du vingtième siècle*, "*The struggle against the rationalization, reification, deification, instrumentalization of reason is the very task of open rationality.*"[26] His feeling for the value and importance of literature, says Morin, was all the more acute once he recognized the limits of the human sciences. For him it was writers such as Dickens and Balzac who did justice to the complexity of everyday life. Indeed, he suggests that it was the "mystical epileptic reactionary," Dostoyevsky, rather than all the great secular thinkers, who had more clearly seen the fanatical spirit of Bolshevism before it came into being.[27]

One of the most potent truths in Morin's book about death concerns the way we live: the human being inhabits the earth not just prosaically but poetically. Myth and the imaginary are not just superstructures, vapors. Human reality is itself semi-imaginary. Myth and the imaginary have a radical place in Morin's complex anthropology, which never sees man principally defined by technique and reason. *Homo sapiens* and *Homo faber* are also *Homo demens et ludens*. Affectivity and the "lived poetry of the surrealists" are at the heart of his anthropology.[28]

At the core of *L'homme et la mort* is the notion of participation, a central activity in *The Cinema, or The Imaginary Man* and what is later to be thought of as complex thought. Morin borrows the term from anthropologist Lévy-Bruhl, who tried to seize archaic man in the infinite cosmic richness of his participations.[29] Before Lévi-Strauss's "cerebral savage" was participating "primitive" man, for whom the risk of death was a part of life, who lived the poetic and the prosaic, who could believe in and act out the crossing of boundaries between separated parts of the world: "Games, dances, are veritable mimes of the cosmos. They imitate the creation of the world, an original unity and indetermination, as Mircea Eliade and Roger Caillois discovered in their different ways."[30] Morin elaborates his conception of anthropocosmomorphism, a conception that will also be fundamental to his work on the cinema:

> Through the subjectivity of participation, man feels himself analogous with the world; and this is what we call the cosmomorphism of the "primitive" or the child; at the same time, he perceives the world as animated by passions, desires, quasi-human feelings, and that is anthropomorphism. Anthropomorphism and cosmomorphism simultaneously and dialectically return man to nature and nature to man.[31]

Myth is the irruption of the cosmos in man. Legends, with their metamorphoses, suppose the analogy of man and the world.

When he later returned to his 1957 book, *The Stars*, Morin repudiated the tone of superior irony he had occasionally adopted, rightly persuaded that one must never be insolent or condescending in regard to a phenomenon studied. He had nevertheless written the original book as "an author who lives in the myths he is analyzing."[32] This is perhaps never more apparent than in his analysis and appreciation of the phenomenon of James Dean. In *L'homme et la mort*, Morin had put forward the notion of the secrets of adolescence and maturity. The mature works of great writers often presented a kind of nirvanian vision, a contemplative wisdom, serenity, an acceptance of the naturalness of death. The secrets of maturity involved "the confident acceptance of cosmic repose, a positive annihilation in Being."[33] But even in maturity a negation can appear, "a youth of spirit and heart capable of silencing the soothing secrets of harmony." Even at the brink of death, "revolt and the secrets of adolescence make themselves heard."[34] "Adolescence" involved movement, the conquering activity of individuality. The poet Rimbaud had illuminated Morin's own adolescence, and Rimbaud was still dear to him. Returning to *L'homme et la mort* in 1970, Morin wrote of the need to restructure the categories of adolescence and age so that we might try to combine the secrets of adolescence and the secrets of maturity, instead of each chasing away the other in the model of the "techno-bourgeois" adult.[35] This techno-bourgeois adult, who has put aside infantile and archaic enthusiasm and wonder, has arguably been the dominant model for the "man of reason."

For Morin, James Dean was "a pure hero of adolescence" in his real and his screen life, expressing the needs of adolescent individuality,

> which, asserting itself, refused to accept the norms of the soul-killing and specialized life that lie ahead. The demand for a total life, the quest for the absolute is every human individual's demand when he tears himself from the nest of childhood and the chains of the family only to see before him the new chains and mutilations of social life.[36]

He quotes critic François Truffaut, who would later help usher in the New Wave of cinema:

> In James Dean, today's youth discovers itself. Less for the reasons usually advanced: violence, sadism, hysteria, pessimism, cruelty, and filth, than for others infinitely more simple and commonplace: modesty of feeling, continual fantasy life, moral purity without relation to everyday morality but all the more rigorous; eternal adolescent love of tests and trials, intoxication, pride, and regret at feeling oneself "outside" society, refusal and desire to become integrated and, finally, acceptance—or refusal—of the world as it is.[37]

In Dean the link between the most intense aspiration to life and the greatest chance of death are lived out. Perhaps one sentence in the James Dean essay in *The Stars* encapsulates Morin's diagnosis of adulthood in the 1950s: "Finally the adult of our middle-class bureaucratized society is the man who agrees to live only a little in order not to die a great deal."[38] Dean the actor died at high speed. Rimbaud the poet turned to trade. It was left to Morin the searcher/researcher to try to combine the secrets of adolescence and maturity.

After World War II, when Rimbaud's "Season in Hell," the desire "to live in intensity and plenitude," had served as Morin's and his comrades' gospel, Morin had faced failure in "normal" adult life. When he had the good fortune to enter the Sociology Section of the Centre national de la recherche scientifique (CNRS) in 1950–51, having excluded himself from the "bourgeois" and Stalinist worlds, he lacked the courage, as he tells us in his preface to the 1977 edition of *The Cinema, or The Imaginary Man*, to take on a "sociologically virulent, directly politicizable subject."[39] He would write about cinema, a "refuge" subject, but far more than that. If cinema was a marginal subject, epiphenomenal for a "sociologist" and seemingly far from the realities of cold war life, it nevertheless brought him back to *his own life*. There was something physical about the possession involved in cinema. He remembered certain films from his teenage years with a hallucinatory intensity.

Beginning with the idea of surveys, audiences, contents, influence, the stuff of sociology, Morin knew that considering cinema as a mass medium and a sociological phenomenon hid the lived aesthetic situation of the film spectator, which was essential to the film experience. We live in the cinema in a state of double consciousness, participating and skeptical. It was not that a "sociological" approach *had to* simplify, reduce, and mutilate films and their spectators. Morin planned

The Cinema, or The Imaginary Man as the first volume of a work whose second volume would be "historico-sociological," inserting the cinema in its "cultural/social problematic." But to consider cinema as a complex phenomenon meant interrogating its very magic. What interested Morin was the modernity of our century and the archaism of our minds.[40]

Homo sapiens/faber/demens was a "producer of fantasies, myths, ideologies, magics"[41]—and the imaginary reality of the cinema and the imaginary reality of man constituted a fertile starting point for Morin. Near the end of *The Cinema, or The Imaginary Man*, he says:

> Effectively, everything enters us, is retained, anticipated, communicates by way of images more or less inflated by the imaginary. This imaginary complex, which assures and disturbs participation at the same time, constitutes a placental secretion that envelops and nourishes us. Even in the state of wakefulness and even outside of any spectacle, man walks, solitary, surrounded by a cloud of images, his "fantasies." And not only in these daydreams: the loves that he believes to be of flesh and tears are animated postcards, delirious representations. Images slide between his perception and himself, they make him see what he wants to see. The substance of the imaginary is mixed up with our life of the soul, our affective reality.[42]

One of the most crucial "complications" in talking about film is the problem of specificity. Attempting to theorize film, we seem impelled to talk about ourselves, those who respond to film. This was no problem for Morin, for whom participation was already a crucial central category, who would later go on, in his complex thought, to stress the importance of considering the *relation* of phenomena and environments, investigator and phenomenon, as opposed to closed systems, distinct essences and substances. In the prologue to *The Cinema, or The Imaginary Man*, he argues that the art of cinema and the industry of film are only the parts that have emerged to our consciousness of a phenomenon we must try to grasp in its fullness. But the submerged part, this obscure obviousness, confounds itself with our own human substance—itself obvious and obscure, like the beat of our heart, the passions of our soul. This is why, as Jean Epstein said, "we do not know all we do not know" of the cinema. Let us add or rather deduce: we do not even know what we know of it. A membrane separates *Homo cinematographicus* from *Homo sapiens*. As it separates our life from our consciousness.

To question the cinema, to envisage it in its human totality, that is the intention of our research. If it seems too ambitious, then it is the need for truth itself that would be too ambitious.

Morin set out on his mission impossible, aided and sustained by companion poets, filmmakers, and original thinkers from various disciplines. He sensed a profound link between the world of cinema and the kingdom of the dead. For him as for many others, the cinema resuscitated the archaic universe of doubles. If the double is the one great universal myth, the latent myth of the cinema is immortality. The threat and promise of death-renaissance comes with this territory of shadow and light. Cinematic vision has its basis in the archaic vision of the world, where "all metamorphoses are possible and effective within an immense fluid relationship where living or active things that are not enclosed in the prisons of objectivity and identity bathe. Metamorphosis triumphs over death and becomes renaissance" (see chapter 3).

The idea that the past does not disappear but takes refuge somewhere is there in every souvenir, says Morin. The most banal photographs can recall a presence, an emotion, a tenderness. We can warm ourselves in the presence on film of those we care for. The image can seem animated with a life more intense or more profound than reality, and even, on the brink of hallucination, in possession of a supernatural life. Then a force as powerful as death radiates from it, sometimes a Proustian power of time recovered, sometimes a spiritualist power. It is as if in man the need that battles against the erosion of time fixes itself in a privileged manner upon the image. (chapter 2)

Projection, or alienation, being fundamental human processes, the difference between "pathological" and "normal" doubling lies in the degree of alienation. There being no "pure" perception, stripped of affect and interpretation, veritable hallucinations can be mixed in with our perceptions (see chapter 5). We can go so far as to project our own individual being into a hallucinatory vision, where a corporeal specter appears to us. The image, suggests Morin, contains the magical quality of the double, but interiorized, nascent, and subjectivized. The double possesses the psychic, affective quality of the image but in an alienated, magical form. Between the poles of the magical double and the image-emotion lies a fluid, syncretic zone that we call the domain of sentiment, the soul, the heart: "In this intermediate zone, so important in our evolved civilizations, ancient magic is ceaselessly reduced to sentiment or the aesthetic; new feeling, in its youthful impetuosity, ceaselessly tends to alienate itself in magic, but without completely succeeding" (chapter 2).

Morin suggests that

the properties that seem to belong to the photo are the properties of our mind that have fixed themselves there and that it sends back to us. Instead of searching in the photographic thing for the so obviously and profoundly human quality of *photogénie*, we must come back to man. The richness of the photograph is in fact all that is not there, but that we project or fix onto it. (chapter 2)

But this is not the end of the story. The *charm* of the image, the phenomenon of *photogénie*, which so compelled earlier French writers, along with the general population, is not explained away. There is still a mystery to the way that everyday objects and persons seem poetic and moving, "made sublime" and "transfigured" by being photographed (chapter 2). Souriau wrote of the "almost congenital" marvelousness of the filmic universe (see chapter 1). For Moussinac, the cinematographic image maintained contact with the real and transfigured the real into magic (see chapter 2). Morin notes that we have the word *magic* surrounded by a cortege of "bubble" words like *marvelous* and *unreal*, words that burst when one tries to grasp hold of them. But this is not because they are meaningless; rather, their meaning cannot be pinned down. They express the helpless desire to express the inexpressible.

Morin mentions commentators for whom film brings a "feeling," a "faith," a "return" toward ancestral affinities of sensibility.[43] The spectator, suggested Epstein, was taken back to "the old animistic and mystical order" (see chapter 3). Bilinsky saw film as "the greatest apostle of animism" (see chapter 3). Once again, Morin invokes Lévy-Bruhl's conception of archaic societies. The foundations of "cinematic" vision share the features of magical visions of the world where the world is in man and man is spread throughout the world. Things can be charged with human presence and man can be charged with cosmic presence. (The cinema "gives a soul," said René Clair, "to the cabaret, the room, a bottle, a wall"! See chapter 3.) It is a commonplace of cinema for the entwined bodies of lovers to metamorphose into waves crashing onto rocks. The human face becomes a medium: "It expresses storms at sea, the earth, the town, the factory, revolution, war. The face is a landscape" (chapter 3). Anthropomorphism and cosmomorphism are two moments or poles of the same *complex*. And at the source of anthropo-cosmomorphism are processes at the heart of the cinema experience.

In the 1950s films *Rebel without a Cause* and *East of Eden*, the characters played by James Dean are relatively good boys who want to respect and be respected by their fathers. In terms of narrative resolution, these films are conservative tales. But through processes of projection and identification, moments of refusal, of vulnerability, youthful beauty and energy garbed in a red jacket, can come to stand for "anthropological revolt," which still means something to cinemagoers in the new millennium. Projection is built into our very perception. In identification, the subject, instead of projecting himself onto the world, absorbs the world into himself. Once again, rather than conceiving of these processes in isolation, we may better think of them in terms of reciprocal transfers—it makes more sense to speak of a projection-identification *complex*:

> Between magic and subjectivity spreads an uncertain nebula, which goes beyond man, without, however, detaching itself from him. We refer to or designate its manifestations with words of soul, heart, feeling. This magma, which has elements of both magic and subjectivity, is neither magic nor subjectivity, properly speaking. It is the kingdom of *projection-identification or affective participation.* (chapter 4)

Neither magic nor subjectivity is an essence. Indeed, any linear, progressive conception of a movement from "magic" to "subjectivity" is problematic. "Evolution" tends to disenchant the universe and interiorize magic, the absorption of magic into subjectivity typifying modernity, but magic remains in private and public life, around taboos in relation to sex, death, and social power. Processes of projection-identification are not only at the heart of cinema but at the heart of everyday life. Sartre, says Morin, saw the way emotion converts itself into magic. All exaltation, lyricism, and élan take on an anthropo-cosmomorphic shading in their outpourings. Lyricism naturally takes on the language of magic, and extreme subjectivity brusquely becomes extreme magic:

"Our life of feelings, desires, and fears, friendships, love, develops the whole range of projection-identification phenomena, from ineffable states of the soul to magical fetishizations" (chapter 4). When we are in love we identify with the loved one and project onto him all the love we carry within ourselves. "His photos, his trinkets, his handkerchiefs, his house, are all infused with his presence. Inanimate objects are impregnated with his soul and force us to love them. Affective participation thus spreads from beings to things and regenerates fetishizations, venerations, and cults" (chapter 4).

The idea that we live affectively, poetically, unsuccessfully fashioned into wholly "secular" beings, "techno-bourgeois" adults in a techno-bourgeois world, has profound implications. A flag and a führer can become the site of sentiments, desires, and fears, symbols of rescue from an ever more rationalizing world. Fortunately, as with his refusal to reduce mass culture to its possibilites for what he calls "low cretinization," Morin does not completely give over the projection-identifications, "magical" participation processes, to their fascist possibilities. But he recognizes their *power*.[44]

A work of fiction is itself "a radioactive pile of projection-identifications," and the cinema offers "cosmic participations at a discount" (chapter 4). The absence of practical participation means an increase in the intensity of affective participation. Isolated and in a group, the spectator is in a situation that is favorable to suggestion:

> So there he is, isolated, but at the heart of a human environment, of a great gelatin of common soul, of a collective participation, which accordingly amplifies his individual participation. . . .
>
> . . . When the charms of the shadow and the double merge on a white screen in a darkened room, for the spectator, deep in his cell, a monad closed off to everything except the screen, enveloped in the double placenta of an

anonymous community and obscurity, when the channels for action are blocked, then the locks to myth, dream, and magic open up. (chapter 4)

For Morin, the cinema star is at the frontier of the aesthetic and magic; she or he is the fruit of a particularly virulent projection-identification complex. He says in *The Stars:*

> The movies, machines for doubling life, summon the heroic and amorous myths to incarnation on the screen, start again the old imaginary processes of identification and projection from which gods are born. The religion of the stars crystallizes the projection-identification inherent in all participation in the film.[45]

While the star is a specific product of capitalist civilization, linked to contemporary individuality, increasing our solitude and participation at the same time, he or she responds to deep anthropological needs that express themselves on the plane of myth and religion. Stars are an integral part of an ethic of leisure, born of needs generated in the twentieth century, affirming the personality "beyond the cursed zone of 'piece-work,' to the exaltation of those activities which counterbalance and cast such servitude into oblivion."[46] In *The Cinema, or The Imaginary Man,* Morin writes of the polymorphous character of projection-identification. The very word *star* indicates the impossible, stellar distances that identification can reach across. He notes:

> I see stuck-up women loving the tramp they would chuck out the door, industrialists and generals full of tender friendship for the vagabond whose real existence is beneath even their contempt. Look at how they all love Charlie Chaplin, Gelsomina, el Matto, and Zampano! This shows that ego involvement is more complex than it appears. It is at play not only in respect to the hero who is like me, but to the hero who is unlike me: him sympathetic, adventurous,

free, and joyful; me sullen, trapped, a servant of the state. It can also apply to the criminal or the outlaw, although, on another level, the worthy antipathy of honest people condemns him when he commits the act that satisfies their profound longings. (chapter 4)

In one of his most knowingly delirious essays in a later edition of *The Stars*, Morin expresses his own fascination with Ava Gardner, "the great mother goddess of *De Rerum Natura*," fabricated in the Hollywood mold but exploding it, "incarnating herself fantastically in the realist genre of western film" but making this realism "explode under her mythic thrust."[47]

In keeping with his complex vision of cinema in which the high and the low, the black and the white, the male and the female cross boundaries, Morin notes that this polymorphous participation goes beyond the framework of the characters. The techniques of cinema plunge the spectator into the milieu and the action of the film. The transformation of time and space, along with movements of the camera and changes of points of view, Morin suggests, pulls objects into an affective circuit:

> "Thus the spectator who sees some faraway automobile race on the screen is suddenly thrown under the huge wheels of one of the cars, scans the speedometer, takes the steering wheel in hand. He becomes an actor." Let us add: he also becomes, just a little, the car itself. The camera is everywhere at the ball: tracking behind columns, pans, high-angle shots, shots of musicians, circling around a couple. The spectator *is* the dance, he is the ball, he is the court. Not only "is this world . . . accepted as the environment in which we temporarily live, thus replacing our real physical environment, the film theater," but we are also ourselves this world, we are ourselves this environment, just as we are the stratospheric rocket, the sinking ship. (chapter 4)[48]

We participate in a totality of beings, things, and actions that the film carries along in its flux. Movement, says Morin, is the key word of his method, but it is not an abstract principle. It is brought back to man. Humanity here is not "a mystical virtue for humanists" (see chapter 8)—projection-identification allows us to bring back fixed things and conceptual essences to their human processes. Long before his work on systems theory, cybernetics, and information theory, and before his advocacy of *la scienza nuova*, in his work on cinema, Morin is arguing for the significance of the fact that all mass comes back to energy. We must "Einsteinize" the sciences of man, he argues here (see chapter 8).

For amateurs who were also theorists of film, it was as if film called for an anti-Cartesian method. For Epstein, the cinematograph represented the universe as a perpetual, mobile continuity, more fluid and agile than directly sensible continuity, where nothing separates mind and matter, where a profound identity circulates between origin and end, cause and effect. On film, metamorphoses of time reveal metamorphoses in the universe itself that generally pass unnoticed. When sped up, noted Blaise Cendrars, the life of flowers is Shakespearean (see chapter 3). Morin draws on Epstein's *Intelligence d'une machine:*

> The acceleration of time vivifies and spiritualizes. "Thus, crystals begin to vegetate . . . plants become animals, choose their light and their support, express their vitality in gestures." The slowing down of time mortifies and materializes. "For example, human appearance finds itself deprived, in good part, of its spirituality. Thought is extinguished from the glance. . . . In gestures, awkwardness—a sign of will, the price of liberty—disappears, absorbed by the infallible grace of animal instinct. The whole of man is no more than a being of smooth muscles, swimming in a dense environment, where deep currents still carry along and fashion this clear descendant of ancient marine animal life, of the

mother waters. . . . Slowed down still more, every living substance returns to its fundamental viscosity, lets its basic colloidal nature rise to its surface." (chapter 3)

Poetic reverie? Morinian myth? In their poetic vision, Epstein and others were expressing the *connections* among the animal, vegetable, and mineral, between the spiritual and the material, with the human being corporeally reinserted in the natural world and the cosmos. When Siegfried Kracauer wrote his theory of film a few years after Morin's was published, he subtitled it *The Redemption of Physical Reality*.[49] Acerbic film critic Pauline Kael brilliantly showed the problematic nature of this intellectual's anthropomorphizing notion of film "gravitating" toward physical reality, having "preferences" or "predilections," having an affinity with the "flow of life."[50] But again, Kracauer, like Morin, was getting at what we might hear, think, see, and feel freshly when involving ourselves in the medium of film—sights, sounds, thoughts, and feelings that remind us we are not strangers to but are a part of the living animal and vegetable world (affirming our "terranian and cosmic" identity, as Morin might later put it). We are conceiving of an *understanding* that protests against the hierarchical and "techno-bourgeois" model of the human and his or her environment. We are conceiving of an *ecology* rather than life as a linear progression of atomized individuals toward death. (What Morin says in *Terre-Patrie [Homeland Earth]* is apt: "Still today, dominant philosophy and anthropology suppress any awareness and any taking into account of the consequences of the living and animal identity of man, denouncing as irrational 'vitalism' or perverse 'biologism' any recognition of our terrestrial, physical, and biological rootedness.")[51] Kael placed Kracauer in "the great, lunatic tradition."[52] Morin knows how easily one gains entry into that tradition by refusing prevailing insanities.[53]

It would be foolish to mistake this enchanted vision, this

reassertion of wonder, for ignorance, for refusal to consider phenomena in their ambiguity. In talking about participation, projection-identification, the soul, magic, and the imaginary, as we are talking about processes rather than essences, we are not talking about good and bad (epiphenomenal) objects. When civilization can no longer adhere to ancient magics, says Morin, it still draws on them and nourishes itself on affective and aesthetic participation. Metaphorically, richly, he evokes the richness of the blossoming of the soul, but he also considers the "hypertrophy," the "complacency" and "hypostasis" of what is an "imprecise zone of the psyche," "a metaphor for us to designate unspecified needs, psychic processes" (chapter 4). When the soul mistakes itself for an essence, it cuts itself off from communication with "the nourishing channels of the universe." "Our civilization is so smeared with soul," suggests Morin, "that the spectator, blinded by a kind of opaque membrane, has become incapable of *seeing* the film, capable only of *feeling* it" (chapter 4). The cinema "overflows" with soul:

> It oozes with it, to the extent that the aesthetic of feeling becomes the aesthetic of vague sentiment, to the extent that the soul ceases to be exaltation and blossoming to become the enclosed garden of inner complacencies. Love, passion, emotion, heart: the cinema, like our world, is all slimy and lachrymal with them. (chapter 4)

The reaction against "crude projection-identification, the dripping soul," on the part of Brecht in the theater, of Bresson in France, Eisenstein in Russia, Wyler in Hollywood, and Welles wherever he could work, is understandable. Our feelings can deform things, deceive us about people and events. "It is not by chance," writes Morin, "that sentiment signifies naïveté or weakness, that magic signifies error, helplessness, dupery" (chapter 8). But this is not the whole story. The imaginary cannot be dissociated from "human nature." *For better and worse*, it is married to material, practical, and rational man. An integrating and vital part of the human, "it constitutes a veritable scaffolding of projection-identification from which, at the same time as he masks himself, man knows and constructs himself" (chapter 8).

Morin's approach to myth may be contrasted with that of Roland Barthes.[54] Concerned to account in detail for the "mystification which transforms petit-bourgeois culture into a universal nature," in *Mythologies* Barthes had argued that the mythologist had to cut himself off from the consumers of myth, his relation to the world being of the order of sarcasm.[55] While he was aware of the simplifications and reductions he was making in relation to the real, his choice was strategic. Desiring a reconciliation of men and the "real," description and explanation, object and knowledge, he nevertheless believed that

> the fact that we cannot manage to achieve more than an unstable grasp of reality doubtless gives the measure of our present alienation: we constantly drift between the object, and its demystification, powerless to render its wholeness. For if we penetrate the object, we liberate it but we destroy it; and if we acknowledge its full weight, we respect it, but we restore it to a state which is still mystified.[56]

Morin refuses the political strategy adopted in *Mythologies*. He shares the notion of powerlessness in relation to totality, and the conception of "navigation" between observer and observed, science and reality, but shrinking or mutilating reality to make it amenable to ideological interpretation and struggle is no solution for him. Such an approach to theorizing phenomena, which are always impure, and the refusal to respect phenomena lest they continue to charm us are alien to complex analysis.[57]

Morin concludes *The Cinema, or The Imaginary Man* by exhorting us to try to question our collectively shared and industrially produced dreams, to reintegrate the imaginary into our reality. In later work he would elaborate on the idea that the problem is not to live in some pure reality purged of myth, but to recognize and elucidate the imaginary reality of myth and live with myths recognized as myths, having a new relationship with them, possessing them as much as they possess us. Combating error is less a process of undertaking naive "demystification" than of "entering the universe of myths with respect, attention, complexity," recognizing *their* reality and *their* truth, which is not the same as *the* truth.[58]

Morin's conception of the human is close to that of his friend and colleague Cornelius Castoriadis, whom he invokes in *Pour sortir du vingtième siècle*:

> Man, as Castoriadis says, is a mad animal whose madness invented reason. The worst madness would be to think that we can suppress madness. The ultimate madness is not to recognize madness. The seeds of the latter are not only in the disorders of the human mind, which make it behave crazily, but they also allow imagination and invention. Madness is also in embryo in the nature of reason itself. Nonetheless, this reason is at the same time what enables us to struggle against this madness.[59]

Like Castoriadis, Morin draws on what have been called romantic and Enlightenment traditions. The "beat of our heart, the passions of our soul" cannot be excised from theory that sees humans as biological and cultural beings, participating beings whose existence is rooted in myth and the imaginary and who are *also* capable of self-understanding.

In *L'esprit du temps*, Morin had argued that it is not only philosophers, writers, or blackshirt thugs who live out contemporary nihilism. Without necessarily knowing it, "the masses" are also confronted with the problems faced by Stirner, Marx, and Nietzsche much earlier. In modern leisure activities, they take part in a kind of game in which it is not always known who plays and who is played. A violence, a "central fire," remains in the "civilized" human, and although mass culture can drug us, make us drunk, it cannot cure our "fundamental furies," only entertain them and project them in films, sensational news headlines, and so on.[60]

Mass culture, which was a product of modern technical civilization that brought with it its own abstractions, was at the same time a reaction against a universe of abstract relations. By technical means, it contested the technical—humanizing, populating, the technical world with the presence of voices, music, images. It dealt with the question of how to live nontechnically in a technicized world. While a kind of prosaic asceticism began to typify many theoretical approaches to the "mystifications" of mass culture, with its happy endings, stereotypes of romantic love, and ideologies of success (all of which Morin himself had identified and acknowledged), Morin brought back emotion, intensity, and activity into the consideration of mass culture in general and film in particular. At the same time, examining their role in cinema meant bringing these elements back into the consideration of everyday life.

Morin is well aware of the dangerous possibilities of participation. If hallucination is a part of perception, even everyday perception, "possession" is an almost "normal" phenomenon at the heart of strong religious/political beliefs and accompanying collective ecstasies.[61] Our "fundamental furies" can make for deadly cocktails when mixed with dispossession, disenfranchisement, and our need for participation and communion.

Morin has often cited Adorno's "totality is nontruth" as a guiding dictum. But in *Introduction à la pensée complexe*, he notes that totality is, at the same time, truth and lie.[62] Adorno, in the wake of Nazism, was allergic to totality, suspicious of collectivity of any kind. A generation of postmodern theorists have taken Adorno further, critical of his "nostalgic" longing for lost wholeness. A longing for unity, myth, the imaginary, and the return of the biological invokes the specter of fascism for many contemporary intellectuals.

But the "romantic" Morin is more tough-minded than many postmodern theorists when he refuses to alter his conception of the human to achieve some kind of imaginary innoculation against tragic outcomes. As Brian Rigby has so aptly put it: "In Morin the Romantic affirmation of the self and the Romantic communion with humanity and the cosmos are combined with the tragic humanism of the Existentialists."[63] The acceptance of human tragedy (and the tragedy of the universe) is for Morin "the condition *sine qua non* of all anthropolitics."[64] His stoic romanticism recognizes that we cannot achieve the dream of eliminating prose and realizing complete happiness on earth, but any complex politics necessitates a "full consciousness of the poetic needs of the human being."[65]

In *The Cinema, or The Imaginary Man*, Morin notes that Lévy-Bruhl endlessly showed that if "archaic" peoples believe that a sorcerer has killed one of their kin, they are nevertheless not ignorant of the fact that the kinsman who had a spell put on him was killed, say, by a crocodile in the river. Although magic is practiced for hunting, there is also fastidious practical preparation of weapons for the kill. It is our own society that breaks "the contradictory unity of the practical and the magical, or, rather, of that which we henceforth call practical and magical," although we and our accoutrements continue to exist and act on both levels (see chapter 6). The modern West officially separates the "poetry" and the "prose" of everyday life, relegating the poetry to "private" life. Technology, which has liberated many human beings from drudgery, subjects them to new servitudes, to the quantitative logic of machines. But if we are expected to live in hyperprose, ignoring the fact that we are going to die, the delineations of our lives fashioned by corporations, technoscience, and bureaucracy, the poetry does not go away. It can take on toxic forms. Morin is not alone in describing the double process of the unification and balkanization of the planet, the return of ancient barbarisms and their alliance with technoscientific barbarism. Statesman/writer Václav Havel evokes our dangerous present and paradoxical situation, in which "civilization" has essentially globalized only the surface of our lives:

> But our inner self continues to have a life of its own. And the fewer answers the era of rational knowledge provides to the basic questions of human Being, the more deeply it would seem that people, behind its back as it were, cling to the ancient certainties of the tribe. Because of this, individual cultures, increasingly lumped together by contemporary civilization, are realizing with new urgency their own inner autonomy and the inner differences of others. Cultural conflicts are increasing and are understandably more dangerous today than at any other time in history. The end of the era of rationalism has been catastrophic: Armed with the same supermodern weapons, often from the same suppliers, and followed by television cameras, the members of various tribal cults are at war with one another. By day, we work with statistics; in the evening we consult astrologers and frighten ourselves with thrillers about vampires. The abyss between the rational and the spiritual, the external and the internal, the objective and the subjective, the technical and the moral, the universal and the unique constantly grows deeper.[66]

As Morin puts it in *Terre-Patrie:*

> The betrayal and collapse of the poetic hope of the universal triumph of fraternity has spread a great blanket of prose over the world. And meanwhile, all around us, on the ruins of the poetic promise of changing our life, ethnic and religious resources strive to regenerate the poetries of communal participation.[67]

This dangerous poetry has become even more apparent at the beginning of this new century.

Not long after writing *The Cinema, or The Imaginary Man* and *The Stars*, while working on *L'esprit du temps*, Morin collaborated with anthropologist and filmmaker Jean Rouch on what was to become a landmark "cinema verité" documentary, *Chronicle of a Summer* (1960). In this project, which was both "ethnographic" and "existential," Morin and Rouch (like a "Jerry Lewis-Dean Martin" team),[68] pulled in different directions. Rouch, Morin has suggested, like a spokesperson for the "life is beautiful" team, veered toward what was "cheerful and light" and he toward what was "sad and sorrowful."[69] Turning ethnography on its head and doing participant observation on Parisians, the filmmakers show them eating, drinking, and being merry; people are bored, dance, cry, argue, hope, and despair. The Algerian war that they had fiercely hoped would end that summer did not end. Instead of harmony, there is discord. Instead of participants coming to affectionate understanding, some become scathingly critical of one another. For Morin, the cutting down of more than twenty-five hours of film to one and a half hours was bitterly disappointing, indeed a mutilation, and yet *Chronicle* remains an unusually powerful document.

The great Hungarian theorist of film Béla Balázs had conceived of the possibility of film as a counter to alienation, believing film might play a role in combating the reductions and occlusions of vital facets of our being. If the discovery of printing had rendered illegible the faces of men and expressive communication had been denigrated among the educated, film might return us to our "aboriginal mother tongue."[70] Eisenstein, Morin notes in *The Cinema, or The Imaginary Man*, had seen cinema as the only concrete and dynamic art capable of "restoring to the intelligence its vital concrete and emotional sources" (chapter 7). So Morin's hopes for what cinema verité might achieve were high. It might bring us to a "lucid consciousness of brotherhood," the viewer might find himself "less alien to his fellow man, less icy and inhuman, less encrusted in a false life."[71] Morin asked: "Can't cinema be one of the means of breaking the membrane that isolates each of us from others in the metro, on the street, or on the stairway of the apartment building?"[72] If people in the film were asked, "How do you live?" this might lead us to ask how we *can* live, what we can do, to question no less than the construction of a new life.[73] An outrageous and impossible expectation.

Chronicle grew out of a particular political and historical moment in Paris, peopled with Left-intellectuals (including a very young Régis Debray), a Renault worker, young African students, concentration camp survivors, and former Resistance militants. Yet when young people in Melbourne, Australia, view the film more than forty years later, people who have never heard of Régis Debray, who know little about French colonialism and nothing of Marxist theories of alienation, they are thankful to see it. They are surprised by their own engagement with the people in the film, their intellectual and emotional involvement—*they talk about their own lives.*[74]

In *L'unité de l'homme*, Morin insists that the unity to which he aspires has nothing to do with unification that destroys variety. It can be achieved only amid the blossoming and the cross-fertilization of differences. A new civilization cannot be founded on the hegemonic image "of the white, adult, Western man; it must on the contrary reveal and revive the civilizational ferment that is feminine, youthful, aged, multiethnic, multicultural. The new society cannot be founded on the homogenizing domination of an empire."[75] Once again, prompted by the viewing of a film, Morin expresses the possibility of people experiencing sameness and difference, the "if not the same, at least common" of which he writes in *The Cinema, or The Imaginary Man*. It is ultimately what his work is about:

Despite the prodigious dispersion of *Homo sapiens* on the planet for the last fifty to a hundred thousand years, a dispersion through which the color of people's skin, the form of the nose, rites, myths, and experiences had diversified to the extreme, still, there remained this fundamental unity of the smile, and of tears. This film made me *live* subjectively this objective finding. I felt profoundly in myself, in terms of kinship, that I was a part of these other humans in other respects so strange; and, to express my feeling, let me say this almost obscene word—love.[76]

The Cinema, or The Imaginary Man

An Essay in Sociological Anthropology

Prologue

A jingling bell summons us. One store among many displays enormous painted faces, photographs of kisses, embraces, horse rides. We enter into the darkness of an artificial grotto. A luminous dust is projected and dances on a screen; our gaze is nourished there. It takes on shape and life; it draws us into an errant adventure: we cross time and space, until some solemn music dissolves the shadows on the screen that has once again become white. We come out, and we talk about the merits and failings of a film.

The strange obviousness of the everyday. The first mystery of the cinema is in this obviousness. What is astonishing is that it does not astonish us. The obvious "stares us in the face," in the literal sense of the term: it blinds us.

"Let everything said to be normal unsettle you," said Brecht. It is here that the science of man begins. It is here that the science of the cinema must begin.

The art of cinema and the industry of film are only the parts that have emerged to our consciousness of a phenomenon we must try to grasp in its fullness. But the submerged part, this obscure obviousness, confounds itself with our own human substance—itself obvious and obscure, like the beat of our heart, the passions of our soul. This is why, as Jean Epstein said, "we do not know all we do not know" of the cinema.[1] Let us add or rather deduce: we do not even know

3

what we know of it. A membrane separates *Homo cinemato-graphicus* from *Homo sapiens*. As it separates our life from our consciousness.

To question the cinema, to envisage it in its human total-ity, that is the intention of our research.[2] If it seems too ambitious, then it is the need for truth itself that would be too ambitious.

The present volume is an attempted elucidation accord-ing to a method of genetic anthropology that suffers from being expounded *in abstracto:* it can be justified only by its effectiveness in rendering the unity and the complexity of the phenomenon studied.

We have only been able to complete this work thanks to the Centre national de la recherche scientifique. We thank the CNRS for having allowed us to undertake it and pur-sue it within the framework of the research of the Centre d'études sociologiques. We thank our colleagues from the CES, Suzanne Schiffman and Claude Frère, for the contin-uous assistance they gave us. We thank those who, with their support, provided us with the most precious gift that could be granted to us—confidence and freedom: Messieurs Max Sorre, Étienne Souriau, and, at the highest level, Georges Friedmann. We are bound by a special gratitude to Georges Friedmann: it is natural that the dedication of this book should go to him.

1 *The Cinema, the Airplane*

As the nineteenth century dies it bequeaths us two new machines. Both of them are born on almost the same date, at almost the same place, then simultaneously launch themselves upon the world and spread across continents. They pass from the hands of the pioneers into those of operators, crossing a "supersonic barrier." The first machine realizes at last the most insane dream man has pursued since he looked at the sky: to break away from the earth. Until then, only the creatures of his imagination, of his desire—the angels—had wings. This need to fly, which arises, well before Icarus, at the same time as the first mythologies, seems to all appearances the most infantile and mad. It is also said about dreamers that they do not have their feet on the ground. Clement Adler's feet, for an instant, escaped the ground, and the dream finally came to life.

At the same time, an equally miraculous machine presented itself: its wonder this time consisted no longer in soaring into the aerial beyond where only the dead, the angels, and gods sojourned, but in reflecting down to earth reality. The objective eye—and the adjective here carried such a weight that it became substantive[1]—captured life to reproduce it, to "imprint" it, in the words of Marcel L'Herbier. Free of all fantasy, this laboratory eye was only finally able to be perfected because it responded to a laboratory need: the decomposition of movement. While the airplane escaped from the world of objects, the cinematograph only attempted to reflect it in order to examine it better. For Muybridge, Marey, Demenÿ, the cinematograph and its immediate predecessors such as the chronophotograph are research instruments "to study nature's phenomena," they "render . . . the same service as the microscope for the anatomist."[2] All the commentaries in 1896 looked toward the scientific future of the apparatus devised by the Lumière brothers, who, twenty-five years later, still regarded the spectacle of cinema as an accident.

While the Lumière brothers still did not believe in the cinema's future, aerial space was civilized, nationalized, made "navigable." The airplane, hobby of the dreamer, hobby-horse of the cavalier of the clouds, let itself be assimilated by the practical and became the *practical* means of traveling, of commerce, and of war. Constantly linked to the earth by radio and radar networks, the "messenger of heaven" has today turned into the courier of the sky, PTT van, public transport, stagecoach of the twentieth century.[3] Still the stuff of dreams, of pioneers and heroes, but each exploit precedes and points to an exploitation. The airplane did not escape the earth. It expanded it as far as the stratosphere. It shrank it.

The flying machine sensibly took its place in the world of machines, but "works created by the cinema, the vision of the world that they present, went beyond the mechanical effects and all the supports of the film in a breathtaking way."[4] It is film that soared, always higher, toward a sky of dreams, toward the infinity of the stars—of "stars"—bathed in music, populated by delightful and diabolical presences, escaping the mundane world, of which it was to be, to all appearances, the savior and the mirror.

This astonishing phenomenon scarcely holds the attention of historians of the cinema, who, with a naive finality, consider the time of the cinema's genesis as an age of apprenticeship where a language and means supposedly predestined to constitute the seventh art are elaborated. They are not astonished that *the cinematograph was, from the time of its birth, radically diverted from its obvious technical or scientific ends, to be seized by spectacle and become the cinema*.[5] And "seized" is the right expression: the cinematograph could just as well have realized boundless practical possibilities.[6] But the rise of the cinema—that is, of film spectacle—truncated these developments that would have seemed natural.

What inner power, what "mana" did the cinematograph possess to transform itself into cinema? And not only transform itself but appear so unreal and supernatural that these two notions can seem to define its obvious nature and essence?[7]

Riciotto Canudo was precisely the first film theorist for having known how to define the art of the objective through subjectivity. "In the cinema . . . art consists in suggesting emotions, and not in recounting facts."[8] "The cinema is the creator of a surreal life," declared Apollinaire back in 1909. In the abundance of texts devoted to the cinema from the 1920s onward, expressions of this sort proliferate: "In the cinema, characters and objects appear to us through a kind of unreal mist in a ghostly impalpability."[9] "The worst cinema remains, in spite of everything, cinema, that is, something moving and indefinable."[10] We constantly come across expressions such as "surrealist eye," "spiritualist art" (Jean Epstein), and above all the key word: "The cinema is a dream" (Michel Dard). "It is an artificial dream" (Théo Varlet). "Is not the cinema also a dream?" (Paul Valéry). "I go to the cinema as I go to sleep" (Maurice Henry). "It seems that moving images have been specially invented to allow us to visualize our dreams" (Jean Tédesco).[11]

But is not everything dreamlike to dreamers and poetic to poets? Theoreticians, scholars, and savants come up with the same words to describe the cinema, the same double reference to affectivity and magic. "In the filmic universe there is a kind of supernatural atmosphere that is almost congenital," says Étienne Souriau.[12] Élie Faure evokes the cinema as "a music which reaches us by way of the eye."[13] For Moussinac and Henri Wallon, the cinema brings to the world a feeling, a faith, the "return to ancestral affinities of sensibility."[14]

This is where the mystery begins. As opposed to most inventions, which become tools and end up being put away in sheds, the cinematograph escapes this prosaic fate. The cinema may be reality, but it is also something else, a generator of emotions and dreams. All the testimonies assure us of this: they constitute the cinema itself, which is nothing without its spectators. The cinema is not reality, *since people say so*. If its unreality is an illusion, it is clear that this illusion is, all the same, its reality. But at the same time we know that the camera lens is devoid of subjectivity, and that no fantasy comes to disturb the look that it fixes on the edge of the real.

The cinema has taken flight beyond reality. How? Why? We can know this only by following the genetic process of this metamorphosis. But first, we have a feeling that, already, the Lumière cinematograph contained in a state of latent power and energy what would transform it into an "enormous strolling player," in the words of G. Cohen-Séat. If it is true that there is something of the supernatural and of the soul in the cinema, this supernatural and this soul were encrypted in the chromosomes of the cinematograph. Can we limit ourselves by logically and chronologically opposing science to the imagination? It was "a science first, and nothing but a science. There was required the grandiose imagination of man."[15] Let us stop there.

Nothing but a science? In 1829, Joseph Plateau stares at the summer sun for twenty-five seconds. He is blinded by it, but, in the meantime, a toy, a simple toy, the phenakistoscope, is born. An eccentric racegoer makes a bet on the gallop of a horse and we have Muybridge's experiments on the Sacramento racecourse. A bricoleur of genius, who goes on to become an industrial potentate, perfects, among other inventions, the Kinetograph. Already its legend has given birth to the ill-fated ancestor of modern "science fiction," Villiers de l'Isle Adam's *Tomorrow's Eve*.[16] "The fanatics, the madmen, the disinterested pioneers, capable, as was Bernard Palissy, of burning their furniture for a few seconds of shaky images, are neither industrialists nor savants, just men obsessed by their own imaginings," says André Bazin.[17] But is not the inventor himself possessed by his imagination before he is hailed as a great scientist? Is a science nothing but a science? Is it not always, at its inventive source, daughter of the dream?

Great inventions are born from the world of pet obsessions, hobbies. They spring forth not from highly developed big business, but from the laboratory of the lone visionary or the workshop of the bricoleur. (It goes without saying that big business rapidly latches onto invention.) If we now generalize at the level of nations, is it perhaps its backwardness on the industrial concentration and rationalization front that made France a country of inventors?

It is certain that if the cinema is an international invention, it is in this "Lepinian,"[18] artisanal France of the bricoleur that the number of discoveries of a cinematographic character was highest (129 patents for the year 1896, as opposed to 50 in England). The birth of the cinematograph could easily lead us to a consideration of the problems of a comparative sociology of invention,[19] but here we want to make this point clear: inventors, bricoleurs, dreamers are from the same family and navigate the same waters where their genius has its source.

The technical and the dream are linked at birth. We cannot at any moment of its genesis and development consign the cinematograph to the camp of dream alone or science alone.

Throughout the nineteenth century, entertainers and scientists send the nascent invention back and forth between them, and, with each of these shuttles, an improvement is added. Plateau's phenakistoscope transforms itself into the

zoetrope (Horner, 1834), the animated magic lantern projecting onto a screen (von Uchatius, 1853), the animated
drawing (Reynaud's praxinoscope, 1887, and the Théâtre
Optique, 1889). At the same time, another toy, associated with
that other game for grown-ups that is photography, through
the extravagant fantasy of the billionaire Leland Stanford,
once again became an instrument of research (Janssen's
photographic revolver, 1876; Marey's chronophotograph,
1882). Better still, the entertainers turn into scientists, and
the scientists turn into entertainers: the professor of natural
sciences Reynaud finds himself director of optic theater and
Lumière director of fairground tours. What is going on? Is
it a question of a toy for "Children's Corner"? Of a rifle for
the scientist off to track down the movements of a butterfly?
Of animated drawings for the Musée Grevin? Of a visual
complement to the phonograph? Of a slot machine? Of a
tool or of a joke?

If we try to delve deeply into its origins, the uncertainty
increases: optical science? Magic shadows? "The invention
of cinema is the result of a long series of scientific works and
of the taste that man has always shown for spectacles of light
and shade," says Marcel Lapierre.[20] The scientific works,
Martin Quigley reminds us, go back as far as the Arab Al-
hazan, who studied the human eye, to Archimedes, who systematically used lenses and mirrors, to Aristotle, who founded
a theory of optics.[21] This pilgrimage takes us back to the
sources, not only of physical science, but also, by way of
phantasmagoria, of religion, magic, and art. The predecessors of the Lumière brothers are the showmen with their
magic lanterns, the most illustrious of whom remain Robertson (1763–1837) and Father Kircher (1601–1682), who are
themselves the heirs of archaic magic:[22] five thousand years
before, on the walls of the caves of Java, the "Wayang"
brought its shadow plays to life. The Greek mystery cults,
originally practiced in caves, were accompanied by shadow
performances, if we follow Jean Przylinsky's hypothesis,

which accounts at the same time for the origin of the platonic myth described in the seventh book of *The Republic*.[23]

So where does the cinema come from? "Its birth . . . has all the characteristics of an enigma and he who asks himself this question will get lost along the way, will abandon the pursuit."[24] To tell the truth, the enigma is not in the facts, but in the uncertainty of a current that zigzags between play and research, spectacle and laboratory, the decomposition and reproduction of movement, in the Gordian knot of science and dream, illusion and reality where the new invention is taking shape.

Does the cinematograph sever this Gordian knot? It springs up in 1895, absolutely faithful to real things through chemical reproduction and mechanical projection, a veritable demonstration of rational optics, and it seems to have to dispel forever the magic of the Wayang, the fantasies of Father Kircher, and the childish preoccupations of Reynaud. It is consequently enthroned in the university, academically recognized. But is not this machine the most absurd that can be, *since it only serves to project images for the pleasure of seeing images?*

2 *The Charm of the Image*

The originality of the cinematograph is relative. Edison had already animated the photograph, Reynaud had already projected animated images on a screen. But the very relativity of the cinematograph—that is, the combination of animated photography and projection in one single device—is its originality.

The cinematograph doubly increases the photograph's impression of reality, on the one hand by restoring natural movement to beings and things, on the other hand by projecting them, liberated from the film as from the Kinetoscope box, onto a surface where they seem autonomous (see chapter 5).

And it is precisely at the moment when the greatest fidelity ever obtained should have directed it toward scientific applications and made it lose all interest in spectacle that the Lumière device presents its images just for contemplation, that is, projects them as spectacle.

Photogénie

This marvel that is exhibited in 1895–96, says Marcel L'Herbier, "like the bearded lady or the cow with two heads" is so wonderful that it shows the cow with only one head and the lady without a beard.[1] Of course, it is not astonishing that each new invention astonishes and elicits curiosity. Of course, from its birth and even before (the Kinetoscope), the filmed image was to be draped in exoticism and fantasy, snapped up by the comic (*l'arroseur arrosé [The Waterer Watered]*), the fantastic (early Méliès), History (the first *L'assassinat du duc de Guise [The Assassination of the Duc de Guise]*), bawdiness (*Coucher d'Yvette, Pierreuse*), Grand Guignol (*Exécution capitale à Berlin*), and festivals, fake newsreels, coronations, naval battles.

But the wide-eyed wonder involved a wonder that was more profound. At the same time as the strange, new, and entertaining image, another image, banal and quotidian, imposed its fascination. The unprecedented craze created by the Lumière tours was not only born from the discovery of the unknown world, as Sadoul rightly insists, but from seeing the known world, not only the picturesque but the quotidian. Unlike Edison, whose first films showed music hall scenes or boxing matches, Lumière had the brilliant intuition to film and project as spectacle that which is not spectacle: prosaic life, passersby going about their business. He sent Mesguisch and Promio out into the streets. He had understood that a primal curiosity *was directed to the reflection of reality*. That people above all else marveled at seeing anew that which did not fill them with wonder:[2] their houses, their faces, the settings of their familiar lives.

Workers leaving a factory, a train entering a station, things already seen hundreds of times, hackneyed and devalued, drew the first crowds. *That is, what attracted the first crowds was not an exit from a factory, a train entering a station (it would have been sufficient to go to the station or the factory), but an image of a train, an image of workers leaving a factory. It was not for the real but for the image of the real that people flocked to the doors of the Salon Indien.* Lumière had sensed and exploited the charm of the cinematographic image.

Was this charm going to wear off after the Lumière showings? One would have thought so. The cinematograph launches itself into the world and becomes a tourist. It transforms itself into a fairy play.[3] Nevertheless, the first reflections on the essence of cinema, twenty years later, begin by being conscious of the initial fascination and giving it a name—*photogénie*.

This quality that is not in life but in the image of life, how should we define it? *Photogénie* is "that extreme poetic aspect of beings and things" (Delluc), "that poetic quality of beings and things" (Moussinac), "capable of being revealed to us only by the cinematograph" (both Moussinac and Delluc).

Hesitant in thought in its infancy, its naïveté of expression, both poor and rich like the babblings of mystical revelation, the great ineluctable truth stamps down its foot: *photogénie* is the quality proper to the cinematograph, and the quality proper to the cinematograph is *photogénie*. Does not Epstein take a step forward when, beyond "the cinematographic property of things, a kind of moving potential," he defines as photogenic "any aspect whose moral character is *enhanced by filmic reproduction*"?[4]

This magnifying quality (it is not shocking to unite the two terms dialectically) cannot be confused with the picturesque, that invitation to painting that pretty things present us with. "Picturesque and photogenic coincide only by chance."[5] The picturesque is in the things of life. The distinctive feature of *photogénie* is to awaken the "picturesque" in things that are not picturesque.

Innocuous scenes, "familiar moments" fixed by the ciné-eye of Dziga Vertov, can find themselves exalted as "a paroxysm of existence" (Chavance) or "made sublime, transfigured" (Agel) to reveal "the secret beauty, the ideal beauty of everyday movements and rites."[6]

What kind of paroxysm, what kind of transfiguration is it? Let us cite Chavance's sentence in its entirety: "I find in this paroxysm of existence a supernatural quality." Let us complete it with Agel's: "The surrealizing power of the cinema realizes itself in the purest fashion."[7] And let us conclude with Valentin: "The camera lens confers on all that comes near it an air of legend, it transports whatever falls within its field away from reality."[8] Is it not astounding that the "legendary," "surrealizing," "supernatural" quality should spring directly from the most objective image that can possibly be conceived of?

Breton marveled at the fact that in the fantastic there is only the real. Let us reverse the proposition and marvel at the fantastic that radiates from the simple reflection of real things. Finally, let us make it dialectical: in the photograph, the real and the fantastic reflect one another while identifying as if in an exact superimposition.

Everything unfolds as if, before the photographic image, empirical sight were doubled by an oneiric vision, analogous to what Rimbaud called *voyance*, not unlike what psychics call "second sight" (nor perhaps that plenitude that "voyeurs" experience by looking): a second sight, as they say, which in the last analysis reveals beauties or secrets ignored at first sight. And it was undoubtedly not by chance that practitioners felt the need to invent, where *to see* seemed sufficient, the verb *to preview*.

Thus, in the words of Moussinac, the cinematographic image maintains "contact with the real and also transforms the real into magic."[9]

What comes back once again, but this time applied to the most faithful of images, is the word *magic*, surrounded by a cortege of bubble words—marvelous, unreal, and so on—that burst and evaporate as soon as we try to handle them. Not that they are meaningless; they cannot say anything. They express the helpless desire to express the inexpressible. They are passwords for what cannot be articulated. We must treat these words with suspicion in their stubborn rehearsal of their nothingness. But at the same time this stubbornness is the sign of a kind of blind intuition, as with those animals who always scratch the ground at the same spot, or bark when the moon rises. What have they sensed?

What have they recognized? Magic? *Photogénie?* What is this genius of the photo?

Genius of the Photo

It is photography that brought the word *photogénie* into being in 1839.[10] It is still used there. We discover before our snapshots whether we are "photogenic" or not, according to a mysterious enhancement or diminishment. Photography flatters or betrays us; it gives or denies us a *je ne sais quoi*.

Certainly the *photogénie* of the cinematograph cannot be reduced to that of photography. But it is in the photographic image that their common source resides. To shed light on the problem it makes sense to set out from this same source.

Although motionless, the photographic image is not dead. The proof of this is that we love photos, we look at them. Yet they are not animated. This falsely naive observation clarifies something for us. With the cinematograph, we could believe that the presence of the characters comes from the life—the movement—that is given to them. *In photography, it is obviously presence that gives life. The primary and peculiar quality of photography is the presence of the person or the thing that is nevertheless absent.* To be assured, this presence has no need for the mediating subjectivity of an artist. The genius of the photo is first of all chemical. The most objective, the most mechanical of all photography, that of the automatic photo booth, can transmit an emotion to us, a tenderness, as if in a certain way, to use Sartre's words, the original had incarnated itself in the image. Moreover, the catchphrase of photography, "Smile," implies a subjective communication from person to person through the medium of film, carrier of the message of the soul. The most banal of photographs harbors or summons a certain presence. We know this, we feel it, since we keep photographs on us, at home, we show them around (significantly omitting to indicate that what we are showing are images—"Here are my mother, my wife, my children"), not only to satisfy a stranger's curiosity, but for the obvious pleasure of once more contemplating them ourselves, to warm ourselves by their presence, to feel them close to us, with us, in us, as small presences in the pocket or the apartment, attached to our person or our home. Deceased fathers and mothers, the brother killed in the war, look out from their large frames, watch over and protect the country home, like household gods. Wherever there is a home, photographs take the place of the statuettes or objects around which the cult of the dead was perpetuated. They play, in an attenuated fashion because the cult of the dead is itself attenuated, the same role as Chinese tablets, those points of connection from which the dearly departed are always available to be called.

Has not the spread of photography partially revived archaic forms of family devotion? Or rather, have not the needs of family worship found in photography the exact representation that amulets and objects achieved in an imperfect and symbolic fashion: the presence of absence?[11]

In this sense, the photograph can be accurately named, and this identification is far-reaching: souvenir.[12] The souvenir can itself be called life regained, perpetuated presence.

Photo-souvenir, the two terms are bracketed together—better still, interchangeable. Let us listen to the prattle: "What great souvenirs for you, what fine souvenirs they will make." The photograph functions as souvenir, and this function can play a determining role, as in modern tourism, which is prepared for and undertaken in expeditions destined to bring back a booty of souvenirs, primarily photographs and postcards. We can ask ourselves what is the underlying goal of these holiday trips, where we go to admire monuments and landscapes that we manage not to visit back home. The same Parisian who ignores the Louvre, has never crossed the portal of a church, and does not go out of his way to contemplate Paris from the top of the Sacré-Coeur will not miss a chapel in Florence, will pace up and down museums, and exhaust himself climbing the Campaniles or getting to the hanging gardens of Ravello. Of course we want to see, and not just take photos. But what we are looking for, what we see, is a universe that, sheltered from time, or at least victoriously enduring its erosion, is already itself a souvenir. Eternal mountains, islands of happiness where millionaires, stars, "great writers," hide away, and of course, above all, "historic" sites and monuments, the realm of statues and colonnades, Elysian fields of dead civilizations. That is to say, a kingdom of the dead, but where death is transfigured into ruins, where a kind of eternity resonates in the atmosphere, that of the memory transmitted from age to age. This is why guidebooks despise a country's industry and work only to present its embalmed mummy within a motionless nature. What we call foreign finally appears in an extreme strangeness, a "ghostliness" accrued from the peculiarity of customs and unknown language (always an abundant collection of "souvenirs"). And just as for archaic peoples the foreigner is a potent spirit, and the foreign world a far frontier of the abode of the spirits, so the tourist travels as if in a world populated by spirits. The camera encased in leather is like his talisman that he carries across his shoulder. And, for certain frenetic people, traveling is a ride broken up only by multiple clicks of the camera. We do not look at the monument, we photograph it. We have ourselves photographed at the feet of giants carved out of stone. Photography becomes the tourist act itself, as if the sought-for emotion is prized only as a future souvenir, the image on film, enriched by a power of remembrance squared.

Every film is a battery of presence that we charge with beloved faces, admired objects, "beautiful," "extraordinary," "intense" events. So the professional or amateur photographer pops up at each of those moments where life leaves its bed of indifference: trips, festivals, baptisms, marriages. Only the funeral—an interesting taboo that we will deal with soon—remains inviolate.

The passions of love charge the photograph with a quasi-mystical presence. The exchange of photos enters into the heart of the ritual of lovers who are united in body or, failing that, in soul. The photo received becomes a thing of adoration as well as possession. The photo given is offered for worship at the same time as appropriation. The exchange of images magically accomplishes the exchange of individualities where each becomes at once the idol and slave of the other, which we call love.

Taking possession, abandoning oneself. Here these terms are rhetorical. But new light is shed on them if we consider extreme cases where the photograph, integrating itself in occult practices, literally becomes a real presence, an object of possession or bewitchment.

Almost from the time of its birth, in 1861, photography has been pressed into the service of occultism, that is, a "digest" of beliefs and practices including spiritualism, clairvoyance, palmistry, and the medicine of quacks, as well as diverse religions and esoteric philosophies.

Healers, sorcerers, and seers, who until that time worked on figurines or mental representations, from then on have used photography. They treat and heal through photographs, they locate a child or a spouse who has disappeared through photographs, they cast a spell or a charm; evil spells of bewitchment are performed on photographs and these are still (and even more and more frequently) practiced, perhaps thanks to photography itself. In other words, the photograph is, in the strict sense of the term, *a real presence* of the person represented; we can read his soul there, his illness, his destiny. Better yet: an action is possible, through the photograph and upon it.

If you can possess through a photo, it is obviously the case that the photo can possess you. The expressions "*to take* a photo" and "to have one's photo *taken*," do they not betray a confused belief in this power?

The fear of this evil possession, still evident some years

ago in China and in numerous archaic cultures, is undoubtedly unconscious for us. It is perhaps no less unconsciously conjured up for us by the restitutive expression "Watch the birdy." The psychosis of espionage brings this fear back to the surface; photographic taboos rapidly go beyond the security objectives that had determined them; one can see everything in a certain foreign city, but one cannot take photographs. An evil hatred surrounds the person taking photographs, even if the latter has only "taken" a wall. He has stripped it of a vital and secret substance, he has taken possession of a power.

Furthermore, it is perhaps not so much their faces as their expressions that the uneducated or the accused hide when they refuse to be photographed. Théophile Pathé cites the case, already cinematographic, of witnesses to a villainous crime, who, having accused one of their acquaintances, subsequently became troubled before the Pathé-Journal camera.[13] Photography can also be endowed with a visionary genius that opens onto the invisible. What we call *photogénie* is only the embryo of a mythical clairvoyance that fixes on film not only the materialized ectoplasms of spiritualist seances,[14] but specters invisible to the human eye. Since 1861, when the Philadelphia photographer Mummler invented "spirit photography"[15]—in other words, superimposition— photos of phantom or divine beings in real landscapes have circulated in occultist and related milieus.

These photographs are, of course, accompanied by stories, always similar ones, that claim to establish their authenticity. Taken by the spectacle of the ruins of an ancient city in Asia Minor, a tourist takes a snapshot. Developing it, he discovers to his amazement three ancient Magi, of great stature, with Assyrian beards, translucent in front of the stones of a defunct temple. We have ourselves witnessed the spontaneous genesis and spread of such legends: a relative showed us a photo taken in a deserted place that revealed a huge smiling face of the prophet. The weekly *Match*, for its part, was able to reproduce, without denouncing it as a hoax, a photograph of the Korean sky with the gigantic face of a Christ superimposed on some bombers in flight.

Photography covers so vast a register, it satisfies needs that are so obviously affective, and these needs are so extensive,[16] that its uses—from the photo-presence and the photo-souvenir to the extrasensory photo—cannot be considered as simple epiphenomena of an essential role, that of archival documentation or scientific knowledge. What, then, is the function of the photo? Multiform and always, in the last instance, indefinable. To be framed, stuck in albums, slipped into a wallet, looked at, loved, kissed? All of that, without doubt. It begins with moral presence; it goes as far as bewitchment and spiritualist presence. Between these two poles, the photo is amulet, fetish. Fetish, souvenir, mute presence, the photo substitutes itself or competes with relics, faded flowers, treasured handkerchiefs, locks of hair, tiny objects, trinkets, miniature Eiffel Towers and St. Mark's Squares. Everywhere, placed on furniture, hung on or stuck to walls, the photograph and the postcard reign over a court of trivial knickknacks, the rear guard of remembrance, combatants of time fighting oblivion and death with their remnants of living presence.

Where does this role come from? Not, evidently, from any property particular to wet collodion, gelatino-bromide, or cellulose acetate, but from what we ourselves place there. Here it is a question of Copernicizing our approach: the properties that seem to belong to the photo are the properties of our mind[17] that have fixed themselves there and that it sends back to us. Instead of searching in the photographic thing for the so obviously and profoundly human quality of *photogénie*, we must come back to man. The richness of the photograph is in fact all that is not there, but that we project or fix onto it.

Everything tells us that the human mind, soul, and heart are profoundly, naturally, unconsciously engaged in the photograph. It is as if this *material* image had a *mental* quality.

In certain cases, it is as if the photo reveals a quality lacking in the original, *the quality of the double. It is at this now radical level of the double and the mental image that we must try to grasp* photogénie.

The Image and the Double

The mental image is an "essential structure of consciousness . . . a mental function."[18] We cannot dissociate it from the presence of the world in man, from the presence of man in the world. The image is their reciprocal medium. But at the same time, the image is only a double, a reflection—that is, an absence. Sartre says that "the essential characteristic of the mental image is a certain way that the object has of being absent even in the midst of its presence." *Let us immediately add the converse:* of being present even in the midst of its absence. As Sartre himself says, "The original incarnates itself, it enters the image." The image is a lived presence and a real absence, a presence-absence.

Archaic peoples, like children, are not at first conscious of the absence of the object and believe in the reality of their dreams as much as in the reality of their daily lives. This is because the image can present all the characteristics of real life, including objectivity. Sartre cites a text by Leroy that shows us that an image, even recognized as a mental vision, can present perfectly objective characteristics: "When I was studying anatomy . . . [l]ying in my bed with closed eyes I would see most vividly and with *complete objectivity* the preparation on which I had worked during the day." Moreover, this objective image can possess a quality of life that the original does not have. Let us complete the quotation: "The resemblance seemed perfect, *the impression of reality* and, if I may say so, of *intense life* which emanated from it was perhaps even deeper than I experienced when facing the real object."[19]

A subjective magnification can thus grow out of simple

objective representation. Let us go further: here subjective magnification is a function of the objectivity of the image, that is, of its apparent material exteriority.

One same movement correlatively heightens the subjective value and the objective truth of the image, to the point of an extreme "objectivity-subjectivity," or hallucination. This movement valorizes the image, which can seem animated with a life more intense or more profound than reality, and even, on the brink of hallucination, in possession of a supernatural life. Then a force as powerful as death radiates from it, sometimes a Proustian power of time recovered, sometimes a spiritualist power. It is as if in man the need that battles against the erosion of time fixes itself in a privileged manner upon the image.

This movement that valorizes the image at the same time pushes it toward the exterior and tends to give it body, depth, autonomy. This involves one particular aspect of a fundamental human process, which is projection or alienation. As Quercy adeptly puts it, "As soon as we have created them, our psychic states are always more or less strange to us. In these so-called subjective states, the subject finds within himself objects. . . . Ideas, memories, concepts, numbers, images, feelings, are subject in us . . . to what the Germans call an *Entfremdung*, an alienation. And if normally only some of our states, called perceptions, are projected into space, this maximum objectivation can, it seems, be generalized to all psychic objects."[20] In the course of this work, we will use almost interchangeably the notion of alienation, with its Hegelo-Marxist ancestry, and that of projection, with its psychoanalytic derivation. One better conveys the nascent movement; the other, the objective concretization of psychic processes.

The more powerful the subjective need, the more the image upon which it fixes itself tends to be projected, alienated, objectivized, hallucinated, fetishized (as many verbs as punctuate the process), the more this image, in spite of and because of its apparent objectivity, is rich in this need to the point of acquiring a surreal character.

In fact, at the hallucinatory encounter of the greatest subjectivity and the greatest objectivity, at the intersection of the greatest alienation and the greatest need, there is the *double*, the image-specter of man. This image is projected, alienated, objectivized to such a degree that it appears as an autonomous specter, endowed with an absolute reality. This absolute reality is at the same time an absolute superreality: the double is the focal point of all the needs of the individual, as if they were realized there, especially his most madly subjective need: immortality.[21]

The double is effectively this fundamental image of man, preceding his intimate awareness of himself, recognized in the reflection or the shadow, projected in the dream, the hallucination, as in painted or sculpted representations, fetishized and magnified in beliefs in the afterlife, cults, and religions.

Our double can appear to us in those Hoffmanesque or Dostoyevskian visions clinically described under the name of autoscopy or heautoscopy. The vision of the double, Dr. Fretet tells us, "is an experience within the reach of everyone." L'Hermitte had the very great distinction of underlining the fact that each of us is "capable, to a greater or lesser degree, of seeing his double."[22] He recognized the anthropological root of the double, "the very vivid experience of one's self."[23] Between the pathological and the normal, the difference is, as always, in the degree of alienation. It is reduced even further when we consider not only our civilization alone, but its origins.

The *double* is effectively universal in archaic humanity. It is perhaps even the single great universal human myth. An experienced myth: its presence, its existence leave no doubt. It is seen in the reflection, the shadow, felt and divined in the wind and in nature, seen also in dreams. Each person lives accompanied by his own double. Not so much a true copy, yet more still than an *alter ego*: an *ego alter*, an other self.

Other and superior, the double possesses magical force. It breaks away from the man who sleeps to go and live the literally surreal life of dreams. In the man who is awake, the double can distance itself, carry out murders and heroic deeds. The archaic person is literally *doubled* (this term is also to be understood in its colloquial sense) throughout his life, to finally be left, as remains, a corpse, upon his death. Once the flesh is destroyed, the decomposition complete, the double frees itself definitively to become a specter, *a ghost*, a spirit. Then, holding man's *amortality*, it possesses a power so grandiose that death changes it to become a god. The dead are already gods and the gods are descended from the dead, that is, from our double, that is, from our shadow, *that is, in the final analysis, from the projection of human individuality into an image that has become external to it.*

In this fundamental image of himself, man has projected all his desires and fears, likewise his spitefulness and goodness, his "superego" and his "ego." When, with evolution, the moral dualism of good and evil emerges and develops, the double (or what remains of it in folklore or hallucinations) is the carrier, sometimes of good (the guardian angel) or, more often, of all evil powers (the ghost).

Before projecting his terrors there, man first of all fixed upon the double all his life ambitions—ubiquity, the power of metamorphoses, magical omnipotence—and the fundamental ambition concerning his death: immortality. He put all his strength there, the best and worst that he has not been able to actualize, all the still-foolish powers of his being. The double is his image, at once accurate and radiating with an aura that goes beyond him—his myth. In a reciprocal way, the primary and original presence of the double, at the most remote threshold of humanity that we can consider, is the first and indisputable sign of the affirmation of human individuality—the fantastic outline of the construction of man by man.

Man's double is the model for innumerable doubles

attached to all living or inanimate things. At the most archaic level, the kingdom of the dead is a universe of doubles that copies the universe of the living in every way. Objects, food, habitat, hunting, passions of the dead are exactly the same as in life, although different in their superior status of double.

The quality of the double can therefore be projected onto all things. It is projected, in another sense, no longer only in spontaneously alienated mental images (hallucinations), but also in and upon images or material forms. It is one of the first manifestations of humanity, this projection of material images—drawings, engravings, paintings, sculptures—through the hand of the artisan. This is anachronistically and improperly called "prehistoric art."

Ever since the origins of graphic or sculpted representation, there appears, at the same time as a tendency toward distortion and the fantastic, a *realist tendency based on faithful outlining and truthfulness of forms*. Les Combarelles, Lascaux, Altamira have preserved the evidence for us. These original and astonishing cave daguerreotypes, played, in magical rites practiced for hunting or fertility, the role of mediating *doubles* that permitted action upon the originals. These realist images are effectively doubles, from the family of the subjective-objective mental image, no longer projected in a hallucinatory fashion, but by the work of the hand. Subsequently, the realist tradition reappears in the paintings and statuettes of cults, offering to prayer or adoration the image that fixes the presence of the god. Still later, *realist* art, *heir of the double*, that is, of the objective mental image, is established through the classicists and the naturalists. Realist art tends toward imitation that is sometimes meticulously detailed and, at its extreme, quasi-photographic (the word should be remembered), sometimes typological or synthetic. Certainly its meanings have evolved since the magic of the caves of Aurignac; artistic realism has developed over several centuries according to complex requirements—through which reality is enriched by the image and the image is enriched by reality. Nevertheless, in the same way that the function of art is not only as a scientific inventory of reality, so *realism is not only the real but the image of the real*. It is precisely on this account that it possesses a particular quality that we call aesthetic, which has the same origin as the quality of the double. Flaubert knew "that it is less a question of seeing things than of representing them to ourselves,"[24] Baudelaire that "remembrance is the great criterion of art," in other words, that the aesthetic of *the objective image tries to revive within itself all the qualities specific to the mental image*.

There is more to this: the simple material image, physically produced by thinking and what we call *reflection*, possesses the same quality. For archaic peoples, it is the double itself that is present in the reflection in the water or the mirror. The universal magic of the mirror, which we have studied elsewhere, is nothing other than that of the double. Numerous superstitions still testify to this: broken mirrors (warning signs of death or luck that the spirit world sends us), veiled mirrors (which prevent the dead person's double from escaping), and so on. For us, used to our mirrors, surrounded by mirrors, their strangeness wears off through everyday use, much as the presence of the double has itself faded from our life. Nevertheless, our image sometimes catches a charming or vaguely puzzled look, a friendly or idiotic smile. We need great sorrow, great shock, misfortune, to be astonished for any length of time by a strange, distraught face that is our own. We need to be caught by a mirror at night for our own phantom to detach itself suddenly, as a stranger, almost an enemy.

As much and even more than in the reflection, the double is localized in these natural and impalpable forms that constitute the shadow. The shadow, which always follows us around, manifests the obvious externality of the double at the same time as its everyday and permanent presence. At night when there is only shadow, curled up in his sleep, man loses his shadow, and it possesses him. The fantastic reigns. Death is like night: it liberates shadows. The dead do not have shadows, they are shadows: we call them that.

Certainly the decline of the double has nowadays reduced the tricks played by the shadow. There remain, nevertheless, those depositories of magic that are folklore, occultism, and art. There remains, in our childhood development, a stage of fascination with shadows, and our parents' hands do their best to represent wolves and rabbits on our walls. There remains the charm of shadow theaters, known to the Far East. There remain the terror and anguish that the shadow can arouse—and that the cinema has admirably been able to exploit, in the same way that it has been able to make good use of the charm of the mirror.[25]

In its decline, the double can both become diabolical—to bear, like the portrait of Dorian Gray, the weight of our hideousness—and bring back the anguish of death that it originally drove away. The radiant double, the incorruptible body of immortality, like that of Christ at Emmaus in the past, is today confronted with the Hoffmanesque specter that heralds the dreadful hour of truth.

Successive layers of beliefs have been superimposed and mixed in the double. From the time of Homeric Greece, the double has just as well, and even simultaneously, brought anguish or deliverance, victory over death or the victory of death. *This quality of debasement or enhancement, born from doubling, can be atrophied or rendered dormant because the double is itself atrophied and dormant; it is no less powerfully present in every being, every thing, in the universe itself, once they are seen through the mirror, the reflection or memory. The mental image and the material image potentially enhance or debase the reality they present to our view; they radiate fatality or hope, nothingness or transcendence, amortality or death.*

The unreal world of doubles is a gigantic image of mundane life. The world of images constantly doubles life. The image and the double are reciprocally models of one another. The double possesses the alienated quality of the image-memory. The image-memory possesses the nascent quality of the double. A veritable dialectic links them. *A psychological power, a projective one, creates a double of everything to make it blossom into the imaginary. An imaginary power doubles everything in psychological projection.*

The double and the image must be considered as the two poles of one reality. *The image possesses the magical quality of the double, but interiorized, nascent, subjectivized. The double possesses the psychological, affective quality of the image, but alienated and magical.* Magic, we will soon have the opportunity to see, is nothing other than the reifying and fetishistic alienation of subjective phenomena. Magic, from this point of view, is the image considered literally as presence and afterlife.

The total alienation of the human *being* into its double constitutes one of the two foundations of magic (we will see the other appear with the metamorphosis of the cinematograph into cinema). If its reign has come to an end, the double still lurks, as we have said, in the ghosts of folklore, the spiritualist astral body, and literary phantoms. It awakens each time we sleep. It springs up in hallucinations, where we also believe these images that are in us to be external. The double is much more than a fantasy from the origins of humankind. It wanders around us and imposes its presence upon our slightest relaxation, at our first terror, in our supreme fervor.

So, at one pole, the magical double. At the other pole, there is the image-emotion, pleasure, curiosity, reverie, vague sentiment. The double dissolves into attractive reflection, entertaining shadow, fond contemplation.

Between these two poles lies a syncretic, fluid zone that we call the domain of sentiment, of the soul or the heart. The germ of magic is there insofar as the image is presence and, what is more, charged with a *latent* quality of time recovered. But this magic is only in a nascent state and at the same time, often, only in a state of decline. For it is enveloped, broken up, stopped short in its place by a lucid consciousness. It is internalized as sentiment. In this intermediate zone, so important in our evolved civilizations, ancient magic is ceaselessly reduced to sentiment or the aesthetic; new feeling, in its youthful impetuosity, ceaselessly tends to alienate itself into magic, but without completely succeeding.

All that is image tends in one sense to become affective, and all that is affective tends to become magic. In another sense, all that is magic tends to become affective. We can now connect the photograph and the cinematograph, or rather their common photogenic quality, to this "fundamental and instinctive urge to create images in living reality [that] goes all the way back to Adam" that Martin Quigley Jr. evoked.[26]

The photograph is a physical image, but rich in the richest psychological quality. If this quality is projected in the photograph in a particularly clear way, that is because of the very nature of photography, a mixture of reflection and shadow. Photography, in color at least, is pure reflection, analogous to that of the mirror. And precisely, insofar as it lacks color, it is a system of shadows. We can already apply to the photo Michotte's essential observation: "The things that we see there are . . . produced for the most part by the obscure portions of the image, by the *shadows*, and we could even say that the more the latter are opaque, the more the objects appear massive. The great bands of light, on the contrary, correspond to the colorless background of thin air. . . . The shadows . . . *appear to be the proper color of the objects*. . . . The dark parts are . . . constitutive of corporeal objects."[27]

Our photographic perception immediately corporealizes shadows: an impression of reality emerges from the shadows. Would this singular fact have been possible if there was not beforehand in the human mind a fundamental tendency to give body to shadows that has led to the belief in these doubtlessly immaterial but corporeal shadows that are specters and phantoms?

The art of the photo—by which we understand not only that of "artists" working in the genre but also the popular art of weekends, vacations, and holidays—reveals through its very aesthetic the affective value that is attached *to the shadow*. It is clear that the framing, the shooting angle, the composition, and so on, are also key elements of the art of the photo. But above all else, what gets called a "beautiful" photo or a beautiful postcard? What are the amateurs at the seaside or the mountains looking for? Never-ending (for us blasé people) backlighting, vivid oppositions of shadows on light backgrounds; or else, on the contrary, the capture of a body, a face splashed with sunshine, devoid of shadows. All the formulas, the tricks—the Vulgate of photography—tend to exaggerate the shadow, to offer it to be seen, or, on the contrary, to exclude it, to make it vanish and make a no less strange shadowless universe appear. At any rate, it is the double that we sense, whether in the universe where we let shadows speak or in the universe that knows nothing of shadows. In other words, art, whose function is to further enrich the affective power of the image (or to enrich the affective power of the real through the image), shows us that one of the moving qualities of the photo is connected to a latent quality of the double.[28] A halo of fantasy surrounds the art of photography. It accentuates the latent element of the fantastic implied in the very objectivity of the image. In truth, we have, before the photo, the impression of contemplating an *analogon*, an *eidolon* that lacks only movement. In fact, it is a mixture of reflection and shadow games that we endow with corporeality and soul, by infecting them with the virus of presence. But let us not yet tackle the problem head-on. What is important is to situate what we examined at the beginning of this chapter: *photography covers the entire anthropological field, which begins with remembrance and ends*

with the phantom because it brings about the conjunction of simul-
taneously related and different qualities of the mental image, the
reflection, and the shadow.

Whence in the first place its admirable aptitude for concretizing memory: better still, for becoming identified with
it, as those family photos and travel postcards, elliptically
but rightly named "souvenirs," tell us. Photography em-
balms time, as André Bazin says in the only genuine and
profound study devoted to the "ontology of the photographic image."[29]

Moreover, the photo can eventually claim to be "truer than
nature," richer than life itself (tourist photos, photogenic faces
and things, artistic photos). Center of small intimate or family rituals, it allows itself to be enveloped, integrated into
the affective-magical zone of everyday fetishizations, amulets, lucky charms. It is an object of worship in the inner
chapels of dream and desire. It accompanies feeling. It finally moves on to the realm of the double in the strict sense
when it gets taken up by occult practices, where archaic magic
is transmitted, consolidated whole, into a secret, permanent
science, with multiple branches. The photograph plays precisely the role of substitute, anchor point, or field of influence of the double. It enables charitable maneuvers as it
does the worst of evil spells. It is enchanted. Ultimately, anything could happen as in the *Mystères du métro* by J. Prévert
and Ribemont-Dessaigne, where the photo sucks in the living to make ghosts of them. It knows no borders between
life and death. Extrasensory, it opens onto the invisible.

An extraordinary anthropological coincidence: technique
of a technical world, physicochemical reproduction of things,
product of one particular civilization, the photograph looks
like the most spontaneous and universal of mental products.
It contains the genes of the image (the mental image) and of
myth (the double), or, if we prefer, it is image and myth in a
nascent state.

But its principal field of influence is, in our modern cultures, that intermediate magico-affective zone where what we call the soul reigns. The two catchphrases of photography are soul words. *Smile*—show your soul through the window of your face; soft, tender, impalpable, trembling, frightened by the slightest thing. And *Watch the birdy*—a strange expression that is perhaps more than a gimmick to attract the attention of children, but (rather) a naive exorcism, a magical restitution that responds to the atrophied fear of being caught.

The affective identification of the bird with the soul is universal. The soul escapes from the dead in the form of a bird in certain African cultures, and that great soul that is the Holy Spirit is incarnated in a bird. "Watch the birdy," then, is addressed to the soul: it will be taken from you but will be liberated and will gently fly away.

Photography transmits all these powers to the cinematograph under the generic name of *photogénie*. And now we can put forward a preliminary definition. *Photogénie is that complex and unique quality of the shadow, of reflection and the double, that allows the affective powers proper to the mental image to fix themselves on the image that arises from photographic reproduction.* Another proposed definition: *photogénie is what results (a) from the transfer onto the photographic image of qualities proper to the mental image, (b) from the involvement of the characteristics of shadow and reflection in the very nature of photographic doubling.*

This *photogénie*, which makes us *look at* the photo rather than use it, has it not played its role in the movement that directed the cinematograph toward spectacle?

Genes and Genius of the Cinematograph

The cinematograph is heir to *photogénie* and at the same time transforms it. Projection offers an image that can expand to the dimensions of a room, while the photo has been able to reduce itself to the size of an individual pocket. The photo cannot dissociate its image from its paper or cardboard material backing. The image projected on the screen is dematerialized, impalpable, fleeting. The photo is, above all, adapted to private use and appropriation. The cinematograph is, above all, adapted to collective spectacle. So most of the fetishizations resulting from private use and appropriation of the photo atrophy or disappear. Thus, for example, there is no cinematic equivalent of the photo that one keeps on oneself or has in a frame at home. Admittedly, 8 mm film permits the affective use of the film souvenir, a thousand times more moving than the photo souvenir. But the film image presents neither that fixed and permanent localization nor that materiality that permits the affective crystallization onto an object, that is to say, to be precise, fetishism. So cinematic fetishisms are forced to pass through the medium of photography (photos of stars) or of writing (autographs).

However, certain phenomena of photographic magic find their cinematic application. The cinematic image cannot be used for bewitchment, but that which in the cinematograph is material and individualized (that is, not the spectacle, but the camera and the projector) can elicit the fear of bewitchment. Iranian nomads protest before the camera, "Why have I been photographed?" and the word betrays the affective equivalence of cinematic and photographic powers. Chinese townspeople, still some twenty years ago, feared their souls would be stolen away. Archaic or naive peoples consider those who show films as "great magicians." It was while crying, "Into the fire, sorcery," that the peasants of Nizhni Novgorod set fire to the Lumière projection booth in 1898. In ancient civilizations and the archaic populations of the five continents, the spread of the cinematograph effectively appeared as a magical phenomenon.

Some years later, in an interview with *Film*, Colonel March- and and General Galliéni took pleasure in contemplating the "pacifying" role of the cinema in the colonies, "which instantly gives its possessors the reputation of sorcerers." At the dinner of the Chambre syndicale de la cinématographie, on March 26, 1914, Monsieur Demaria recalled the "salutory terror" elicited by films projected the year before at the palace of the sultan of Morocco. In short, if the cinematograph was not seriously used by spiritualism, it at least transformed itself into cinema by utilizing spirit photography's trickery.

All the latent affective and magical powers are thus just as present in cinematography as in photography. But the photographic image was adapted to individual particularities. Unlike the photo addict, the film addict cannot consider himself the owner of the image. The cinematograph *is thus purified*, in comparison to photography, of numerous fixations stemming from private appropriation.

Projection and animation jointly accentuate the qualities of shadow and light involved in the photographic image. If the screen image has become impalpable, immaterial, it has, at the same time, acquired an increased corporeality (thanks to movement, as we shall see). The phenomenon, already photographic, of the corporealization of shadows is amplified accordingly. Michotte, in the article previously cited, has drawn attention to this paradox: "We project on the screen no more than flecks of light, the dark parts having to be considered, from the physical point of view, as a sort of negative, corresponding to those regions of the object that do not stimulate the retina. However, it is exactly the inverse that is produced in the perceptive field (of the spectator)."

Cinematographic vision takes shape from the shadows that move on the screen. The substantialization is therefore directly connected to the density or, rather, the a-density of nonbeing, of the great negative emptiness of the shadow. If we add that the conditions of darkness, favorable to projection, are correlatively favorable to the magic of the shadow at the same time as to a certain para-oneiric relaxation, we must note that the cinematograph is much more marked by the quality of the shadow than is photography. At least it was so up until the arrival of color, and since then, it still hesitates between using shadow and pure reflection. Perhaps, let us say even without doubt, the quality of reflection will finally eat away that of the shadow. But despite the enrichment that color brings, the resistance of black and white is significant. Moreover, color cinema and black-and-white cinema are as much isotopes as isomers of one another. In view, then, of its chromatic possibilities, the cinematograph became part of the lineage of shadow spectacles, from the Javanese Wayang to Robertson (1763–1837). Now we can better grasp the relationship indicated above: from cavern to cavern, from the caves of Java, those of the Hellenic mysteries, the mythical cave of Plato, up to the movie theaters, the fundamental shadows of the universe of doubles have been found lively and fascinating.

We understand that even before 1914, a particular shadow technique appeared and took on the eloquent name of photography. Like the art of the still photo, that of animated photography deals with, accentuates, and exaggerates shadow and light, but this time in accordance with increased means, artifice, and systematization.[30] The cameraman filters, channels, or casts shadows and light in order to charge the image with maximum affective powers: "No horror can be so horrible, no beauty so enchanting, if really seen, as the horror or enchantment suggested by its shadow."[31] Conversely, the cameraman can, in eliminating all traces of shadows, make radiant the soul and the spirituality of faces. At one extreme, the shadow can even be substituted for actors and play a primary role in films.[32] At the other extreme, there suddenly appears the image of a universe that has lost its shadows and that, by that very loss, equally possesses the qualitative power of the double. Color, without changing the aesthetic nature of the image, orients it in a different direction: the quality of reflection becomes dominant. The cinema gains in enchantment, but loses in charm.

Finally, animation brings to light phenomena that were embryonic or even unknown in photography. Cinematographic vision of oneself is much more moving and rich than photographic self-contemplation. Epstein said: "Is it not worthy of attention that on the screen no one resembles himself? That on the screen nothing resembles itself?" The same remark has already been made about hearing recordings of our own voices, always strange, that is, semiforeign. We are in fact gripped by the profound, contradictory feeling of our resemblance and our difference. We appear at the same time outside and identical to ourselves, me and not-me, that is, in the end, *ego alter*. "Whether for better or worse, the cinematograph, in its recording and reproduction of a subject, always transforms it, re-creates it as *a second personality, whose appearance can trouble one's consciousness to the point of leading it to ask: Who am I? Where is my true identity?*"[33]

It happens that the double feeling of alterity and identity can be clearly perceptible, as in the attitude of the Iranian nomad who sees himself for the first time on the screen. He gets up and waves, exclaiming, "Look everyone, here I am." In the space of an instant, from the greeting to the exclamation "here I am," he has managed to be astonished by his alien double, admire it, and at once proudly assimilate it. We are already able to divine this sentiment in the surprise and exclamations with which we greet our image on the screen. The first sign of doubling is indeed reacting, however slightly, to ourselves. Most often, we laugh, and the laughter indicates more than surprise. It is the polyvalent reaction of emotion. It can successively or at the same time signify childlike wonder, embarrassment, concealed shame, the sudden feeling of our own ridiculousness. Pride and shame, shame about this pride, irony about our candid expression of wonder; in our auto-cinematographic laughter there is a complex of astonishment, admiration, embarrassment, strangeness.

Sometimes embarrassment and shame dominate this complex. Epstein once again draws our attention to the fact that the screen reveals the "vulgarity of an attitude, . . . awkwardness of a gesture, . . . shame of a look."[34] We often react, in fact, as if the extrasensory camera were able to tear off our socialized mask and uncover, before our eyes and those of others, our unavowed soul. Is this not demonstrated by the fact that, as soon as we are called before a photographic or film camera, we "pose," that is, adjust a mask, our most hypocritical mask: a smile or a look of dignity?

Those pompous attitudes we assume in the cardboard cabins of fairground stalls, those triumphant poses of urchins in Teheran, their foot on a friend on the ground, illustrate our desire to display ourselves in an image inflated to the proportions of our vanity. The pose equally tries to mask the fear and intimidation that arise due to the camera. It is the expression of this difficulty, this quasi-impossibility of being natural before an extrasensory gaze. (We have already cited the case where two witnesses for the prosecution were suddenly afraid to repeat their accusation before the Pathé-Journal cameraman.) Monsieur Caffary tells us that Iranian nomads, during the projection of a film that portrays them, straighten their clothing, take on a dignified pose. Is this not the pose that they were unable to assume when they were being filmed? At the same time as trying to make up for an awkwardness or a sloppiness, is it not their soul that they are attempting to disguise? Ultimately, have they not felt, just a little, the disquieting presence of the double, which is what shames them?

For my part, I have strongly felt, on hearing myself on the radio and seeing myself on the screen, a brief, shameful embarrassment, as if my little Mr. Hyde had suddenly appeared before me. It is likely that in such cases, a kind of auto-ghostliness, related to autoscopic hallucination, is awakened. Of course the difference is essential: the hallucinatory double, although at the limit of normal perceptive phenomena, is seen by a subject in a neurotic state. On the other hand, the auto-spectator sees himself in a psychologically normal state. So his double cannot cinematographically display its strangeness, its fantastic side, its fatality. It very rarely provokes horror and only sometimes sorrow, as in those cases Epstein cites, like the one of Mary Pickford, who, "incredulous, disappointed, scandalized . . . cried when she saw herself on the screen for the first time."[35] There is no equivalence, then, between auto-cinematographic experience and autoscopic vision, but the first can present the nascent characteristics of the second.

Indeed, it is a double in the nascent state that reveals itself to our eyes on the screen; that is why, more than the double of hallucination, it is close to the double the child discovers in the mirror or the archaic person in the reflection—strange and familiar, affable and protective, already slightly enhanced but not yet transcendent. That is why our ordinary reactions are richer in pleasure and wonder than in embarrassment and shame within the affective complex where the surrealistic surprise and disturbance of the discovery of the double are mixed with the realistic surprise and disturbance of the discovery of oneself. That is why the people filmed in the street by Lumière cameramen rushed to the projection rooms.

Another type of auto-cinematographic experience is that of the star. The star has two lives: that of his films and his real life. In fact, the first tends to command or take over the other one. It is as though stars, in their everyday life—and we will come back to this—are condemned to ape their cinema life devoted to love, dramas, holidays, games, and adventures.[36] Their contracts even oblige them to imitate their screen personae, as if the latter possess the authenticity. The stars then feel themselves reduced to the state of specters who outwit boredom through "parties" and diversions, while their true human substance is sucked out by the camera; whence the spleen, depressions, blues that characterize Hollywood.

"It is you who are nothing but a shade; it is the phantom's living lips that fondly smile at the love for him revealed [in the fan letter]," Adams, the star hero of René Clair's novel murmurs to himself.[37]

The idea often comes up in Ramón Gomez de la Serna's *Movieland:* "And the deceitful cocktails . . . are poured profusely every day . . . to excite all those who have concluded that they are becoming ghosts and are driven to despair." A star says: "Screen figures! . . . I feel as though I were doomed to be a shadow without a soul." And again: "'You are not interested in the hereafter?' Edna Blake asked Elsa. 'No. Poised as we are, half way between shadow and reality, we know no hereafter.'"[38]

An admirable reply, which suddenly gives us insight into the profound nature of the cinematograph, like the profound nature of the afterlife: memory, intermediary between shadow and reality. Which also reveals that the *magnification* of the double can devalue our real life. In the apologue of Silenus to Midas, the discourse of Croesus, the myth of the cave, it is we who become ghosts in comparison to ghosts who have ceased to be mortal. In the same way, before the *cinematographic double, charged* with an affective-magical magnification, the flesh-and-blood spectator perhaps feels that he is going to "see the positive proofs of a world whose endless negative he will always resume." In this sense, in Paul Valéry's admirable formulation, the cinematograph "criticizes life."[39]

A hint of reverie, imagination, anticipation, is sometimes enough for the moving cinematic image to be suddenly exalted to the mythic dimensions of the universe of doubles and death. Let us consider the cinema of the future imagined in science fiction. We see the ultimate myth of cinematography take shape, which is at the same time its original myth. *The total cinema*, which catapults into the unfathomable future that which is in embryo in the very nucleus of the image, reveals its latent powers.

The first wave of science fiction begins by conferring all the sensory characteristics on projected images. Aldous Huxley describes, in *Brave New World*, the singing, speaking, synthetic film, in color, stereoscopic, scented. All the spectators' senses are enticed by the "feelies."

This timid science fiction is only one or two steps ahead of CinemaScope. More interesting are the imaginings that utterly get rid of the room and project the cinema into "the beautiful screen that the sky offers us, the night. We look for an inventor who can bring this idea to life."[40] After René Clair, in 1931, Dovzhenko prophesied a cinema without a screen, where the spectator would take part in the film as if he were at the center of the cinematic action.[41] In the meantime, Barjavel imagines the credits for a film of Sinbad the Sailor projected into the sky. The spectators recline in their seats. Waves are born, and die. In the waves a ball swells up, opens, and blossoms into a lotus flower. "At the heart of the flower squats the roc. It rises, spreads its immense wings, and circles the room three times. A tiny man hangs from one of its legs, which are larger than a thousand-year-old oak." Better still, Barjavel describes the telecinema of the future: "Waves will carry the images throughout space. Receiving sets will materialize them at will."[42] And Henry Poulaille: "Tomorrow . . . the image will be before us, woven from threads of luminous rays, without the aid of the screen, staggering."[43]

At this stage of oneiric science fantasy, the world of film has already become, very precisely, the world of spirits or ghosts, much as it appears in a great number of archaic mythologies: an aerial world, which omnipresent spirits navigate. The screen has dissolved into space. Ghosts are everywhere. But let the imagination go even further or, rather, let it rediscover its source, and the ghosts are brought back down to earth. They are among us, corporeal specters, identical to ourselves. It is in its pure archaism, in its chimerical presence in the midst of the real world, that the total cinema finally doubles our universe. The evolution of the cinema will be complete "when it is able to present us with characters in the round, colored and perhaps scented; when these characters free themselves from the screen and from the darkness of the theaters to go and walk in public spaces and the apartments of each and every person"[44]—like the men and women of the Island of Morel, like the lions cinematographico-psychologically projected in Ray Bradbury's all-too-perfect nursery.[45]

This imagining is not random. This is proved by the fact that it is modeled fairly accurately on the mythic archetype that the genius of Villiers de l'Isle Adam was able to dream up, taking off from the inventions of Edison, even before the birth of the Kinetograph. In *Tomorrow's Eve*, the "sorcerer of Menlo Park" creates a perfect copy—except on the level of foolishness, which is the inimitable peculiarity of man—of the superb and foolish Alicia Clary.[46] This radiant double, Hadaly, is of the same essence as the Faustine of Bioy Casares. Within seventy years, dreams that preceded the cinema and the dream of the cinematic end of man meet in the world of doubles. This world rediscovers its original charm and even exalts its essential magical quality: a world of immortality—that is, a world of the dead.

As a little boy said to Max Jacob, "They make the cinema with dead people. They take dead people and make them walk and that's cinema."[47] The dead are incarnated, what is more, naturally, in Barjavel's total cinema. "The ghosts of great men will precede memorial processions. The image of the Bastille will drive each Fourteenth of July back into the heart of Paris. . . . On the battlefields, impalpable Bayards will lead hesitant men to heroic ends."[48]

But we are not yet at the end of our journey. This *doubled world* finds itself trying to absorb the real world. In *Movieland*'s new invention, the spirits of the spectators will be sucked in through the absorbing funnel of the projector of reality.[49] The sleeping bodies remain in the theater, under

the surveillance of police officers. Just as the occultist photograph "drains" the living, the total cinema will draw out
our own double to make it live an organized collective dream.
Morel's invention is still more grandiose. It is to suppress
death that the brilliant Morel has entirely "sucked" the living onto his island, committed, from then on, to eternity.[50]
Total cinema, which finally engulfs humans in its impalpable and concrete, unreal and real substance, in the midst of
tragic, playful, and eternal adventures, merges death and
immortality in the same act.

Morel's invention proposes the final cinematographic
myth: the absorption of man into the universe of doubles
so that—at last—eternity saves him just as he is. This way,
it shows us that if the latent myth of the cinematograph is
immortality, the total cinematograph is itself a variant of
imaginary immortality. Is it not in this common source, the
image, the reflection, the shadow, that the first and ultimate
refuge against death lies?

The Birdy

The image. The Lumière cinematograph carries within it
all the powers that, since time immemorial, men have attrib-
uted to the image. There is, even only in the strict reflection
of nature, something more than nature. The cinematograph
enhances the real, transfigures it without transforming it,
through its own automatic power, which some people have
named *photogénie*, as one could have spoken in the past of
the soporific power of opium. This photogenic power covers the whole field extending from the image to the double,
from subjective emotions to magical alienations. Effectively,
the Lumière cinematograph, limited as it is, is already a
microcosm of total cinema, which is in a sense the complete
resurrection of the universe of doubles. It animates shadows
that bear the magic of immortality as well as the terrors of
death. But, in fact, these tricks and these powers are in a

nascent, embryonic, atrophied, unconscious state. *They are the extreme phenomena of auto-cinematographic vision, of photographic or cinematic occultism, of the mythology of total cinema that allows us to shed light on the undifferentiated complex of normal phenomena.* Reciprocally, normal phenomena—that is, the curiosity and pleasure attached to cinematographic projections precisely intended for this pleasure and curiosity—allow us to divine their magical potentialities. The double is potentially there, invisible on the screen, in a viral state, to use Malraux's word. It needs only the naive look of the archaic person, a little abandon on our part, in order to reveal it.

Photography was already the chemical Saint John the Baptist for a cinematograph that delivered the image from its chains, purified it of the fetishizations into which every encounter between pleasure and private appropriation hardened, and brought it the movement of life. The cinematograph is truly the image in the elementary and anthropological state of the *shadow-reflection*. It revives, in the twentieth century, the originary double. *It is an anthropological marvel, precisely in this capacity to project as spectacle an image perceived as an exact reflection of real life.*

We understand then that all the currents of past inventions were naturally directed toward it. We can get a sense of why it was not necessary to change the device to allow its prodigious future developments. *The cinematograph was a necessary and sufficient machine to give focus to divergent investigations, then to effect its own transformation into cinema.*

It necessarily carried this transformation within itself. For the ciné-eye, the ciné-mirror of Lumière, was only to be a trend, like Vertov's ciné-eye. *The cinematograph was to be only a unique and brief moment of transition when the realist fidelity of reflection and the virulence of human powers of projection were in equilibrium.* Something else had to be born. And this something else was precisely implicated in this force projected in the image and capable of taking it as far as the magic

of immortality. The most astonishing magical-affective complex, enclosed in the image, had to try to free itself, to clear
its own way toward the imaginary. Effectively, the cinematograph changed its form according to an astounding
half-affective, half-magical process. A remarkable thing took
place: "The strange exaltation of the power proper to images in its turn improvised spectacles that were buried away
in the invisible."[51] The birdy, always promised in vain by the
photographer, was about to come out at last.

3 Metamorphosis of the Cinematograph into Cinema

There were investigations not only into the movements of bipeds, quadrupeds, and birds at the origins of the cinematograph, but also into the charm of the image, of the shadow and reflection. This charm takes command of a device essentially destined for spectacle. The flow of inventions that meandered right through the nineteenth century has now found a bed and settles there. The device and the system of projection stabilize. As early as the Exposition of 1900, the cinematograph apparently had at its disposal the technical means necessary to enlarge the image to the dimensions of the giant and even circular screen (the Ciné-cosmorama of Grimoin-Sanson and Baron's Cinématorama), to enrich it with sound (the talking films of Baron in 1898, the Phonorama, the Phono-Cinéma-Théâtre, cinéphonography, and so on), to present it in color—in short, to present a more faithful and more complete reflection of things.[1] But it will set aside these foreseeable developments for several decades in order to effect an unexpected, unbelievable transformation. This evolution—revolution, we will soon call it—involves not the filming device, but, as Arlaud says, the way in which it is used.[2]

Ontogenesis

An extraordinary metamorphosis, which goes, nevertheless, almost unnoticed. For—among other reasons—those who effect the transition from the cinematograph to the cinema are not honorable professionals, certified thinkers, or eminent artists, but bricoleurs, autodidacts, failures, fakes, entertainers. For fifteen years, in making films, they make the cinema, without worrying about art other than as a pompous justification for the curious. The revolution that these anonymous people effect, in isolation and simultaneously, through little tricks, naive ideas, and booby traps, is the fruit of an obscure pressure, quasi-unconscious, but, for this very reason, profound and necessary.

It is in fact impossible to pinpoint the paternity of the cinema to one name, one man, one country: in England, in France, in Italy, in the United States, in Denmark, in Sweden, in Germany, in Russia, everywhere films are produced, almost the same discoveries spring up. As Sadoul has shown, before Griffith and even Porter, Méliès and the English filmmakers at Brighton invent the first techniques. The latter are reinvented on multiple occasions. Montage is the product of twenty-five years of inventions and reinventions, audacity and luck, in order at last to find its master, Eisenstein.

Sparked off by bricoleurs, the metamorphosis blossoms after the 1914–18 war with expressionism and the German *Kammerspiel* and, in 1925, the year of *Battleship Potemkin*, the ascendance of Soviet film.

But as soon as it passes from the entertainer's hands of Méliès, the Brighton photographers, and directors like Zecca into the enclave reserved to artists, the cinema, ignored until then, finds itself annexed by the avant-gardes of aesthetics.

Retrospectively, in the same way that we look for ancestors and a lineage for someone elevated, we baptized as art the alchemy of the studio at Montreuil; this art Canudo identified as the seventh, and we forgot its common origins, that is, the nature of the cinema.

Certainly an art was born, but at the same time as an art, much more than an art. To recognize this art, we must consider what precedes, foreshadows, and effects its birth; to understand the cinema, we must follow the transition from the cinematograph to the cinema, without prejudging the intimate or ultimate essence of the total phenomenon, of the *ontogenesis* that occurs.

How does the birth of the cinema come about? One name lets us crystallize the whole mutation: Méliès, that great naive Homer. What kind of mutation is it? Is it the passage from the animated photograph taken from real life to scenes of the spectacular? It is believed we can sum up Méliès's contribution—and Méliès himself believed this—by saying that he launched film "along the path toward theatrical spectacle." But, by its very nature and from its first appearance, the cinematograph was essentially spectacle: it displayed what it shot to spectators, for spectators, and in this way implied the theatricality that it was to subsequently develop with mise-en-scène. Moreover, the first Kinetoscope films were already presenting boxing matches, music hall shows, little playlets. The cinematograph itself, from its first day, showed *l'arroseur arrosé* (the waterer watered). So scenic "spectacularity" appeared at the same time as the cinematograph.

It is true that in inventing the mise-en-scène of cinema, Méliès even more profoundly committed film to the "path toward theatrical spectacle." It is, however, not in theatricality but through it that we must look for the source and the essence of the great mutation.

Special effects and the fantastic are the two faces of the revolution that Méliès brings about. A revolution within the spectacle, but one that transforms it. Moreover, the historians know this. They marvel at the "great Méliès," "whose magic spells actually constituted the germs of the cinema's syntax, language, and means of expression."[3] But if they marvel at it, they are not at all astonished that instead of increasing the realist fidelity of its image by enlarging it (the giant or circular screen), endowing it with sound and color as the Exposition of 1900 heralded, from 1896, the cinematograph involved itself in phantasmagoria. Effectively, the fantastic immediately sprang up from the most realistic of machines, and Méliès's unreality was deployed as flagrantly as was the reality of the Lumière brothers.

Absolute lack of realism (Méliès) answers absolute realism (Lumière). An admirable antithesis that Hegel would have loved, from which the cinema was to be born and developed, the cinema that is a fusion of the Lumière cinematograph and the Méliès fairy play.[4]

The Metamorphosis

In the same year, 1898, in Paris and Brighton, Méliès, with *La caverne maudite (The Cave of the Demons)*, *Rêve d'artiste (The Artist's Dream)*, *Les quatre têtes embarrassantes (The Four Troublesome Heads)*, and *Dédoublement cabalistique (The Triple Lady)*, and G. A. Smith, with *The Corsican Brothers* and *Photographing a Ghost*, introduce the ghost and the double into film by superimposition and double or multiple exposures.

This trick, which Méliès ranked fourth among the various techniques in his major text of 1907, "Cinematographic Views,"[5] immediately inspires imitation, and doubles proliferate on screens: doubles of the dead (ghosts) as of the living, doubles to the power of two in the case of a phantom twin as in *The Corsican Brothers*. Specters spring up in superimposition with disturbing spontaneity as if to inscribe the cinematograph unequivocally in the lineage of the shadow spectacles of Father Kircher and Robertson. Indeed, the magic lantern enlightens us with its magic and illuminates its magic with our understanding. One year after its birth, the cinematograph follows in the footsteps of this "little machine" that delights in skeletons and ghosts and "makes us see in the darkness, on a white wall, a number of hideous specters, in such a way that those who do not know the secret believe that it is done through magical art."[6] So true is this that the shadow, any shadow, immediately summons up fantasy and surreality. The sudden apparition of the ghostly opens up the magic enclosed in the "charm of the image."

The ghost is not a simple efflorescence. It plays a genetic and structural role. It is remarkable that where the genesis of the cinema occurs, in Brighton and in Paris, the double is immediately summoned up, mobilized, and provides the point of departure for one of the key techniques of film: superimposition.[7]

We have given ghostly superimposition and doubling pride of place because they have for us the familiar traits of that "magic" already evoked, but also because they possess the characteristics proper to the new world of the cinema: *they are tricks whose effect is first of all fantastic, but that subsequently go on to become techniques of realist expression*. They integrate in an amalgam where Méliès adds his original formulas to those of the Théâtre Robert-Houdin and the magic lantern. They are part of this systematic insertion of trick effects into the heart of the cinematograph. They are a part of this cluster of illusions that, once the fantastic recedes, will constitute the elementary and essential rhetoric of all film.

In fact, all Méliès's conjuring tricks take root in *key techniques* of the art of film, including, and above all even, the art of documentary and newsreels. Superimposition, the close-up, the fade, the dissolve, are, so to speak, the distilled products of the imaginings of Star Film.[8]

Historians—even the Anglo-Saxons—are aware of the genetic importance of Méliès. But these same historians are like half-dumbfounded, half-shrewd spectators who would have gone backstage to find out how things were done. "Tricks, these are tricks, only tricks." And in turn addressing the public, they solemnly announce: "These little magic formulas actually constitute the germs of the syntax, language, and means of expression which enabled the cinema to translate the reality of life."

They know that these tricks changed the soul of the cinema, but they know nothing of the soul of these "tricks." Sadoul's sentence, cited once again, evades the true question while posing it. How were simple tricks, unbelievable fairy plays, able to play this driving, genetic, and structural role? *Why, in what way*, did they revolutionize the cinematograph? How is it that the father of a new language and art was only an entertainer who hid a pigeon up his sleeve? Why did such small and comical machinations have such great and moving effects? Why does the cinema go by way of these "magic spells" in order to be able "to translate the reality of life"?

We should first of all examine the common nature of Méliès's various tricks. They are those of the theater of fantasy and the magic lantern: although enriched by innovations, they all aim for effects that are precisely magical and fantastic, to use once again the terms associated with these spectacles that preceded the cinema and that have nourished it.

Magical and fantastic, these tricks, like these spectacles, are of the same family as sorcery or occultism. Prestidigitation, like sorcery, produces apparitions, disappearances, and metamorphoses. But the sorcerer is believed to be a sorcerer, whereas the conjurer is known to be a trickster. Conjuring spectacles, like Méliès's tricks, are decadent and fairground offspring in which the fantastic has ceased to be taken literally. The fantastic, nevertheless, constitutes the lifeblood of these spectacles. And, although aestheticized and devalued, it is the magical vision of the world that is perpetuated through them.

We still cannot provide the essential characteristics of this magical vision of the world, for the cinema will illuminate them as they will illuminate it. Let us make it clear in the meantime that we are referring to magic not as an essence, but as a certain stage and certain states of the human mind. If, in order to describe it, we refer to the vision of the archaic world, it is because there alienation is manifest, fetishized. If, furthermore, we grant a preeminence to the archaic vision of *death*, it is because no empirical veneer, none of the sludge of reality, prevents us from considering its fantastic nature.

In the preceding chapter, the study of the image-reflection led us to one of the two poles of magic: the double. It stopped at that moment where the image remains a faithful mirror and is not yet transformed under the flux of desire, of fear, or the dream. Yet the universe of magic is not only populated by shadows and ghosts: it is, in essence, open to all metamorphoses. All that is fantastic comes back finally to the double and to metamorphosis.[9]

In the archaic worldview, all metamorphoses are possible and effective within an immense fluid relationship where living or active things that are not enclosed in the prisons of objectivity and identity bathe. Metamorphosis triumphs over death and becomes renaissance. Death-renaissance is a second immortality, parallel and related to the survival of the double. Doubles move freely in the universe of metamorphoses, and the latter is animated by spirits, that is to say, doubles.

Metamorphoses have remained alive and active in childhood fairy tales, in the tales and fantastic stories of young children, and, on the other hand, in prestidigitation, which, although reduced to exhibition at fairs, is precisely a magical art, not only of transfers from the visible to the invisible and vice versa (apparitions, vanishings), but also, and above all, of transmutations and transformations.

Now, if we go back to Méliès, that is, to the transition from the cinematograph to the cinema, *not only do we find prestidigitation (trick effects) with the resulting fairy play at the origin of his films, but we discover that the first trick, the operative act, even, that initiates the transformation of the cinematograph into cinema is a metamorphosis.*

At the end of 1896 (in October, Sadoul surmises)—that is, scarcely one year after the first presentation of the cinematograph—Méliès, like any Lumière cameraman, films the

Place de l'Opéra. The film gets jammed, then, after a minute, starts running again. In the meantime, the scene has changed; the horse-drawn Madeleine-Bastille trolleybus has given way to a hearse. New pedestrians traverse the field taken in by the camera. Projecting the film, Méliès suddenly sees a trolleybus transformed into a hearse, men changed into women. "The substitution trick had been discovered."[10]

In 1897, the year when "he becomes conscious of his mission," as they say in the naively definitive language that biographers affect,[11] Méliès exploits the process. The first transformations meet with great success *(Le manoir du diable [The Devil's Manor], Le diable au couvent [The Sign of the Cross], Cendrillon [Cinderella], Faust et Marguerite [Faust and Marguerite], Le carrefour de l'opéra, Magie diabolique [Black Art])*. As one "effect leads to another," Méliès seeks and finds new processes, and only then goes on to employ the machinery and prestidigitation of the Théâtre Robert-Houdin and the magic lantern. Still with the aim of creating fantasy, he will invent the lap dissolve and the tracking shot.

There is no doubt about it: the fairy play and the fantastic, the magical vision of the universe, and the technical processes of the cinema merge in their nascent state in the genius of Méliès. More precisely still, metamorphosis was not only chronologically the first effect, but the essential one.

Ten years later and after many many tricks, Méliès still emphasized the fundamental role of metamorphosis in distinguishing films according to two categories, one of composed subjects or genre scenes and the other of *so-called transformation views*. But it is not in the first category that he innovated and became famous. Edison had already dreamed of making film into a sort of mirror of the music hall production. Méliès leaped headfirst through the looking glass held out by Edison and the Lumière brothers and landed in the universe of Lewis Carroll. The great revolution was not only the appearance of the double in the magic mirror of the screen, but also this crossing through the mirror. If origally, essentially, the Lumière cinematograph is doubling, the cinema of Méliès is originally, essentially, metamorphosis. But by the same token, we can grasp the profound continuity at the heart of this profound difference. In the same way that in magical vision there is continuity and syncretic unity from the double to metamorphosis, the dual nature of the cinematographic image already summoned or let us preview the fantastic world of metamorphosis. Whence the almost immediate transition from one to the other. "The magician's wand is in every camera and the eye of Merlin the Magician turned into a lens."[12] Or, rather, the eye of Merlin the Magician only turned into a lens when Méliès the magician's lens turned into Merlin.

The Other Metamorphosis: Time

Tricks, the supernatural, the fantastic, metamorphosis, are so many faces of the same Mélièsian reality that transforms the cinematograph into cinema. But after Méliès, the domain of the fantastic and of the supernatural shrinks: the tricks lose their conjuring powers. And above all, although metamorphosis was the driving force behind the transition, it was not its indispensable means. This revolution that Méliès admirably symbolizes was not the work of Méliès alone and does not end with Méliès alone.

Like their respective political histories, the evolutionary (English) phenomenon and the revolutionary (French) phenomenon confront each other. In the first case, there is a continuum of small qualitative mutations; in the other, a radical transfiguration. But in both cases, as Sadoul has shown, the same techniques emerge.

Once again we note that these discoveries are simultaneous, spontaneous, that is, necessary. We also note that the history of the cinema could possibly have done without

Méliès, but that the magic of metamorphoses, although not necessary, proved at any rate sufficient to create the cinema. On the one hand Méliès, the magician, puts the cinematograph into a hat to pull out the cinema. But on the other hand, in Brighton, brain waves of fantasy are empirically grafted onto film and transform it from within, slowly and imperceptibly. The cinema is produced not only from the action of the magic of metamorphoses, but by undergoing an internal, profound metamorphosis. For us, it is a question of reciprocally illuminating the evolutionary and the revolutionary phenomenon.

The techniques of the cinema—the differentiation of shots according to the distance from the camera to the object, camera movements, use of sets, special lighting effects, fades, dissolves, superimposition, and so on—are joined, or rather combine, and take on their meaning in the supreme technique: *montage*. Our aim here is not to take an inventory or examine, in the manner of a catalog, these techniques or formulas, which have been very well described elsewhere.[13] Moreover, we will have the opportunity to turn our attention to each of them successively. What is important is to bring to light their *revolutionary* and *structural* traits.

Film stops being *an* animated photograph to break up into an infinity of heterogeneous animated photographs or shots. But, at the same time, it becomes a *system* of animated photographs that has acquired new spatial and temporal characteristics.

Time in the cinematograph was precisely real chronological time. The cinema, by contrast, expurgates and breaks up chronology; it puts temporal fragments in harmony and continuity according to a particular rhythm, which is one not of action but of images of action. Montage unites and arranges the discontinuous and heterogeneous succession of shots in a continuum. It is this rhythm that, starting from a temporal series of tiny, chopped-up morsels, *reconstitutes a new, fluid time*.

This fluid time is subject to strange compressions and elongations. It is endowed with several speeds and eventually reverse motion. Films expand and slow down the intense moments that streak across real life like a flash of lightning. "What happens in ten seconds you can hold on the screen for one hundred and twenty seconds," said Epstein. Lovers' looks, catastrophes, collisions, explosions, and other supreme moments tend to bring time to a standstill. By contrast, empty moments, secondary episodes, are compressed to the point of volatilization. Certain special effects related to acceleration even literally represent time's flight: calendar leaves flying away, clock hands spinning around. Moreover, a fundamental technique, the fade, functions to dissolve a great deal of time by implying it, like suspension points, little pearls of time that fall, or rather dark dwarf stars, which compress within them the density of a nebula.

Compression and expansion of time are *general principles and effects of the cinema* that are put into practice even in the speed of shooting the images. Time is literally cheated by what we call accelerated and slow motion. Fast and slow motion are not uniquely destined to render visible and scientifically analyzable what the excess or insufficiency of natural speed kept invisible. Like the superimposition and the fade, they take their place among the *tricks* with fantastic or comic effect and, at the same time, among the elementary techniques that govern the universe of the cinema. They reflect, at the level of recording the image, the great metamorphosis of time by compression and dilation.

This metamorphosis in time entails a metamorphosis of the universe itself, which generally goes by unnoticed, but which fast and slow motion, in their optical exaggeration, render perceptible. In fast motion, the life of flowers is Shakespearean, said Cendrars.[14]

In fact, a page from Epstein admirably expresses it for us. The acceleration of time vivifies and spiritualizes: "Thus, crystals begin to vegetate . . . plants become animals, choose their light and their support, express their vitality in gestures." The slowing down of time mortifies and materializes:

> For example, human appearance finds itself deprived, in good part, of its spirituality. Thought is extinguished from the glance. . . . In gestures, awkwardness—a sign of will, the price of liberty—disappears, absorbed by the infallible grace of animal instinct. The whole of man is no more than a being of smooth muscles, swimming in a dense environment, where deep currents still carry along and fashion this clear descendant of ancient marine animal life, of the mother waters. . . . Slowed down still more, every living substance returns to its fundamental viscosity, lets its basic colloidal nature rise to its surface. . . .
>
> Something whose essence remains completely inaccessible to us is found to be sometimes angel and sometimes beast, sometimes plant and sometimes mineral, according to the conditions of time and space in which it appears.[15]

Thus fast and slow motion, by exaggerating the fundamental fluidity of cinematic time, give rise to a universe that is itself fluid, where everything undergoes metamorphosis.

Can we not assume a kinship between this metamorphosis and Méliès's fantastic metamorphosis?

Cinematic time is not only compressible and expandable. It is reversible. It flows unhindered from the present to the past, often by way of the fade, which then compresses time— no longer time that is passing, but time that has passed. In the same way that it makes us move forward, the long fade to black or dissolve that precedes the coming of memory makes us move back in time. The fade certainly conveys to the spectator "that the pictures shown are not those of real objects but of images of the mind."[16] Effectively, the longer it lasts, the more it gives a visionary character to the process of recollection, analogous in this way to the usual symbolic methods of introducing memory: soft focus, whirlpools, swirls, and the like. But, at the same time as it points to its mental nature, the fade corporealizes vision until the latter achieves the objectivity and actuality of present temporality. Soft focus and fade are at the mental turning point between the present and the past: directly afterward, the past becomes *solid*, present. Thus their function in these cases is to smooth the transition to facilitate a reversal of time that Western minds only cautiously accept. By contrast, Japanese films often evoke the past without transitions: present and past are juxtaposed without a break; they are of the same essence.

The flashback and cutback, with or without fades, show us the normal character, obvious at the cinema, of the insertion of the past into present temporality, and, except for rare exceptions where the memory is kept in soft focus,[17] memories are made present. The past and the present are of the same time.

This time, which makes the past present, conjointly makes the present past: if past and present merge in the cinema, it is also because, as we have already seen, the presence of the image has already, implicitly, the moving character of the past. Time in film is not so much the present as a past-present.

The art of montage culminates precisely in parallel actions, the flashback and cutback, that is, the cocktail of pasts and presents in the one same temporality. Indeed, since *The Power and the Glory*, there have been numerous films beginning with their ending, in a moment of meditation where the whole of the past reemerges, and that exploit the ability of the cinema to play on multiple registers of time (*Le jour se lève [Daybreak]*, *Le diable au corps [The Devil in the Flesh]*, and others).[18]

It is undoubtedly a quality of the cinematic image to actualize the past—to recuperate it, as Étienne Souriau says—better than any other art has been able to do.[19] The idea that the past does not dissolve but takes refuge somewhere is there in every souvenir, as we have seen. Magic gives body to it. This past that flees and remains is the world of doubles: of the dead. Between the subjective quality of the image-memory and the alienated quality of the survival of specters slides a myth that blossoms in the modern science fiction novel, which is the search for lost time. The psychological writer searches for lost time in the depths of his soul, in the mental source of memory. The adventure writer searches for it somewhere in the ethers, and *with a camera*.

Numerous science fiction stories have as their subject *the cinematic recovery of time*, to the point of recapturing an incorruptible fragment of the past. Élie Faure develops an analogous vision when he imagines the inhabitants of a distant planet, living at the time of the crucifixion of Jesus, sending us by missile a film that would make us actual witnesses. This recovery of the fleeting past is of the same essence as the immortality realized by the invention of Morel.[20] At its limit, then, time in the cinema jointly opens onto the magic of the double and that of metamorphoses.

The desire to go back in time made its call heard from the first Lumière sessions in the strangest way. The projectionist's arm spontaneously, unconsciously, finds itself moved, as soon as the screening is over, by an astonishing desire: to show the film backward. Already at the Musée Grevin, Émile Reynaud had amused himself by inverting the movement of the praxinoscope. Already in 1895, Louis Lumière had created the first retroactive film, *La charcuterie mécanique (The Mechanical Butcher)*, in which a pig comes out of a machine that takes in sausages.

Mesguisch tells us how, in the course of a triumphant tour in the United States, before a crowd filled with wonder, he suddenly had the supreme inspiration, the "wait and I'll show you," the height of cinematic exaltation: to show the film backward. Since then the trick has been ceaselessly imitated. Like the myth of the cinematic search for lost time, it exalts and exaggerates what is the very essence of the cinema: the movement in all directions and at different speeds through a time "reduced to the rank of a dimension analogous to [that] of space," where present and past are identical.[21]

Equivocal time: some variations of speed or of movement, and here it is transforming the universe according to the magic of metamorphoses and even going so far as to reverse the course of the world, bringing sausages back to their state of pig. Magical time, in a sense. But, in another sense, *psychological* time, that is, subjective, affective time whose dimensions—past, future, present—are found undifferentiated, in osmosis, as in the human mind, where past memory, the imaginary future, and the lived moment are simultaneously present and merged. This Bergsonian *durée*, this indefinable lived experience—it is the cinema that defines them.

Metamorphosis of Space

At the same time as the metamorphosis of time, the cinema brought about the metamorphosis of space by getting the camera moving and endowing it with ubiquity. The camera leaves its immobility behind with the pan and the tracking shot. The latter, invented at the same time by Promio in Venice, by Méliès in *L'homme à la tête de caoutchouc (The Man with the Rubber Head)*, and by the Brighton filmmakers, is brought up to date by Pastrone in 1913 in *Cabiria*. The camera loses its rigidity, becomes progressively more flexible to the point of the extreme acrobatic agility of Murnau's *The Last Laugh* (1925). At the same time as these continuous movements take place, the camera leaps in discontinuous bounds, or changes of angle, whether on the same object or moving from object to object (long shot, medium shot, medium close shot, close-up, shot/reaction shot, and so on).

From now on it goes everywhere, perches and nestles where no human eye has ever been able to perch or nestle. It leaps from the cabin of the truck onto the wheel spinning around, from the wheel to the rock that overhangs the road; it takes flight, falls back to ground level, and goes under a locomotive. It can position itself in any angle of one same place, in no matter what point in space. It even breaks through the infinite ocean of the interstellar night, as in the first, unforgettable images of *Superman*. The whole layout of the film studios is designed to allow ubiquity, like the houses visited by the limping devil, but better still, dwellings are deprived of their roofs and gutted.[22]

This spatial ubiquity, which complements temporal ubiquity (movement in a reversible time), is for Agel what is "most fascinating at the cinema."[23] Most constant and obvious in any case. It has been said that it is the role of the camera to transgress the unity of place. The film, at the level of the shot as at the level of the montage as a whole, *is a system of complete ubiquity that allows the spectator to be transported to any point in time and space.*

Let us note that neither the spectator thus transported nor the screen moves: it is the objects that we effectively see moving on the screen according to the advances, retreats, and leaps of the camera. They appear and disappear, expand and shrink, pass from the microscopic to the macroscopic, and so the optical effect of ubiquity is the *metamorphosis of objects*. The screen is literally a magician's handkerchief, a crucible where everything is transformed, appears, and vanishes. We can immediately grasp the strange yet indubitable kinship that can exist between these elementary effects of the cinema, unknown to the Lumière cinematograph, and the tricks, apparitions, disappearances, substitutions, and magnifications of G. A. Smith and, above all, Méliès. What distinguishes the fantastic from the realist film is that in the first case we perceive the metamorphosis, whereas in the second we experience it without perceiving it. But sometimes, on the other hand, a naive look is enough for us to be struck by the apparent (that is, real on the screen) movement of things. "Show an uneducated man a pan of a house," says

M. Sellers, "and he will tell you that he has seen the build-ing run away. Show him a tilt and he will tell you that the building is sinking into the ground."[24]

The relationship between manifest metamorphosis (the fantastic film) and latent metamorphosis (the realist film) becomes one of filiation when one thinks of the dissolve. The dissolve compresses space as the fade compresses time. It is in some way the "anti-comma" of the language of film (the comma in written language marks a certain break in the continuity sustained by the sentence: the dissolve, on the contrary, works to establish an urgent continuity within an inevitable rupture). "[A] dissolve between two shots always and inevitably produces the feeling of an essential connec-tion between them."[25] The dissolve assures this continuity by the *metamorphosis* of objects, living beings, landscapes, which it effects right before our eyes. The dissolve is more-over one of the *tricks of metamorphosis* used by Méliès, who transformed himself into a skeleton by the lap dissolve in *L'oeuf magique prolifique (The Prolific Magical Egg)*. It still sometimes retains a whiff of its ancient magic: a slow dis-solve of a landscape "produces the effect of a dream, or of magic."[26]

The transformation of space by the cinema, like that of time, can thus ultimately open onto the magical universe of metamorphoses.

Fluid Universe

Of course, with the exception of the genre of the fantastic, this transformation (as we will see) does not destroy the realism and the objectivity of the universe. *But the realist universe of the cinema is no longer the former universe of the cin-ematograph*. As Epstein says, it is a "new nature, another world."[27] Time has acquired the movable nature of space and space the transformative powers of time. The double transmutation of cinematic time and space has produced a kind of unique symbiotic dimension, where time is incorporated in space, where space is incorporated in time, where "space moves, changes, turns, dissolves and recrystallizes,"[28] and where time "becomes a dimension of space."[29] This double transmutation results, as Francastel rightly says, in a "space-time."

Space-time, such is the total and unique dimension of a *fluid universe* that Jean Epstein defined in a passage where we only ask that the reader read "cinema" instead of "cinematograph":

> Through its construction, in an innate and ineluctable fashion, the cinematograph presents the universe as a perpetual and completely mobile continuity, *much more . . . fluid and more agile than directly sensed continuity.* . . . [L]ife comes and goes through matter, disappears, reappears as vegetable where it was believed to be mineral, animal where it was believed to be vegetable and human; nothing separates matter and spirit . . . a profound identity flows between beginning and end, between cause and effect. . . . *[T]he cinematograph possesses the power of universal transmutations.*[30]

From the first metamorphosis on the Place de l'Opéra to the montage of *Battleship Potemkin*, all the foundations of the cinematograph that seemed solid and fixed forever were swept away by a flood to make way for an ocean of movement.

Inanimate Objects, Now You Have a Soul

Within this ocean, as we have said, objects spring up, leap, slip away, blossom, shrink, are diminished. These phenomena are not perceived (in the strict sense of the term) although visible, but although they are not perceived, they make their effects felt.

What effects?

At the theater we know and feel that objects and scenery, often symbolically represented, are props, accessories that can even disappear. In the cinema, by contrast, the decor has none of the appearance of decor; even (and above all) when it has been reconstructed in a studio, it is a thing, an object, nature.

These things, these objects, this nature, gain not only a body, which, at the studio, they lack, but a "soul," a "life," that is, subjective presence. Certainly in real life, glass menageries, knickknacks, handkerchiefs, pieces of furniture charged with memories, are already like little presences watching over us, and we admire landscapes sprinkled with soul. The cinema goes further still: it takes hold of things scorned in everyday life, handled as tools, used out of habit, and it kindles new life in them: "Things were real, they now become present."[31]

The Lumière cinematograph already imbued with a certain soul everything at the limit of materiality, visibility, and palpability, precisely at the border of a nature that is fluid, frothy, nebulous, gaseous, or aqueous. Sadoul notes that spectators in the years 1895–96 never tired of marveling at "smoke, froth on beer, leaves trembling in the wind" along with "pounding waves."

Lumière recognized and exploited the mysterious attraction of fluid substances and particularly smoke (*L'arrivée d'un train à la Ciotat [The Arrival of a Train at La Ciotat]*, *Les forgerons [The Blacksmiths]*, *Un incendie*, the puff of the cigar in *La partie d'écarté [The Card Party]*, *Les brûleurs d'herbes*, or even the cloud of dust from a wall being demolished). Perhaps we can link this attraction to latent magical beliefs attached to winds and smoke, where ethereal spirits, ghostly doubles, are incarnated in proportion to their disembodiment, to the visible limit of their invisibility. Of course the Lumière cinematograph did not revive ancient magic but *reanimated*, without making us conscious of it, an animist or vitalist sensibility with regard to all that is animated by the "dynamogenic powers" of which Bachelard speaks—that is, with regard to all that is at once fluid and moving.

The cinema itself extends this particular fluidity to all objects. It puts these immobile things into motion. It expands them and reduces them. It breathes into them those dynamogenic powers that secrete the impression of life. If it does not deform them, it paints them with shadows and lights, which awaken or quicken presence. Finally, the close-up, this way of "interrogating" objects (Souriau), achieves a blossoming of subjectivity in response to its macroscopic fascination: the rotten meat in *Battleship Potemkin*, like the glass of milk in *Spellbound*, suddenly cries out to us. "Good close-ups are lyrical; it is the heart, not the eye, that has perceived them."[32]

Thus things, objects, nature, under the combined influence of rhythm, time, fluidity, camera movement, magnifications, games of shadow and light, gain a new quality. The term "subjective presence" is inadequate. We can say "atmosphere." Above all, we can say "soul." Balázs again says of the close-up that it "reveals the soul of things." Epstein, Pudovkin, all those who have spoken about film have expressed the same feeling. It is not only the close-up: it is the cinema as a whole that, as René Clair says, "gives a soul to the cabaret, the room, a bottle, a wall."[33]

This soul, of course, we must understand in a metaphorical sense, since it is a question of the state of the spectator's soul. The life of objects is obviously not real: it is subjective. But an alienating force tends to extend and externalize the phenomenon of soul into an animistic phenomenon. Objects hoist themselves up between two lives, two levels of the same life: external animistic life and internal subjective life. There are in fact two meanings to the word *soul*, the magical (alienated) sense, where the soul is transferred onto the contemplated object, and the subjective sense, where it is experienced as internal emotion. The cinema is expert at simultaneously saturating things with diffuse sentiment and eliciting a particular life from them. Thus scenery is mixed with action, as Barsacq notes. Mallet-Stevens goes further:

"architecture performs." Landry expresses the same idea: "The cinema asserts its superiority over all other arts in all cases where the framing must be considered as an actor or even as a protagonist." Béla Balázs speaks of dramatization of natural phenomena: "A new personage is added to the *dramatis personae* of the photographed play: nature itself."[34]

Objects begin to live, to play, to speak, to act. Balázs cites this scene from a silent American film: an engaged woman suddenly tears herself away from her future husband and runs through a long room where wedding presents are set out. The objects smile, call her, reach out to her with their arms. She slows down, stops, and finally retraces her steps.

Hero objects, comrade objects, comic objects, objects that are moving; a special attention "must be paid to the special part played in pictures by objects," says Pudovkin.[35] From the first Othello in art film, "the principal roles appear to belong to the handkerchief and the daggers of Iago and Othello" (Max Nordau). "On the screen no more still life: it is as much the revolver as the murderer's hand and his tie as much as him that commit the crime" (Bilinsky).[36] The avant-garde of 1924–25 had such a feeling for this life of things (in part, under the influence of painters) that we see in this period films about objects, *ballets méchaniques*. Since then, numerous objects have acceded to stardom, such as the snow dome in *Citizen Kane* or the statuette in *The Maltese Falcon*. This animation of objects takes us back, in a sense, to the universe of archaic vision, or to the gaze of a child. Epstein, like Landry, moreover, perspicaciously noted that the spectacle of things brings the spectator back "to the old animistic and mystical order."[37]

The animating power of the close-up can be exercised not only on the total object, but on one of its parts. At the extreme, a drop of milk (in *The General Line*) is endowed with a power of refusal and adherence, with a sovereign life.

A curious operation is performed on certain parts of the human body: the close-up reveals various little local

souls, related to those pupil souls and thumb-high souls that
E. Monseur studied in archaic religions and magics.[38] Epstein
had already foreseen this: "It no longer seems to me a fable
that there is a particular soul of the eye, of the hand, of the
tongue, as the vitalists believed."[39] The nose, the eye, the
mouth are endowed with autonomy, or, rather, soul. "Did
you know what a foot was before having seen it live in a
shoe, under a table, on the screen?"[40] Epstein even recognized the grim reaper, waiting in ambush behind the gaze
(the traditional window of the double): "In the pit of the
pupil, a spirit forms its oracles. One would like to touch this
boundless gaze, were it not charged with so much force that
is perhaps dangerous."[41]

For archaic peoples as for children, subjective phenomena are alienated in things that become carriers of soul. The
feeling of the spectator at the cinema tends toward this animism. Étienne Souriau put it aptly: "Universal animism is a
filmological fact that has no equivalent in the theater."[42] Let
us add, "that has no equivalent in any contemporary art":
"The cinema is the greatest apostle of animism."[43] Everything effectively takes on a soul, "the orange peel, the gust
of wind, a blunder."[44] Inanimate objects, now you have a
soul in the fluid universe of the cinema.

It is obviously the cartoon that completes, expands, exalts the animism implied in the cinema, to such a degree that
this animism blossoms into anthropomorphism. The farm-
yard speaks and sings to us, flowers leap about on their little feet, tools open their eyes, stretch out, and start dancing.

The cartoon only exaggerates the normal phenomenon:
film "reveals this anthropomorphous physiognomy in every
object."[45] Everything bathes in a latent anthropomorphism,
and this word signals well the profound tendency of the cinema in regard to animals, plants, and even objects: at different stages and strata, the screen is at once infused with soul
and populated with souls. Objects radiate with an astonishing presence, with a kind of "mana" that is simultaneously

or alternately subjective richness, emotive power, autonomous life, particular soul.

The Landscape of the Face

In addition to anthropomorphism, which tends to charge things with human presence, there is more obscurely, more weakly, cosmomorphism, that is, a tendency to charge man with cosmic presence. Thus, for example, the bodies of two lovers in an embrace metamorphose into a wave breaking on a rock, and are only returned to, their desire appeased, in the following shot. The cinema makes use of these cosmomorphic representations in extreme cases, precisely such as this one of human coupling. Most often what comes across is an attenuated cosmomorphism, where the human face is the mirror of the world that surrounds it. The Russians have made great use of the cosmographic powers of the face. "You want to show a great civilization, great technical progress?" said Balázs, "Show them in the men who work: show their faces, their eyes, and then we shall be able to tell what that civilization means and what it is worth."[46] In yet another way, the face is the mirror, no longer of the universe that surrounds it, but of the action that takes place offscreen, that is, out of frame. Agel puts it very well: "If it is a question of a physiognomy, the camera is at once a microscope and a magic mirror."[47] The face has become a medium: it expresses storms at sea, the earth, the town, the factory, revolution, war. The face is a landscape.

In actual fact, it is later on that we will be able to envisage in all its fullness the cosmomorphism implied by the cinema, when we will no longer consider only film, a universe saturated with soul, but also the spectator, a soul saturated with the universe.

For now, however, we can understand, without going back to the very crux of the problem, that film implies anthropomorphism and cosmomorphism, not as two separate functions, but as two moments or two poles of one same complex. The fluid universe of film supposes unceasing reciprocal *transfers* between the microcosm man and the macrocosm. Alternately substituting an object for a person is one of the most common processes in the cinema; film derives its most effective results from precisely such transfers: "A shot in close-up of a door slowly moving is more disturbing than a shot of a character making it move."[48] Equally, a distraught face can be more moving than a door closing. To express the same feeling, directors always have the choice between a person and a thing, and they express it by passing from the one to the other. Moving—more moving than anything in my memory—is the drop of milk, where, through the human drama that is tearing apart and uniting a kolkhoz, the very future of the revolution trembles. Close-ups alternate, from the milk separator to the faces of the peasants, anxious or attentive, suspicious or sly, from these faces to that of the woman who is working the machine. There is a transfer, a flow from the faces to the machine, from the machine to the faces, until finally a drop forms, trembling, a drop of soul, substance born of hope, carrier of all the promise of a world in its infancy.

The great current that carries each film along gives rise to the interchangeability of men and things, faces and objects. Ceaselessly, the face of the earth is expressed in that of the plowman, and, reciprocally, the soul of the peasant appears in the vision of wheat fluttering in the wind. In the same way, the ocean is expressed in the face of the sailor, and the face of the sailor is expressed in the ocean. For the face, on the screen, becomes landscape and the landscape becomes face, *that is, soul*. Landscapes are states of soul and states of soul landscapes. Often the weather, the ambience, the scenery are in the image of the feelings that animate the characters: we see alternate, then, shots of nature and shots of humans, as if an affective symbiosis necessarily connects the anthropos and the cosmos. Cosmomorphic men and anthropomorphic objects are a function of one another, becoming symbols of each other, according to the reciprocity of the microscosm and the macrocosm. On a drifting sheet of ice, Lillian Gish, an abandoned girl, is swept along as the river thaws (*Way Down East;* Griffith, 1920), "the human drama combining closely with the drama of the elements whose blind force took the part of a character in the cinematic tragedy."[49] Thus the heroine becomes a thing adrift. The thaw becomes an actor.

In this to-ing and fro-ing, the drama is sharply concentrated on an object, the drop of milk, the revolver, "dark like the temptations of the night (that is, cosmomorphized) . . . taciturn like passion, brutal, hard, heavy, cold, mistrustful, threatening" (that is, anthropomorphized). These incessant conversions of the soul of things to things of the soul correspond, on the other hand (as we will see in a subsequent volume),[50] to the profound nature of the fiction film, where subjective imaginary processes are concretized in things—events, objects—that spectators in turn reconvert into subjectivity.

The metamorphosis of the trolleybus into a funeral hearse one autumn day in 1896 was the beginning of fundamental metamorphoses. Méliès's tricks are the "keys to a new world," as M. Bouman expresses it. The characteristics of this new universe are, *apart from metamorphosis (and its negative, ubiquity), the fluidity of a circulable and reversible space-time, incessant transfers between the microcosm man and the macrocosm, and finally anthropomorphism and cosmomorphism.*

Fluidity, metamorphoses, micro-macrocosm, anthropocosmomorphism are the very foundations of cinematic vision. *Furthermore, if we add to these the qualities proper to the double, as defined and presented in the preceding chapter, we rediscover in their integrity and their nascent essence the fundamental characteristics of every magical vision of the world.*

Magical Vision

Indeed, if we consider magic in its pure state, that of death, it appears that the survival of the double is only one of two forms of immortality, the second being that which, immediately or later, makes the dead person be reborn as a new living being, child or animal.

The survival of the double and death-renaissance are found, at every level of belief, always symbiotically associated, according to variable combinations where one or another of the two immortalities predominates. Most often, the phantom-double lingers for a determinate time around the living, then goes to the dwelling place of the ancestors, whence come the newborn.

Like the survival of the double, death-renaissance is a universal of archaic consciousness. It is, as we have shown elsewhere, a universal of oneiric consciousness, a universal of poetic consciousness, a universal of infantile consciousness.

Death-renaissance is present at the very heart of the vision of life: the latter is a perpetual movement where death fertilizes life, where man fertilizes his action upon nature through death (sacrifice) and accedes to different stages of his existence through these veritable death-renaissances that are called initiations. Finally, the very mechanism of the perpetual metamorphoses that govern the universe is that of death-renaissance. In this sense, death-renaissance is a particular, or internal, aspect of the universal law of metamorphoses.

Metamorphoses imply, and here we agree with L. Lévy-Bruhl, *a fluid universe* where things are not hardened in their identity, but participate in a great cosmic unity that is in motion. This fluidity explains and accounts for the reciprocity between the microcosm man and the macrocosm. The analogy of man and the cosmos is the magic fulcrum where the fluidity of the universe and anthropo-cosmomorphism are articulated.

It has long been noticed that animals, plants, and things

seem, for archaic peoples as for children, animated by human feelings. In some cases, they are believed to be inhabited by spirits, they are spirits themselves: in other words, *doubles* (the dead) are found installed in the very heart of the fluid universe. At a certain stage of evolution, the universe is nothing other than a vast tribe of spirits nestled in the bosom of all things. This is what has been called animism. *This animism is deeply rooted in a fundamental process through which man experiences and recognizes nature by projecting himself into it: anthropomorphism.*

Reciprocally, archaic man is inhabited by nature. It is not the presence of a "self" that he feels within him. His "self," the double, is outside. Inside him the world is swarming. Thus the Kanak, as Maurice Leenhardt points out in *Do Kamo*, sees the sap flow in the veins of his arms.[51] Archaic language, conduct, masks, ornaments, possession phenomena, show us that men, while knowing themselves to be men, feel inhabited, possessed, be it by an animal or by a plant, at any rate by cosmic forces. In the same way, children who mimic animals, the storm, the wind, the airplane, *are*, without ceasing to know that they are children, animal, storm, wind, or airplane. Cosmomorphism, through which humanity feels itself to be nature, corresponds to anthropomorphism, through which nature is felt to have human features. The world is inside man and man is spread throughout the world.

Leenhardt quite correctly insisted on the importance of cosmomorphism, but he distinguished it chronologically and logically from anthropomorphism. In our opinion, these two terms cannot be separated; that is why we will be compelled (very often, unfortunately) to use the word *anthropocosmomorphism*. The totem animal, the parrot of the Bororos, for example, is one of man's cosmomorphic fixations. Man, acting in good faith (he continues in other respects to act practically as a man, but does more than perform, he lives his identification with the bird), believes himself, feels himself to be a parrot; he mimics the bird in his festivals. At the same time, the totem parrot is anthropomorphized: it is the ancestor, it is man. Thus it is in relation to this anthropo-cosmomorphism, where man simultaneously feels analogous to the world and experiences the world under human conditions, that we must conceive of the magical universe.

Totemism is only a stage of crystallization in a much more general process. In fact, the micro-macroscopic analogies flow on naturally from anthropo-cosmomorphism. The cosmomorphized man is a miniature universe, mirror and summary of the world: the anthropomorphized world teems with humanity. In the midst of this immense fluid relationship bathe all things that have become living, colloidal. All metamorphoses—that is, death-renaissances—are possible and real, from microcosm to macrocosm and within the macrocosm itself.

Thus magic appears to us: a vision of life and a vision of death, common to the infantile part of archaic peoples' vision of the world and the childish part of modern peoples' vision of the world, and to neuroses and psychological regressions like the dream. We have, since Freud, often compared the vision of the child, that of the "primitive," and that of the neurotic. Without entering into the dispute that has arisen around the validity of this comparison, let us say that it is not our intention to identify the primitive, the neurotic, and the child, but to recognize, in what is analogous in them, a common system, which we precisely call magic. *This common system is determined by the double, metamorphoses and ubiquity, universal fluidity, the reciprocal analogy of the microcosm and the macrocosm, and anthropo-cosmomorphism. That is, exactly the characteristics constitutive of the universe of the cinema.*

Dziga Vertov, in defining the ciné-eye, in his own way recognized the dual and irreducible polarity of the cinema: the charm of the image and the metamorphosis of the universe—*photogénie and montage.*

From the Image to the Imaginary

In a manner corresponding to its spatiotemporal metamorphosis, the cinematograph enters into the universe of fiction.

This obvious point, however, needs to be amended. We have already said that the first films of Edison, even before those of Lumière, portrayed scenes of fantasy, playlets, music hall shows. Moreover, the era of the cinematograph is as much that of the music hall or of filmed theater as documents taken from real life. In the end, it is conceivable that, without being transformed into cinema, the cinematograph could have been used to spread those works of the imagination that are theater pieces.

Conversely, Vertov's ciné-eye and all the great documentary movements, from Flaherty to Grierson and Joris Ivens, show us that the structures of the cinema are not necessarily tied to fiction. Better still: it is perhaps in documentaries that the cinema utilizes its gifts to the maximum and manifests its most profound "magical" powers.

Granted these reservations, fiction remains the dominant trend in the cinema: it spreads with the cinema and the cinema spreads with fiction. Méliès's discoveries are, as we have seen, inseparable from the fantastic film. Those of the Brighton school are made in the framework of fantasy scenes and equally fantastic. From Edison on, it can be said, an irrepressible push precipitates the new invention toward fiction. In 1896–97, the very year of its baptism, comedy, love, aggression, fictionalized history, are introduced into film from all over the place. The cinematographic image is literally immersed, carried along in an imaginary stream that will not cease to swell. The cinema has become synonymous with fiction. This is astoundingly obvious. The currents and the contents of this fiction are of such importance that we will devote another study to the great trade winds of the imaginary.

Here again it is noteworthy that the fantastic was the first, decisive, and great wave of the imaginary through which the passage from the cinematograph to the cinema (Méliès and G. A. Smith) was accomplished. The fantastic is certainly going to recede, to be reduced to a genre. But this reflux leaves the techniques of the cinema and an imaginary deposit on the shore: fiction.

We enter into the kingdom of the imaginary when aspirations, desires, and their negatives, fears and terrors, take up and mold the image to order according to their logic, dreams, myths, religions, beliefs, literatures, precisely all fictions.

Myths and beliefs, dreams and fictions, are the burgeonings of the magical vision of the world. They put anthropomorphism and the double into action. The imaginary is the spontaneous magical practice of the dreaming mind.

So we see, here again, how the objective cinematograph and the fiction cinema are opposed and linked to each other. The image is the strict reflection of reality; its objectivity contradicts the extravagance of the imaginary. But at the same time, this reflection is already a "double." The image is already saturated with subjective powers that are going to displace it, distort it, project it into fantasy and dream. The imaginary casts a spell on the image because the latter is already a potential sorceress. It proliferates on the image like its natural cancer. It is going to crystallize and deploy human needs, but always in images. The imaginary is the place common to the image and the imagination.

Thus, with the same continuity, the world of doubles blossoms within the world of metamorphoses, the image is heightened in the imaginary, and the cinema deploys its distinctive powers in cinematic techniques and fiction.

Dream and Film

Henceforth, the objective image is going to resemble that of the dream—the imaginary museum of our childhood thought: magic.

While the connections between the structures of magic and those of the cinema have only been felt intuitively, or allusively, or aesthetically, or in a fragmentary way (due to the lack of an anthropological conception of magic), by contrast, the relationship between the universe of film and that of the dream has been frequently perceived and analyzed. Let us recall the quotations in our first chapter: "Cinema is dream. . . . It is an artificial dream. . . . Is the cinema not also a dream? . . . I go to the cinema as I go to sleep." The expression repeated by Ilya Ehrenberg and Hortense Powdermaker is used again and again: "dream factory." Manvell speaks of the "popular dream market." Rosten nicely says that "the makers of films are paid to dream their dreams and exploit their reveries." And all of us, habitués of the cinema, have vaguely identified dream and film.

"In short, it is like a scene in a film"—a sentence that psychologists and psychoanalysts know well from people relating the visions from their dreams or when they were half asleep. "It was like something you see at the cinema." "I did nothing, I watched as in a film." Dr. S. Lebovici notes "this frequent slip of the tongue during sessions of analysis, a number of subjects speaking of a film while meaning a dream."[52] Moreover, the same clinicians are themselves brought around to discover profound analogies between the universe of film and the oneiric universe. Dr. Heuyer declares that the delirium of daydreaming resembles cinematic vision.[53] Dr. Desoille notes that in the daydream, there are *scenarios*.[54] From the first daydreams directed according to his method, Desoille notes the appearance of metamorphoses, of mirrors, that is, of the same magical elements that were present at the birth of the cinema. Lebovici clarified and defined these connections already found all over the place,[55] and that Jean Epstein summed up in this way: "The processes used by the discourse of dream that allow it its profound sincerity find their analogues in cinematic style."[56] The dynamism of film, like that of the dream, disrupts the boundaries of time and space. The enlargement and expansion of objects on the screen correspond to the macroscopic and microscopic effects of the dream. In dreams and in film, objects appear and disappear, the part represents the whole (synecdoche). Equally, time expands, contracts, is reversed. Suspense, frantic and interminable chases, situations typical in the cinema, have the character of a nightmare. Many other oneiric analogies could be noted; in dreams as in film, images express a latent message, which is one of desires and fears.

Film rediscovers, then, "the dreamed, weakened, shrunken, enlarged, brought closer, distorted, haunting image of the secret world we withdraw to in the waking state as in sleep, of this life greater than the life where crimes and heroics that we never accomplish lie dormant, where our disappointments are drowned and our maddest desires take root."[57]

The cinema introduces the universe of the dream within the cinematic universe where one is awake. Is the cinematograph negated by the cinema in the classical sense of the term, that is, abolished, or in the Hegelian sense, that is, overtaken but conserved? And to what extent? To confine oneself to the oneirism of the cinema is to ignore this problem whose subsequent elucidation must necessarily make apparent to us, if it exists, the "specificity" of the cinema.

Music (Prelude)

It is also to ignore the scope of the unreality that blossoms in the cinema. As if some ultimate realist propriety prevented it, our dreams are not accompanied by music. Music, on the other hand, reigns in the universe of the cinema.

Although it seems so obvious that it can be forgotten,[58] film music is without doubt the most implausible element in the cinema. What is more unreal than these rhythms and these melodies that are ever present, in the town and the countryside, in the sea and on land, in privacy as in a crowd?

And yet music imposed itself on film at the same time as the cinema freed itself from the cinematograph: it is one of the moments of this transformation. Without waiting for the sound track, pressured by a mysterious urgency, pianos and orchestras accompanied silent films. Was it to conceal the hum of the projector, as a tenacious legend would have it? (A contingent incident always explains something whose logic escapes us.) And why not? What matters is that music went beyond, far beyond, this protective role. Very soon "incidentals" appeared, all-purpose pieces written to accompany silent films, original scores,[59] then leitmotifs relating to heroes.[60] In 1919, Guiseppe Becce was able to bring together in one "Kinothèque" a thousand pieces classified according to atmosphere and situations, admirable material for a sociology of the categories of musical affectivity. So even before the sound film, music appeared as a key element, that is, something the cinema needed.

One could perhaps think that music was only a substitute for the voices and sounds that the silent film lacked. But the sound film, although it speaks and makes sounds, still, and always, needs music. It lives in music, bathes in music. Let us not even speak of film operettas from the *The Road to Paradise*[61] to *Les belles de nuit (Night Beauties)*, or of what Maurice Jaubert calls "real" film music (jazz in a nightclub, an organ in a church). The cinema is not satisfied with this external music, which it nevertheless makes abundant use of. Above all, it needs music that is integrated, "mixed" into the film, inherent to it, that it can bathe in and be nourished by. The cinema is musical, like opera, although the spectator is not at all aware of this.

Films without music are extremely rare, and they do without it only to substitute a symphony of sounds, as in *Jetons les filets*. There is no film without music, and in a ninety-minute film, the average length of the screen score is from twenty to forty-five minutes.

What does music do in film? It is not yet time to answer

this question. Let us just say what it is: an affective presence. All-purpose scores for silent films (incidentals) are veritable catalogs of states of the soul. Cheerful, sad, and sentimental scenes constitute their main categories. It is interesting to note that these incidentals have a latent anthropo-cosmomorphic character: they express an inner feeling at the same time they describe a natural spectacle. In other words, the scene is permeated with emotion and the emotion is projected onto the scene: "*Dramatic chase—Despair—Amoroso cantabile––Visions of horror—A walk in the country*." These titles are revealing of the descriptive-affective (micro-macrocosmic) complex that governs film music. One of the most utilized incidentals, *Storm*, accompanies equally well "the forest fire, the turbulence of a wounded heart, the railroad catastrophe," and thus reveals the anthropo-cosmomorphic equivalence of torment and storm, of the tempest inside a skull and the tempest out at sea, of the storm in the atmosphere and the storm of the passions.

So there is an anthropo-cosmomorphic complementarity between music (at least descriptive music) and cinema. This complementarity, is it not also kinship?[62]

Élie Faure says that film "is a music that reaches us through the medium of the eye." In fact, the peculiarity of the cinema is to have introduced, in place of simple animated photography, fluidity, continuity—a fluid continuity based on the discontinuity of shots, just as musical continuity is based on the discontinuity of notes; a concrete fluidity constructed by the most abstract means—a temporality that accelerates, slows down, or goes backwards; a set of themes, leitmotifs, flashbacks, and so on.

A kind of analogy seems to preside over the fraternization of the cinema and music. This fraternization sometimes even goes as far as confusion and reciprocity. Cohen-Séat points to certain cases of equivalence where "the literal significance of the images is in fact extremely flimsy . . . the sensation becomes musical to the point that, when music really accompanies it, the image really draws the best of its expression, or rather suggestion, from the music."[63] Among the most heartrending cinematic *visions* (the word came of its own accord) that haunt us are those moments where a refrain evokes a past image without this image being reintroduced by a flashback or a superimposition. The tune *Nous irons à Suresnes* revives the image of the crime committed in the past by the legionnaire (*La bandera* [*Escape from Yesterday*]). The *Violettera* evokes the painful and radiant memory of love when Charlie Chaplin, out of prison, suddenly sees the little blind girl again *(City Lights)*. Vision has become music, and this music has become vision; it takes the place of superimpositions or flashbacks, since by its charm alone it revives the image memory for us. In the course of this alchemy, the quintessence of music is identified with the quintessence of memory—its unique and irremediable character, its timid promise of eternity—its magic.

During recent projections of silent films without music, once the unpleasant phase of adaptation had been overcome, we still seemed to perceive by synesthesia a kind of internal music, an inner orchestra. It is as if the cinema expressed the music included, implied, in things. As if in the cinema, everything sang. As if the role of music was to underline this song to bring it up to a perceptible level.

We will return, necessarily, to film music, which illuminates the cinema as if from inside. Let us note for the moment that the cinema breaks away from the cinematograph, completes its first revolution, to blossom bathed in music—in complete unreality.

Unreality, Magic, Subjectivity

Beyond music, which is only one aspect of it, it is indeed unreality that the cinema brings, and it is indeed through unreality that it contradicts the cinematograph. But, as we have seen, the cinematograph already carried within it the genes of this unreality. The cinema gave momentum to what was latent in the cinematographic mother image; it was this élan itself, and as a result the unreal blossomed into the real.

Unreal: that is the negative, empty label. We must unravel the structures of this unreality, its logic, its system. Then the magical vision of the world appears, just beneath the surface, under the cinema, as it had already under the cinematograph—but this time in its totality, in all its fullness.

No—we have not meandered away from our subject. Establishing the magical system allows us to get away from the soporific power of a word that has become a catchall. It allows us to see that the passage from the cinematograph to the cinema did not come about by chance. Automatically, certainly, but once more, logically. The "enchantment of vulgar matter" of which Apollinaire spoke had commenced secretly within the invisible, beneath the objective image. Méliès liberated the chrysalis. Film was subjugated, gobbled up, digested, transfigured.

Magic is our frame of reference, or rather, better, our *blueprint*, our *pattern*. For, we have often said, but we must reiterate, we do not at all identify the cinema with magic: we are bringing out analogies, correspondences.

In fact, we wander from the spectator to the image, from the interior soul to the fantastic exterior. The universe of the cinema possesses magic genetically, structurally, yet is not magic; it possesses affectivity but it is not subjectivity either. Music, dream, fiction, fluid universe, micro-macrocosmic reciprocity—so many terms, each of which is slightly applicable, yet none entirely so.

It is a veritable magical-affective flow that pushed and animated the camera in all directions, opened huge gaps in the objective image from shot to shot. It swells and overflows, surges and gushes forth; it carries along and mixes the subjective quality of memory and the magical quality of the double, the Bergsonian *durée* and metamorphosis, animism and state of the soul, music and real objects. Carried along by what need?

To recognize the depth of this need, we must go deeper into the subjective structures of magic.

But the truth is we are already starting to recognize ourselves: however opposed they seem, magic always appears as the other pole of subjective sentiment, the alienated, externalized, solidified, recognizable pole. Sentiment, music, dream, magic: there is something unique in them, but at diverse moments of differentiation. Have we not seen that there was always a connection between the most fantastic of Méliès's tricks and the most elementary, quasi-subjective structures of the cinema?

4 *The Soul of the Cinema*

Magic has no essence: a sterile truth if it is simply a question of noting that magic is illusion. We must look for the processes that give body to this illusion.

We have already glimpsed some of them; they are anthropomorphism and cosmomorphism. Reciprocally, they inject humanity into the external world and the external world into the inner man.

Projection-Identification

If we go back to their source, anthropomorphism and cosmomorphism progressively reveal their original energizing nature to us: projection and identification.

Projection is a universal and multiform process. Our needs, our aspirations, our desires, our obsessions, our fears, project themselves not only into the void as dreams and imaginings, but onto all things and all beings. Contradictory accounts of one occurrence, a catastrophe at Le Mans or a traffic incident, the battle of the Somme or a domestic scene, betray distortions that are often more unconscious than intentional. A historical or psychological review of testimony shows us that even the most elementary of our perceptions, like the perception of other people's size, are at once muddled up and fashioned by our projections.[1]

However diverse its forms and objects may be, the process of projection can take on the appearance of automorphism, anthropomorphism, or doubling.

At the automorphic stage—the only one, moreover, that has interested cinema observers up until now—we "attribute to a person whom we are judging character traits, tendencies that are our own."[2] Everything is pure to the pure, and everything is impure to the impure.

Anthropomorphism appears at another stage, where we fix on material things and living beings "character traits or tendencies" that are properly human. At a third stage, a purely imaginary one, we come to doubling, that is to say, to the projection of our own individual being into a hallucinatory vision where our corporeal specter appears to us. In a way, anthropomorphism and doubling are moments where projection crosses over into alienation: these are magical moments. But already, as Fulchignoni has noted, the seeds of doubling are present in automorphic projection.

In the process of identification, the subject, instead of projecting himself into the world, absorbs the world into himself. Identification incorporates the environment into the self and integrates it affectively.[3] Identification with others can end up in "possession" of the subject by the foreign presence of an animal, a sorcerer, a god. Identification with the world can broaden into cosmomorphism, where man feels and believes himself to be a microcosm. This last example, where anthropomorphism and cosmomorphism blossom in a complementary fashion, shows us that projection and identification reflect one another within a global complex. Already the most banal "projection" onto another—the "I am putting myself in his place"—is an identification of myself with him that facilitates and calls for the identification of him with me: he has become assimilable.

So it is not enough to isolate projection on the one hand, identification on the other hand, and finally reciprocal transfers. We must also consider *the projection-identification complex, which involves these transfers.*

The projection-identification-transfer complex commands all so-called subjective psychological phenomena, that is, phenomena that betray or distort the objective reality of things or that deliberately locate themselves outside of this reality (spiritual states, reveries).

It also commands—in its anthropo-cosmomorphic form —the complex of magical phenomena: the double, the analogy, metamorphosis.

In other words, the subjective state and the magical thing are two moments of projection-identification. One is the nascent moment, blurred, hazy, "ineffable." The other is the moment where identification is taken literally, made substantial; where the alienated projection, lost, fixed, fetishized, becomes a thing: doubles, spirits, gods, bewitchment, possession, and metamorphosis are truly believed in.

Dreams show us that there is no solution of continuity between subjectivity and magic, since they are subjective or magical depending on whether they occur by day or at night. Until we wake up, these projections of images seem real to us. Until we go to sleep, we laugh at their unreality. Dreams show us how the most intimate processes can become alienated to the point of reification and how these alienations can reintegrate subjectivity. The essence of the dream is subjectivity. Its being is magic. It is projection-identification in its pure state.

If our dreams—our subjective states—detach themselves from us and become one with the world, it is magic. If a fault line prevents this or they do not manage to hold on there, it is subjectivity: the magical universe is subjective vision that believes itself to be real and objective. In a reciprocal way, subjective vision is magical vision in its nascent state, latent, or atrophied. It is only the alienation and reification of the psychic processes in question that differentiate magic from interior life. The first provokes the second. The second extends the first. Magic is the concretization of subjectivity. Subjectivity is the lifeblood of magic.

Historically, magic is the first stage, chronologically the first vision of the child or of humanity in its infancy and, to a certain extent, of the cinema: everything begins, always, with alienation.

Evolution—that of the individual like that of the race—tends to disenchant the universe and internalize magic. Certainly enormous expanses of magic live on in public life as in private lives, clustered around taboos related to sex, death, and social power. Certainly psychological regressions (individual and collective neuroses) endlessly resuscitate ancient magic. But, in the main, the double dematerializes, shrivels up, dims, reenters the body, is localized in the heart or the brain: it becomes the soul. Animistic objects become objects charged with soul. Magic is no longer belief taken literally, it has become feeling. Rational and objective consciousness makes magic recoil into its den. At the same time, "interior" and affective life hypertrophies. So magic corresponds not only to the preobjective vision of the world, but also to a presubjective stage of man. The melting of magic liberates enormous fluxes of affectivity, a subjective flood. The stage of the soul, affective blossoming, succeeds the magical stage. Anthropo-cosmomorphism that no longer manages to cling on in the real flaps its wings into the imaginary.

Affective Participation

Between magic and subjectivity spreads an uncertain nebula, which goes beyond man, without, however, detaching itself from him. We refer to or designate its manifestations with words of soul, heart, feeling. This magma, which has elements of both magic and subjectivity, is neither magic nor subjectivity, properly speaking. It is the kingdom of *projection-identification or affective participation*. The term *participation* coincides exactly, to our mind, on the mental and affective plane, with the notion of projection-identification. So we will use these terms interchangeably.

Subjective life, the interior soul on the one hand, and alienation, the animistic soul on the other, polarize affective participations, but the latter can encompass both of these in various ways. Magic is not entirely reabsorbed into the soul, as we have said, and the latter is itself a semifluid, semireified residue of magic.

After the magical stage comes the stage of the soul. Entire fragments of magic remain, which the stage of the soul does not dissolve but integrates in a complex way. On the other hand, the intensity of subjective or affective life revives the old magic, or rather gives rise to a new magic. A violent burst of energy, and the solfataras once again become volcanos and hurl out matter. Sartre indeed saw that emotion converts itself into magic. All exaltation, all lyricism, all élan take on an anthropo-cosmomorphic shading in their effusion. As poetry shows us, lyricism naturally follows the pathways and the language of magic. Extreme subjectivity brusquely becomes extreme magic. In the same way, the height of subjective vision is hallucination—its objectivation.

The zone of affective participation is that of mixed, uncertain, ambivalent projection-identifications. It is equally that of magico-subjective syncretism. We have seen that where magic is manifest, subjectivity is latent, and where subjectivity is manifest, magic is latent. In this zone, neither magic nor subjectivity is completely manifest and latent.

Thus our life of feelings, desires and fears, friendships, love, develops the whole range of projection-identification phenomena, from ineffable states of the soul to magical fetishizations. We need only consider love, the supreme projection-identification; we identify with the loved one, with his joys and misfortunes, experiencing feelings that are properly his. We project ourselves onto him, that is, we identify him with ourselves, cherishing him, what is more, with all the love that we carry within ourselves. His photos, his trinkets, his handkerchiefs, his house, are all infused with his presence. Inanimate objects are impregnated with his soul and force us to love them. Affective participation thus spreads from beings to things and regenerates fetishizations, venerations, and cults. A dialectical ambivalence binds phenomena of the heart and fetishizations. Love is the everyday example of this.

Hence affective participation carries within it a residual magic (not yet totally internalized), a renewed magic (provoked by affective exaltation), a depth of soul and of subjective life. We can also compare it to a colloidal solution where a thousand magical concretions would be found in suspension. Here too we must turn to the notion of a *complex*.

We can now reciprocally elucidate magic, subjectivity, and affective participation. We can cast some light in this enormous zone of shadow—ruled by reasons that the reason does not know, that the sciences of man still prefer to despise through ignorance rather than ignore with spite.

We can now add to our accepted understanding a new understanding of the metamorphosis of the cinematograph into cinema. Manifest magic, that of Méliès, G. A. Smith, and their imitators, appears to us not only as a naive moment of childhood, but also *as the original and natural effusion of affective powers within the objective image*.

On the other hand, we can now unmask the magic of cinema, recognize in it the projected shadows, the hieroglyphs of affective participation. Better still: the magical structures of this universe make us unequivocally recognize its subjective structures.

They show us that all cinematic phenomena tend to confer the structures of subjectivity on the objective image. They call into question all affective participation. It is the scope of these phenomena that we should evaluate, it is the mechanisms of excitation that we should analyze.

Cinematographic Participation

As brief and lengthy as it may be at the same time, such an analysis was necessary so as to avoid certain all-too-common puerilities. The processes of projection-identification that are at the heart of the cinema are evidently at the heart of life. So we should spare ourselves the Jourdainesque joy of discovering them on the screen.[4] Naive commentators, and even a mind as penetrating as Balázs, think that identification and projection (what is more, always examined separately) were born with film. In the same way, no doubt, each person thinks he has invented love.

Projection-identification (affective participation) plays a continuous role in our daily life, private and social. Already Gorky had admirably evoked "the semi-imaginary reality of man." If we follow Mead, Cooley, Stern, we will even mix up imaginary participation and social participation, spectacle and life. Role taking and personation control person-to-person relations. Our personality is a confection, ready-made. We put it on like an item of clothing, and we wear our clothing like a role. We play a role in life, not only for others but also (and above all) for ourselves. The costume (that disguise), the face (that mask), the talk (those conventions), the feeling of our own importance (that comedy), maintain in ordinary life this spectacle offered to self and others— *that is, imaginary projection-identifications*.

To the extent that we identify the images on the screen with real life, our projection-identifications peculiar to real life are set in motion. In fact, to a certain extent, we are going to rediscover them there, which seemingly dissipates the originality of cinematographic projection-identification but in fact reveals it. Indeed, why "rediscover" them? There are only games of shadow and light on the screen; only a process of *projection* can *identify* shadows with things and real beings, and attribute to them this reality so obviously lacking on reflection, although scarcely obvious to sight.

So a first and elementary process of projection-identification confers enough reality on cinematographic images for the ordinary projection-identifications to enter into play. In other words, a mechanism of projection-identification is at the very origin of cinematographic perception.

In other words still, subjective participation, with the cinematograph, goes by way of objective reconstitution.

But we are still not sufficiently equipped to tackle this essential problem directly (see chapters 5 and 6). Let us get around it provisionally by limiting ourselves to observing that the impression *of life and of reality* proper to cinematographic images is inseparable from a first rush of participation.

It is obviously to the extent that spectators of the Lumière cinematograph believed in the reality of the train charging toward them that they were frightened by it. It is to the extent that they saw "astonishing scenes of realism" that they felt themselves to be actors and spectators at the same time. As far back as a screening on December 28, 1895, H. de Parville noted the phenomenon of projection-identification with definitive simplicity: "One asks oneself if one is a simple spectator or actor in these astonishing scenes of realism."

However slight it was, this uncertainty was experienced at the time of the first sessions: people fled screaming because a vehicle was rushing toward them; women fainted. But they recovered immediately; the cinematograph appeared in a civilization where the awareness of the unreality of the image was so deeply rooted that the vision projected, realistic as it was, could not be considered as *practically* real. Unlike archaic peoples, who would have totally adhered to the reality, or rather the practical surreality, of vision (doubles), the developed world could only see an image in the most perfect image. It "felt" only the "impression" of reality.

So the "reality" of cinematographic projections, in the practical sense of the term *reality*, is devalued. The fact that cinema is only a spectacle reflects this devaluation. The quality of spectacle—let us say, more broadly, the aesthetic quality in its literal sense, which is the felt (or affectively lived as opposed to *practically lived*)—avoids and emasculates all the practical consequences of participation: there is no risk or commitment for the public. In every spectacle, even if there is a real risk for the actors, the public is in principle out of danger, out of harm's way. It is out of reach of the train that is arriving, that is arriving right now, but in a present that is itself out of the spectator's reach. Although frightened, the latter is at ease. The spectator of the cinematograph is not only practically outside of the action, but knows that the action, however real, is *actually* outside the realm of practical life.

The attenuated reality of the image is better than no reality at all, when the cinematograph offers, as Méliès said, "the world within arm's reach." Foreign capitals, unknown and exotic continents, bizarre rites and customs arouse, on the cheap, perhaps, cosmic participation that would be more pleasant to live practically—by traveling—but that is practically out of reach. Even though practically devalued, the attenuated reality of the image is better in a sense than a dangerous reality—a storm at sea, an automobile accident—because it allows us to taste, moderately, of course, but inoffensively, the intoxications of risk.

But there is more, as we have seen. The cinematographic image, which lacks the probatory force of practical reality, possesses an affective power that justifies a spectacle. *An eventually heightened affective reality—which we have called the charm of the image—balances its devalued practical reality.* Mixed and linked to each other, cosmic participations at a discount and the affective enhancement of the image proved themselves powerful enough to set up the new invention as spectacle from the beginning. Thus the cinematograph is not only spectacle, but it is spectacle.

The cinematograph has *the charm of the image* at its disposal; that is, it renews or exalts the vision of banal and everyday things. The implicit quality of the double, the powers of the shadow, a certain sensitivity to the ghostliness of things, combine their age-old tricks in the midst of photogenic enhancement and often summon imaginary projection-identifications better than practical life would do. The flights of enthusiasm provoked by the smoke, steam, winds, and the naive joys of recognition of familiar places (already discernible in the joys of the postcard and the photo) clearly betray the participation that the Lumière cinematograph excites. After *L'arrivée d'un train à la Ciotat*, notes Sadoul, "spectators evoked their excursions, saying to their children: you will see, it's just like that." From the first screenings, Lumière discovers the pleasures of identification and the need for recognition; he advises his cameramen to film people in the streets, and even to pretend to shoot, "to attract them to the show."

As proof of the intensity of the cinematographic phenomenon of projection-identification, we can cite Kuleshov's experiment, which was still not dependent on cinematic techniques. Kuleshov successively placed close-ups of Mosjoukine "which were static and which did not express any feeling at all" before a plate of soup, a dead woman, a laughing baby; the spectators "raved about the acting of the artist," seeing him express, in succession, hunger, pain, and gentle paternal emotion.[5] Of course, there is a distinction only in degree between these projective effects and those of everyday life and of the theater: we are used to reading hate and love in the blank faces that surround us. But other phenomena confirm for us that the Kuleshov effect is particularly strong.

Thus we can already attribute to the cinematograph false recognitions where identification goes as far as an error in identity, such as when the king of England recognized himself in the newsreels of his coronation fabricated in a studio.

The cinematograph established a spectacle because it already aroused participation. As institutionalized spectacle, it aroused it even more. The power of participation has had a snowball effect. It has revolutionized the cinematograph and at the same time projected it toward the imaginary.

In any spectacle, as we have said, the spectator is outside of the action, deprived of practical participation. The latter is, if not totally annihilated, at least atrophied and channeled into symbols of accompaniment (applause) or refusal (hisses) and, in any case, powerless to modify the internal course of the picture. The spectator never enters the action; at the very most he makes gestures or signs.[6]

The absence or the atrophy of motor, practical, or active participation (one of these adjectives is more suitable than the others depending on the particular case) is closely linked to psychological and affective participation. Unable to express itself in action, the spectator's participation becomes internal, felt. The kinesthesia of the spectacle is engulfed in the coenesthesia of the spectator, that is, in his subjectivity, and brings about projection-identification. Thus the absence of practical participation establishes an intense affective participation: veritable transfers take place between the soul of the spectator and the spectacle on the screen.

Correlatively, the passivity of the spectator, his impotence, places him in a regressive situation. The spectacle illustrates a general anthropological law: we all become sentimental, sensitive, tearful, when we are deprived of our means of action: the disarmed SS officer sobs over his victims or over his canary, the ruffian in prison becomes a poet. The example of the surgeon who faints before the film of an operation reveals the sentimentality that impotence suddenly arouses. It is because he finds himself outside of practical life, stripped of his powers, that the doctor then feels the horror of flesh laid bare and tortured, *exactly as a layman would do when faced with a real operation*. In a regressive situation, infantilized, as if under the effect of an artificial neurosis, the spectator sees a world handed over to forces that escape him. That is why, in a spectacle, everything passes easily from the affective to the magical level. It is moreover at the limit of passivity—sleep—that the projection-identifications we then call dreams become magnified.

As spectacle, the Lumière cinematograph stimulates projection-identification. In addition, the cinematograph already presents a spectatorial situation that is particularly pure because it establishes the greatest possible physical segregation between the spectator and the spectacle. In the theater, for example, the presence of the spectator can have an effect on the performance of the actor, it participates in the uniqueness of an event subject to risks: the actor can forget his role or feel badly. The "ambience" and the ceremonial cannot be dissociated from the actual, lived character that theatrical representation takes on. With the cinematograph, the physical absence of actors as of things renders all physical accidents impossible; no ceremonial, that is, no practical cooperation of the spectator in the spectacle.

In constructing itself, notably in constructing its own theaters, the cinema has amplified certain para-oneiric characteristics favorable to projection-identification. Darkness was one element not essential (one sees this in the advertising during intermissions) but energizing for participation. Darkness was organized, isolating the spectator, "wrapping him up in black" as Epstein said, dissolving diurnal resistance and accentuating all the fascinations of the shadow. People have spoken of a hypnotic state; let us say, rather, imitation-hypnotic state, since in the end the spectator is not asleep. But, if he is not asleep, his seat is granted an attention not accorded in other spectacles, spectacles that avoid a numbing comfort (theater) or even despise it (stadiums): the spectator can be half stretched out in an attitude propitious to "relaxation," favorable to reverie.

So there he is, isolated, but at the heart of a human environment, of a great gelatin of common soul, of a collective participation, which accordingly amplifies his individual participation. To be isolated and in a group at the same time: two contradictory and complementary conditions favorable to suggestion. Television in the home does not get the benefit of this enormous resonance chamber; it presents itself in the light, among practical objects, to individuals whose number has difficulty making up a group (that is why in the United States people invite each other to TV parties).

The spectator in the "dark room" is, on the contrary, a passive subject in a pure state. He can do nothing, has nothing to give, even his applause. Patient, he endures. Enthralled, he submits. Everything happens a long way away, out of his reach. At the same time and as a result, everything happens inside of him; we could say, in his psychological coenesthesia. When the charms of the shadow and the double merge on a white screen in a darkened room, for the spectator, deep in his cell, a monad closed off to everything except the screen, enveloped in the double placenta of an anonymous community and obscurity, when the channels for action are blocked, then the locks to myth, dream, and magic open up.

The Aesthetic Imaginary and Participation

The irruption of the imaginary in film would have brought with it, at any rate, an increase in affective participation even if there had not been a metamorphosis of the cinematograph into cinema.

The work of fiction is a radioactive pile of projection-identifications. It is the product, objectivated in situations, events, characters, actors, reified in a work of art, of the "reveries" and the "subjectivity" of its authors. Projection of projections, crystallization of identifications, it presents itself with all the alienated and concretized characteristics of magic.

But this work is aesthetic, that is, destined for a spectator who *remains conscious of the absence of the practical reality of what is represented:* the magical crystallization thus reconverts itself, for this spectator, into subjectivity and feelings, that is, into affective participations (see Figure 1).

A veritable energy circuit allows a high dose of reified participations to be relayed to the public. Thus *a to-ing and fro-ing of magical reconstruction through feeling, a to-ing and fro-ing of magical destruction through feeling* occurs at the heart of the aesthetic universe, by and through imaginary works. We see how the work of fiction revives magic but at the same time transmutes it, and consequently how all we have said about the magic of the cinema comes within the framework of the general law of aesthetics.

The aesthetic imaginary, like any imaginary, is the realm of man's needs and aspirations, incarnated, put in place, taken care of within the framework of a fiction. It is nourished at the most profound and intense sources of affective participation. In the same way, it nourishes the most intense and profound affective participation.

In the years between 1896 and 1914, the charm of the image, cosmic participation, the spectacular conditions of projection, the imaginary tide, carry each other along to create and exalt the great metamorphosis that will give the cinematograph the very structures of affective participation.

The cinematographic image had gorged itself on affective participations to the point of bursting with them. It burst, literally. This enormous molecular explosion gave birth to the cinema. From now on, the extreme mobility of the image will be added to the extreme immobility of the spectator to constitute the cinema, spectacle among spectacles.

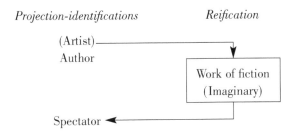

Figure 1. The circuit of transmutation.

The Processes of Acceleration and Intensification

The techniques of the cinema are provocations, accelerations, and intensifications of projection-identification.

The cinematograph restored the original movement of things. The cinema brings other movements: camera mobility, rhythm of action and editing, acceleration of time, musical dynamism. These movements, rhythms, tempos, themselves accelerate, combine, superimpose themselves upon one another. Every film in the cinema, even the most banal, is a cathedral of movement. The powers of participation, already awakened and provoked by the spectacular situation, are spurred along by the thousand deployments of movement. From then on, all the machinations of kinesthesia rush toward coenesthesia. They *mobilize* it.

Almost every cinematic means can be brought back to a modality of movement, and almost all the techniques of movement tend toward *intensity*. The camera, in fact, whether it be by its own movements or those of successive shots, can never allow itself to lose sight of, and must always frame and give star billing to, the moving element. It can always focus according to the highest intensity. On the other hand, its convolutions, its multiple takes (different shooting angles) around the subject, effect a veritable affective envelopment.

Together with kinesthetic techniques and determined by them, techniques of intensification by temporal dilation (slow motion) or spatial dilation (the close-up) have been brought into play. The emphasis on the duration of the kiss (divine "eternity of the instant") and the insistence on close-up vision of this same kiss exercise a kind of engulfing fascination; they take hold of and hypnotize participation.

To move and put things to our mouths: these are the elementary processes by which children start to participate in things that surround them. To caress and to kiss, the elementary processes of amorous involvement—these are also the processes through which cinema involves us: kinesthetic envelopments and close-ups.

Completing the intensifying devices of kinesthesia, slow motion and the close-up, the techniques of mise-en-scène, also tend to excite and prefabricate the spectator's participation. The *photograph* exaggerates shadows or isolates them to engender anguish. Kilowatts of electric light surround the pure face of a star with a halo of spirituality. The lights are there to direct, orient, and channel the affective lighting. In the same way, the shooting angles, the framings, subject the forms to contempt or respect, to exaltation or disdain, passion or disgust. After he has been put forward for admiration by the low-angle shot, the high-angle shot humiliates the porter deposed to the washroom. He has become the last of men, *Le dernier des hommes*.[7] *Skanderbeg*, while shot from below, imposes legendary grandeur.

Thus the machinations of the mise-en-scène call forth and color emotion. The machinations of kinesthesia hasten toward coenesthesia to mobilize it. The machinations of affective intensity tend to mutually engulf the spectator in the film and the film in the spectator.

Film music in itself epitomizes all these processes and effects. It is, by its very nature, kinesthesia—affective material in movement. It envelops, imbibes the soul. Its moments of intensity have a certain equivalence to the close-up and often coincide with it. It establishes the affective tone, gives the starting note, underlines in a stroke (a rather large one) the emotion and the action. Film music is, moreover, as Becce's "Kinothèque" showed us, a true catalog of states of the soul. Thus, at once kinesthesia (movement) and co-enesthesia (subjectivity, affectivity), music bridges the gap between the film and the spectator; it joins in with all its élan, it adds all its binding quality, its perfumes, its resonant protoplasm, to the grand participation.

Music, said Pudovkin, "expresses the subjective appreciation" of the objectivity of film.[8] We can extend the formula

Affective excitation
established by the
animated photograph
(the Lumière
cinematograph)

{

Image

Shadow—reflection—double

World within arm's reach

Real movement

Imaginary

Affective
excitation established
by cinema techniques

{

Camera mobility

Succession of shots

Persecution of the moving element

Acceleration

Rhythms, tempos

Music

Assimilation of a milieu, of
a situation by prehension

Encirclements (movements and
positionings of the camera)

Slowing down and suppression
of time

Macroscopic fascination
(close-up)

lighting { shadows
          lights

shooting { high-angle shot
           low-angle shot

Figure 2. Techniques of excitation of affective participation.

to all the techniques of the cinema. They tend not only to establish subjective contact, but to create a subjective current. "The rhythm of this universe is a psychological rhythm, calculated in relation to our affectivity."[9]

This flux of images, feelings, and emotions constitutes a current of ersatz consciousness that adapts itself and adapts to it the synesthetic, affective, and mental dynamism of the spectator. It is as if the film develops a new subjectivity that carries that of the spectator along with it, or, rather, as if two Bergsonian dynamisms adapt to each other and carry each other along. Cinema is exactly this symbiosis: *a system that tends to integrate the spectator into the flow of the film. A system that tends to integrate the flow of the film into the psychic flow of the spectator*.

The film carries within it the equivalent of a *choke* or starter for participation that imitates its effects in advance. Hence, to the extent that it performs a whole portion of his psychological work for the spectator, it satisfies him at minimum cost. It does the work of an auxiliary feeling machine. It motorizes participation. It is a projection-identification *machine*. The distinctive feature of any machine, without wanting to play on words, is to mash up man's work for him.

Whence the "passivity" of the cinema public, which we will take care not to bemoan. Of course there is passivity in the sense that the cinema ceaselessly opens up channels where participation has only to be engulfed. But in the end, the irrigating torrent comes from the spectator, it is in him. Without it, the film is unintelligible, an incoherent succession of images, a puzzle of shadow and light. The passive spectator is also active, as Francastel says: he makes the film as much as its authors do.

This active passivity means that "we can without boredom (and even with joy) follow appalling nonsense on the screen that would never have been tolerated in reading."[10] Not only does film have the presence of images at its disposal (which is not sufficient: static documentaries are boring), but it titillates participation in the right spot, like a clever acupuncturist; the mind of the spectator, thus appealed to and active, is swept along in this dynamism that is also its own.[11] This is why a critic has confessed, putting it in plain language, that he would have been profoundly moved at the cinema by this same *Ordet* that he finds execrable at the theater. This is why it has been able to be said: "But even in the most obnoxious picture, I can feel the . . . hypnosis." "The worst cinema remains, in spite of everything, cinema, that is, something moving and indefinable."[12] "A silly film is less silly than a silly novel" (Daniel Rops). The first films, foolish but marvelous (Blaise Cendrars). And the whole world: "It's stupid but it's funny." A key turn of phrase about filmic participation.

The Anthropological Range of Projection-Identifications

We have already listed some of the participations proper to the Lumière cinematograph. Let us recall in particular: wonders, vanities, fears, pleasures of self-recognition and of the recognition of familiar things, the Kuleshov effect.

Let us now add phenomena more particularly elicited and stimulated by the cinema. The first, the most banal and most conspicuous, is that which we call "identification" with a character on the screen. Here again we can cite phenomena of extreme identification or false recognition, noteworthy above all among archaic peoples, children, and neurotics. My daughter Véronique, aged four and a half, exclaims when she sees the dwarf jockey in *The Greatest Show on Earth:* "There's Véronique." In 1950, M. Caffary tells us, the Bakhtiari, nomads of Iran, were shown a film made in 1924 on the exodus of their tribes (*Grass*, by Merian C. Cooper and E. Schoedsack). Numerous spectators boisterously recognized themselves in the adults while they were no more than children at the time of filming. Nevertheless, as soon as the cinematograph arrives, as we have seen, false recognition appears.

It is clear that the spectator tends to incorporate himself and incorporate into himself characters on the screen according to physical or moral resemblances he finds there. That is why, according to Lazarsfeld's inquiries, men prefer masculine heroes, women feminine stars, and the elderly mature characters.[13] But this is only *one* aspect of projection-identification phenomena—and not the most important one.

What is important, in fact, is the movement of fixation of this tendency onto personalities called *stars*. It is the constitution in and by the cinema of a permanent system of characters to identify with:[14] the "star system," whose study we will undertake elsewhere.[15] What is important, above all and in the end, are *polymorphous projection-identifications*.

If the spectator's projection-identification settles on characters who are assimilable to him because they are like him, already the example of the stars, the very word, reveals to us the impossible stellar distances that identification can cross. In fact the power of identification is unlimited.

Kids in Paris and Rome play cowboys and Indians, cops and robbers. In the same way that little girls play mommy, little children murderers, at the cinema good women play the whore and mild civil servants the gangster. The cinema's force of participation can bring about identification even with those held in low regard, the ignored, despised, or hated of everyday life, such as prostitutes. Blacks can identify with whites, whites with blacks, and so on. Jean Rouch, who has frequented cinemas on the Gold Coast, has seen blacks applaud George Raft, the slave trader, who, to escape his pursuers, hurls his cargo of black gold into the sea.

An exotic example? But I see stuck-up women loving the tramp they would chuck out the door, industrialists and generals full of tender friendship for the vagabond whose real existence is beneath even their contempt. Look at how they all love Charlie Chaplin, Gelsomina, el Matto, and

Zampano! This shows that ego involvement is more complex than it appears. It is at play not only in respect to the hero who is like me, but to the hero who is unlike me: him sympathetic, adventurous, free, and joyful; me sullen, trapped, a servant of the state. It can also apply to the criminal or the outlaw, although, on another level, the worthy antipathy of honest people condemns him when he commits the act that satisfies their profound longings.

Thus identification with the like and identification with the foreign are both stimulated by film, and *it is this second aspect that breaks very cleanly with real-life participations.* The damned take their revenge on-screen—or rather the damned part of ourselves does. The cinema, like the dream, like the imaginary, awakens and reveals shameful, secret identifications.

The polymorphous character of identification sheds light on this original, yet often forgotten, sociological finding: the diversity of films and the eclecticism of taste in the one same public. Ego involvement is as much affected by films we call escapist—legendary, exotic, incredible—as by realist films. In another sense, the universal enthusiasm for cowboy films, combined with the fact that "westerns are most popular in the Rocky Mountains"[16] attests to the same double reality: to escape from oneself, to find oneself again. To find oneself again in order to escape (the inhabitants of the Rocky Mountains), to escape in order to find oneself again (the entire world).

Finally, polymorphous participation goes beyond the framework of characters. All the techniques of cinema converge to plunge the spectator into the environment as well as into the action of the film. The transformation of time and space, the movements of the camera, the incessant changes of points of view, tend to carry the objects themselves into an affective circuit.

"The rails in the documentary enter my mouth."[17] "Thus the spectator who sees some faraway automobile race on the screen is suddenly thrown under the huge wheels of one of the cars, scans the speedometer, takes the steering wheel in hand. He becomes an actor."[18] Let us add: he also becomes, just a little, the car itself. The camera is everywhere at the ball: tracking behind columns, pans, high-angle shots, shots of musicians, circling around a couple. The spectator *is* the dance, he is the ball, he is the court. Not only "is this world . . . accepted as the environment in which we temporarily live, thus replacing our real physical environment, the film theater,"[19] but we are also ourselves this world, we are ourselves this environment, just as we are the stratospheric rocket, the sinking ship.

This polymorphous participation that cinema brings with it in an incomparable fashion thus embraces and unites not only *a* character, but *the* characters, the objects, the landscapes, the universe of the film in its entirety. We participate, beyond the passions and adventures of the heroes, in a totality of beings, things, actions, that sweep the film along in its flow. It is into an anthropo-cosmomorphic and micro-macrocosmic brew that we are snapped up.

We had gone back from anthropo-cosmomorphism right up to the source of projection-identifications. Now we go back down the current and once again come upon the animism of objects, faces that are mirrors of the world, incessant transfers from man to things and things to man. *Anthropo-cosmomorphism is the crowning achievement of the cinema's projection-identifications.* It reveals its formidable affective power. We reach the magic, or rather we pass through it, transforming, energizing, and it restores to us an increased participation. It is the phenomenon itself, the original, that the Lumière cinematograph was incapable of eliciting, except at the edges of haze and smoke.

The Soul of the Cinema

Magic is integrated and reabsorbed into the vaster notion of affective participation. The latter determined the fixation of the cinematograph into spectacle and its metamorphosis into cinema. It still determines the evolution of the "seventh art." It is at the very heart of its techniques. In other words, we must conceive of affective participation *as a genetic stage and structural foundation* of the cinema.

It would be interesting, from the genetic point of view, to follow through film history affective participations that progressively free themselves from their fantastic (magical) coating: phantoms become *Fantomas*, ubiquities transform themselves into wild adventures. The torrential current broadens from 1910 onward: the stage of the soul blossoms.

The stage of the soul emerges in its own right with the dramatic use of the *close-up* by Griffith (1912), the introduction of hieratic Japanese acting by Sessue Hayakawa in *The Cheat* (1915), and the exalting of faces in Soviet films.

Having truncated the body and eliminated the lower limbs (medium shot), silent cinema privileged and magnified the human face. "On the screen, heads two meters long look at us, heads that have no equals other than those of the Egyptian columns or the mosaics of Christ Pentocrator filling the apse of a Byzantine basilica."[20] The face attains erotic, mystical, supreme cosmic dignity.

The close-up fixes dramatic representation onto the face; it focuses upon it all the dramas, all the emotions, all that happens in society and nature. One of the greatest dramas of history and of faith is played out in a confrontation of faces, a combat of the soul, a struggle of consciences against a soul (Dreyer's *Jeanne d'Arc [The Passion of Joan of Arc]*).

From then on, the face ceased to grimace in deaf-mute mimicry to let projection-identification be engulfed in it (Sessue Hayakawa). Kuleshov's experiment allows us to become fully conscious of the phenomenon that Pudovkin and Eisenstein will systematically broaden out into micro-macrocosmic participation.

The face has become a medium. Epstein said quite rightly

that the close-up is "psychoanalytic." It makes us rediscover the face and allows us to read in it—that is Balázs's great idea in *Der sichtbare Mensch*. We plunge into it as into a mirror where "the bottom of the soul" appears.[21] The grandeur of Griffith and Pudovkin was to reveal, quasi-radiographically, that this foundation was the cosmos: the face being mirror of the soul, the soul itself being mirror of the world. The close-up sees much more than the soul in the soul, it sees the world at the root of the soul.

The cosmic richness of interior life—reciprocally, the inner richness of cosmic life, that is, the blossoming of soul. And just as the states of soul are landscapes, landscapes are states of soul.[22] Filmmakers entrust to landscapes the task of expressing states of soul: rain evokes melancholy, storm, torment. The cinema has its catalog of landscapes, incidentals of soul, its "exteriors" that correspond to so many inner registers: light comedy takes place on the Côte d'Azur, dramas of solitude in the North Seas.

The world impregnated with soul, soul impregnated with world: projection-identification, which tends toward anthropo-cosmomorphism, does not literally end up there, but blossoms out into a state of soul. Hence the soul state corresponds to a moment of civilization, where the latter can no longer adhere to ancient magics but feeds on their sap in the midst of affective and aesthetic participations.

We must also consider the other aspect of this civilization of soul: the hypertrophy, the complacency, the hypostasis of the soul.

What is the soul? It is this imprecise zone of the psyche in its nascent state, in a state of transformation, this mental embryogenesis where all that is distinct is confounded, where all that is confounded is in the process of becoming distinct, in the midst of subjective participation. Let the reader who wears his soul on his sleeve forgive us. The soul is only a metaphor for us to designate unspecified needs, psychic processes in their nascent materiality or decadent residual state. Man does not have a soul. He has soul.

A moment comes where the soul swells and becomes hardened; it ceases to blossom in order to become a refuge. Comes the moment when the soul is happy with its own emanations; it mystically exaggerates its reality, which is to be an intersection of processes; it takes itself for an essence, cloaks itself in its exquisite subtlety, encloses itself like a private property, displays itself in a shop window. In other words, the soul destroys itself by wanting to pass itself off as autonomous reality. It degrades itself in exaggerating itself. It loses communication with the nourishing channels of the universe. And now we have the soul, isolated, on offer, obscene, so gelatinous, so soft, a Medusa-like jellyfish abandoned on the beach. It bemoans living in a world without soul, while it is drowned in it, and, as the drunkard calls for his drug, it naively calls for "soul supplement."

Our civilization is so smeared with soul that the spectator, blinded by a kind of opaque membrane, has become incapable of *seeing* the film, capable only of *feeling* it. Ombredane carried out a very significant experiment when he compared the accounts of blacks from the Congo and Belgian students about the same film, *La chasse sous-marine*.[23] The former were purely descriptive, precise, teeming with concrete details. This goes to show that, and we will see it again, magical vision does not obscure practical vision among archaic peoples. The white students' accounts displayed a poverty of details, an extreme visual indigence. They were, on the contrary, riddled with literary effects, general, vague, and they had a tendency to relate the events in a manner at once abstract and sentimental, with aesthetic considerations, subjective impressions, states of soul, value judgments. The civilization of soul internalizes vision that has become blurred, affective, obscured. Harpoon fishing is no longer an actual hunt, but a system of emotive signs, a drama, a story, a "film." It is not the game and the hunting technique that interest us, but the intoxications of risk, the surprises or wonders in the face of the unknown of the aquatic depths. We are shown tuna fishing, "men of Aran" and "Nanooks" of the great North in their practical life, but these awaken in us great shivers of the soul. "What counts is not the image; the image is only the film's accessory. What counts is the soul of the image" (Abel Gance). Here we can already sense the fundamental determination of the contemporary sociological context on our cinema psyche, that is, our psyche, *tout court*.

It is at the level of the film score that we clearly see the effects—or damages, as Jaubert claims—of soul music or "expressive" music, "a kind of musico-cinematic language combining the least commendable of Wagnerian recipes with pseudo-Debussy-like-banalities," which underlines the emotion, the action, the meaning, in one large stroke, and carries participation along toward the whirlwind of soul.[24]

On the other hand, decorative music (that of *The Third Man*, for example, or indeed the traditional music that still often accompanies the Hindu or Egyptian film, more rarely the Japanese film) is reiterative, without confusion. It does not faithfully espouse the events in the story. It is contrapuntal.[25] It organizes the story into a great rhythm that goes beyond it and gives it something like a superior or esoteric sense. It is like a kind of necessary cosmic order within which what happens in the film is integrated or moves. Laid on the film, this music superimposes an epic backdrop to the romantic (soul) event.[26] When the film is itself epic, then a superior synchronism between sequence and music, music and film can be established, as in the battle on the ice in *Alexander Nevsky* (Eisenstein, 1938).

Decorative music tends to broaden the soul's participation toward cosmic participation. Expressive music tends to direct cosmic participation toward the exaltation of the soul. Without entering into the problem, let us note that in the

West, decorative music comes about in reaction to the crudeness of the effects of ordinary film music *(The Third Man, Les jeux interdits [Forbidden Games], Touchez pas au grisbi [Hands off the Loot])*. In the East, by contrast, the Western screen score is infiltrating the film, particularly to transform the tempests, fires, and upheavals of nature into tumultuous soul states. We often see two kinds of music overlap, the one native, the other an importation, as in *Pamposh* (India, 1954) and *Le ciel d'enfer (The Blazing Sky)* (Egypt, 1953). Western music reigns supreme in *Love Letter* (Japan, 1954)—as much a sign of a troubling correspondence between romantic music and current cinema as of the conquering spread of the romantic civilization of soul specific to the bourgeois West.

Does the cinema have a soul, the Philistines wonder. But it has only that. It overflows with it; it oozes with it, to the extent that the aesthetic of feeling becomes the aesthetic of vague sentiment, to the extent that the soul ceases to be exaltation and blossoming to become the enclosed garden of inner complacencies. Love, passion, emotion, heart: the cinema, like our world, is all slimy and lachrymal with them. So much soul! So much soul! One understands the reaction that has emerged against crude projection-identification, the dripping soul, in the theater with Bertolt Brecht, in film, in diverse forms, with Eisenstein, Wyler, Welles, Bresson, and others.

Technique of Affective Satisfaction

Inflated and overflowing with soul to such an extent, and, more broadly, structured and determined by affective participation to such an extent, the cinema responds to needs.

And we already feel the needs, which are those of any imaginary, of any daydream, any magic, any aesthetic: *those that practical life cannot fulfill.*

The need to escape oneself, that is, to lose oneself in an elsewhere, to forget one's limits, to better participate in the world. That is, in the end, to escape in order to find oneself again. The need to find oneself again, to be oneself even more, to rise up to the image of this double that the imaginary projects in a thousand incredible lives. That is, the need to find oneself again in order to escape. To escape to find oneself again, to find oneself again in order to escape, to find ourselves elsewhere than in ourselves, to escape into our inner selves.

The "specificity" of cinema, if we can put it this way, is to offer the potentially infinite range of these flights and reunions: the world within arm's reach, all the cosmic fusions—and also the excitement on the spectator's part of seeing his own double incarnated in heroes of love and adventure.

The cinema has opened itself up to all kinds of participation: it has adapted itself to all subjective needs. That is why it is the ideal technique of affective satisfaction, as Anzieu put it, and has effectively become so at all levels of civilization, in all societies.

Does the transformation of a technique of the real into a technique of affective satisfaction not merit study?

It is in developing the latent magic of the image that the cinematograph filled itself up with participations to the point of transforming itself into cinema. The point of departure was photographic *doubling*, animated and projected onto the screen. From here on, a genetic process of chain reactions immediately started up. The charm of the image and the image of the world within arm's reach established a spectacle, the spectacle excited a prodigious imaginary unfolding; image-spectacle and imaginary stimulated the formation of new *structures* within the film: the *cinema* is the product of this process. The cinematograph roused participation. The cinema intensifies it, and projection-identifications blossom, exalting in anthropo-cosmomorphism.

In the course of these revolutionary processes, magic, subjectivity, affectivity, and aesthetics were called into question and remain so. It is here that analysis becomes difficult. Are these notions not themselves reified, semimagical, in their acceptance and use? It is absolutely vital to understand that magic, affectivity, and aesthetics are not essences, but moments, modes of the process of participation.

We have seen that magic structures the new affective universe of the cinema, that affectivity establishes the new magical universe, that the aesthetic transmutes magic into affectivity and affectivity into magic.

Cinema, while it is magic, is aesthetic, and while it is aesthetic, is affective. Each of these terms comes back to the other. A mechanical metamorphosis of the spectacle of shadow and light, the cinema appears in the course of an age-old process of internalization of the ancient magic of our origins. Its birth takes place in a new magical blaze, but like the tremors of a volcano on its way to becoming dormant. Above all, we must consider these magical phenomena *as hieroglyphs of an affective language*. Magic is the language of emotion, and, as we shall see, of the aesthetic. Therefore,

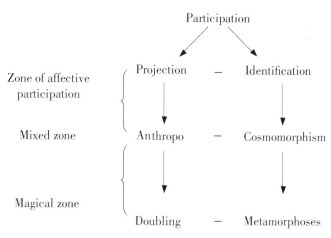

Figure 3. From participation to magic.

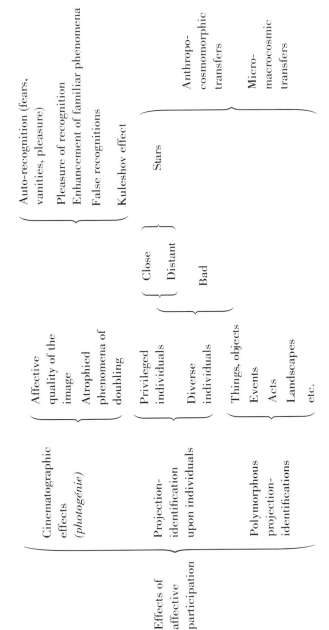

Figure 4. Effects of affective participation.

we can define the concepts of magic and affectivity only in relation to one another. The concept of the aesthetic inserts itself into this multifaceted reciprocity. The aesthetic is the great oneiric festival of participation, at that stage where civilization has kept its fervor for the imaginary but has lost faith in its objective reality.

Paul Valéry, with an admirable turn of phrase, said: "*My soul* lives on the all powerful and animated screen: it *participates* in the passions of the *ghosts* that are *produced* there." Soul. Participation. Ghost. Three key words that unite magic and affectivity in the anthropological act: participation. The processes of participation—in their characteristics specific to our civilization—reveal the extraordinary genesis. What is most subjective—feeling—has infiltrated *what is most objective: a photographic image, a machine*.

But what has become of objectivity?

5 *Objective Presence*

Subjective life structures the cinema and brings it under the influence of the great trade winds of the imaginary.

What, along the way, has become of *the objectivity* of the image that made H. de Parville say, "It has an extraordinary truth"?

Must we not, however, pose the preliminary question: What is this objectivity, and what is it founded on?

Why was it not noticed, on December 28, 1895, that the cinematograph had no sound, color, depth, and so on? Why was a global and objective reality immediately present on a screen merely brushed by a beam of twenty-four flashes of pretense a second? By what ultimate principle of reality was the impalpable luminous dust able to remain a depository to be turned into "extraordinary truth," into "astonishing scenes of realism"? What first principle of objective reconversion have we, the spectators, ourselves set in action?

Cinematographic Objectivity

The first supports of reality are *forms*, called real, although they are only apparent, and, precisely because they are faithful to appearances, they give the impression of reality. These are the same forms that show up on the photographic image and that the latter restores to sight.

117

This is why the photograph, as flat and as immobile as it is, already brings with it an impression of objective reality.

The image of the cinematograph is the photographic image itself. Film has become the common name for the two kinds of film. If photography, in order to be formally objective, is less real than the cinematograph, without, nevertheless, being more unreal (the reverse is true, as we shall see), it is because the latter increases its reality through movement and projection on the screen.

The projection of movement restores physical and biological mobility to beings and things. *But, in the same stroke, it brings much more*.

The photograph was frozen in an eternal moment. *Movement brought the dimension of time: film unfolds, it lasts. At the same time, things in motion produce the space that they measure and traverse, and, above all, become real within space*. As Michotte pointed out in his first-rate article, movement restores to forms brought to life on the screen the autonomy and the corporeality that they had lost (or almost lost) in the photographic image. "The opposition between the movement of the figure and the immobility of the screen acts . . . as an agent of segregation and frees the object from the shot in which it was integrated. It becomes substantial in some way. . . . It becomes a corporeal thing."[1] The moving image extracts itself from the screen: movement completes its corporeal reality. Cinematographic projection frees the image from the plate and the photographic paper as from Edison's box, launches the bodies released from all entanglements other than those impalpable ones of luminous rays that cross the room, and in this way accentuates the segregations and substantializations created by movement. But projection only puts the finishing touches to the work of movement. Movement is the decisive power of reality: it is in it, through it, that time and space are real.[2]

The conjunction of the *reality* of the movement and the *appearance* of the forms brings about the feeling of concrete life and the perception of objective reality. The forms provide their objective framework to the movement, and the movement gives body to the forms.

Together, they immediately establish an objective truth much more lively than not only forms stripped of movement but also movement accompanying approximate or stylized forms (cartoons) would do.

This objective truth awakens certain affective participations connected to real life—sympathies, fears, and so on (what Michotte calls "really experienced emotions")—and these participations consolidate and, in their turn, increase the objective truth. Things have body, so they exist, so they *truly* have body.

Whence the first excitement at the arrival of the train or the galloping horse. Proof of the instant dazzling sight of reality provoked by the cinematograph had just been demonstrated.

Objective truth, impression of reality: let us be precise.

This means that the processes of practical or objective perception are at play in the perception of cinematographic images. Practical perception considers things fixed and constant in their corporeal materiality, that is, irrevocably identical with themselves. Objective things obey not retinal images, where they appear, disappear, grow, and shrink, not ubiquities and metamorphoses, but their essence and their permanence, their own *identity*. And we have just come out with the key word of the universe "civilized" by man (equally the key word of the policed universe where man, equipped with an identity card, becomes an object). This permanent identity of things with themselves is at the same time their objectivity and their rationality, within a universe itself rational because *one*, identical with itself and constant in its laws.

The fundamental process of objective perception is that of the law of constancy that brings back visible forms, always variable according to the distance or position of the observer, to a kind of average height gauge that is none other than their rational scale of perception and form. The gestalt has made us recognize that the dimension, form, orientation, the position of objects in the visual field, tend to remain constant despite our proximity or distance, the ceaseless movements of our eyes, the rotation of our head, or the changes in the comportment of our body. "A man seen from a distance of ten meters keeps his height as a man in our eyes and the ostensible height that science concedes him, around 15 centimeters, is unconscious."[3]

Consistency operates immediately and unfailingly on the visible forms of the real world. It is these that the cinematograph reproduces. That is why they are immediately converted to objective perception. *That is why they even impose an objective perception.*

In fact, from the time it appeared, the cinematograph immediately responded to the essential exigencies of practical perception, and the law of consistency automatically applied.

Even before the cinematograph, H. de Parville had already enlarged the few centimeters of the minuscule image of Edison's Kinetoscope to this "standard" vision, this psychological average that we call real vision: "The washbasin, the hairdresser and his clients. We are there. It is extraordinarily real. One could almost enter to have a shave." The same H. de Parville—and all the spectators with him—a little later shrank to the same objective average the enormous faces looming in the first shot *(L'arrivée d'un train à la Ciotat).*

Is there, in other respects, a difference between microscopy and macroscopy for the spectator from the last and the first row? "The figures on the screen seem to have the dimensions of reality . . . even when we see them from the back of the room."[4] Yet a box of matches held at arm's length before one eye, the other being closed, entirely covers the screen for the spectators at the back of the room, and for those in the first rows, it covers a scarcely visible fragment of the screen. Thus, although in other respects the size of the image, apparent or real, can be important, objective consistency withstands the distance from the spectator to the screen, as it does the dimensions of the screen.

Photography is much less favorable to restoring consistency; it must avoid the acromegalies or apparent monstrosities created by the excessive closeness of a hand, a foot (low-angle shot), a head (high-angle shot). On the other hand, the movements of a limb toward the cinematographic lens, as in high-angle or low-angle shots on people moving, create neither discomfort nor displeasure: the distortions are not, or are scarcely, perceived. Consistency does its job, almost as in practical life, where we always see the average shape of people viewed from ground level or a height. Its abatement before the screen is more or less the same as in practical life: from the height of a plane, apparent size is finally substituted for "true" size and we discover little men, dolls' houses, and toy railways.

Because with the cinematograph consistency was reestablished without fail, its naïveté was immediately exploited, presenting it with naval battles filmed in the pond at the Tuilleries and eruptions of Mount Pelée in a wood fire. These first special effects were still cinematographic in essence: they did not metamorphize the objective universe; they were addressed, on the contrary, to the sense of objectivity that sees in their "truthful" dimension warships in the harbor in Cuba and the volcano in Martinique. The cinema, subsequently, was able to systematically take advantage of our consistency: models and miniature objects represented the most grandiose monuments, settings without depth opened up the most distant perspectives.

Thus a faultless perception imperturbably confers on odds and ends of make-believe, still faithful to apparent forms, substance, body, rational identity, practical objectivity.

Here we once again encounter the paradox discussed in chapter 2. The cinematograph provokes an objective perception, but this objective perception has as its reverse side, if we can put it this way, the quality proper to the double, to the image. Reciprocally, cinematographic reflections and shadows are themselves supports of corporealization and reality. The *real* original is perceived, but through its double. So at the same time as real-life participation, the participation proper to *photogénie* is awakened. Movement, which accentuates objective perception, equally accentuates the "charm of the image" and animates the winds and smoke of a latent fantastic.

Thus one process is doubly turned toward objectivation and subjectivation, affective projection-identification and the *projection* of rational frameworks onto apparent forms that go on *to identify themselves* with the consistent forms of objective perception.

It is this contradiction within the one process that the cinema will explode.

Perception in the Cinema

The cinema breaks the objective spatiotemporal frame of the cinematograph. It captures objects from uncommon viewing angles, subjects them to prodigious enlargements, makes them subject to unreal movements.

The camera leaps from place to place, from shot to shot, or else, in one shot, circles, advances, pulls back, navigates. We have linked this ubiquity and this movement to a system of affective intensification. *We can just as well say (and the whole significance of the problem is in the "just as well") that the camera imitates the processes of our visual perception.*

The workings of the gestalt have revealed that the human gaze, in its perceptive deciphering of reality, is always mobile. As Zazzo very accurately puts it, "The camera . . . has empirically found a mobility that is . . . that of psychological vision."[5]

The mobility of the camera and the succession of partial shots on one center of interest bring into play a double perceptive process that goes from the fragmentary to the totality, from the multiplicity to the uniqueness of the object.

Fragmentary visions converge in a global perception: practical perception is a reconstitution of the whole taking off from signs. The perception of a landscape or of a face, for example, is a partial and intermittent operation of discovery and decoding—we know that reading is a succession of visual leaps from fragment to fragment of words—from which comes an overall vision. The reading of a shot fixed on the screen is also done, of course, in fragments and jolts.

But it is performed from within another deciphering through fragments and jolts, a mechanical one, carried out by the film itself. The latter is nothing other than a succession of partial shots around a location that then often has no need of a shot of the whole. Thus a sequence can still show us separately three characters in the cab of a truck, but the spectator will see them together.[6]

Five-year-old Irène, whom I take to the cinema for the second time, perceives one single scene where three fragmentary shots succeed one another: (1) Bing Crosby puts croissants on the end of his cane, (2) this cane goes down through the window along the side of the carriage, and (3) Bob Hope, hidden under the carriage, grabs the croissants (*The Road to Bali*).[7]

The partial points of view are often multiple points of view of one object or one situation. This multifocal mobility of the camera leads us toward a prehension and an objective assimilation. An object is an object because it is psychologically seen from all angles. "We must *learn* objects, that is to say, multiply upon them the possible points of view," says Sartre. We must "*make a tour* of objects."[8] In other words, objective perception is the *end*, the conclusion, the globalization of partial shots, enveloping images, as in those naive or cerebral paintings that try to assemble all the perspectives of one object on the canvas. This process, for familiar objects, is already preconstituted, ready-made.

We recognize the cube at a glance and from a single angle because we have already concretized its "cubicity" in previous engaging experiences. Otherwise, it would only be a hexagon.

The moving camera combines and mixes fragmentary and multifocal apprehensions. It ferrets, flits about everywhere, and the spectator's eye reconstructs and condenses. Fraisse's experiment, which everyone can reconstitute for himself each time he goes to the cinema, shows us that the sight of a truck racing along as fast as possible is determined by multiple shots of details (i.e., inserts): wheels, speedometer, rearview mirror, a foot on the accelerator.

We always reestablish not only the consistency of objects, but that of their spatiotemporal frame. The spectator converts parallel actions to simultaneous ones although they are presented in alternation in successive shots. This "although" is also a "because": succession and alternation are the very modes through which we perceive simultaneous events and, better still, one unique event.

In real life, the homogeneous spatiotemporal milieu, its objects and its events, are given; perception, in this framework, decodes recognitions and envelopments in multiple stages. At the cinema, the work of decoding is prefabricated, and, from these fragmentary series, perception reconstructs homogeneity, the object, the event, the time and space. The perceptive equation is finally the same, only the variable changes. This similar perceptive outcome appears when we confront the two spectacles, so alike and so different—cinema and theater.

The limits of the theater stage, from the seventeenth century up until a quite recent period, determine the coordinates of a fixed space (like that of the Lumière cinematograph). The screen itself hovers in space. At the theater, the spectator clearly sees the whole spatial field; his viewing angle does not change; his distance from the stage remains constant. But carried along by projection-identification, although the latter may be less violently excited than at the cinema, he is psychologically plunged into an environment and into the middle of a performance. He psychologically destroys and rebuilds, chooses, makes particular shots succeed one another within the vision and the development of the whole. His psychological viewing angle, his psychological distance from the stage, ceaselessly change. His attention travels like a camera, mobile, free, ceaselessly adjusting itself in quasi close-ups, medium shots, master shots, tracking shots, pans.[9] Moreover, a whole theater tradition demands that the actors never remain in place, so their perpetual movements never cease to excite the perceptive mobility of the spectator and create, in some way, a psychological equivalent of camera movements. Conversely, the ceaseless mobility of the camera in Cocteau's film *Les parents terribles (The Terrible Parents)* makes very precise use of the psychological processes of the theater spectator, and in this way becomes "specific" to the cinema.

So there is a secret cinema in the theater, in the same way that a great theatricality envelops each cinema shot. In the first case, psychological vision cinematomorphizes the theater; in the second case, rationalization and objectivation theatricalize the cinema. In the first case, the rational and objective frames are *given* by the theater (unity of place and time); in the second case, it is psychological vision that is *given* by the cinema. In the first case, the little cinema that we have in our head begins to function on its own; in the second, it is our own little theater that deploys its stage and its space.

The spectator often does not know that it is he, and not the image, who brings the global vision. In the same way, he is unconscious of what profoundly differentiates the cinema film from the cinematograph's film (the theater film): the mechanized takeover of perceptive processes. But at the same time, he is obscurely conscious of what finally brings cinema and theater back to the same denominator: the unity of psychological vision.[10]

Perception is modeled, regulated, by a psychological vision whose mobility and independence in relation to the retinal image constitute one of the great mysteries of the human mind, often skimmed over by psychiatrists and psychologists, but which Farigoule was one of the rare ones to tackle in his work on extraretinal vision.

Imaginary processes, veritable hallucinations, says Quercy, are mixed up in our perception. Let us say in another way that doubling and *vision* (in the visionary sense of the term) are in embryo in perception.

Psychological vision seems to be driven by an eye that would free itself from the body, pedunculated, roving, circling away from its mooring post while nevertheless tied to it. It is as if there were a taking off beyond the limits of ocular vision, outside of our material being, of another self, who was precisely recorder and bearer of psychological vision. *"I suddenly had the impression of being outside my body."*[11]

Likewise, it is as if this *alter ego* were potentially endowed with an external sight that, from some meters in the distance, sees us from our head to our knees. This distance from self to self, which seems secretly to accompany us, is a sort of auto–medium shot. We can ask ourselves if the medium shot is not the locus of a meeting between the projection of our own alterity and identification with another, whence its systematic use in certain films.

We now understand that autoscopic hallucination and doubling are the pathological extreme—the magical reification—of a normal phenomenon, unnoticed but guiding perception.

Between the doubling of the mad or the possessed and everyday perception, dream and memory ensure continuity. Within the dream, each person can experience the incredible freedom of ambulant sight, with strange viewing angles, which goes as far as us contemplating ourselves. In the same way, the image of a memory goes beyond the angle of vision that was that of our eye and often also incorporates our own person.

We look at ourselves and we look with apparently doubled eyes, in reality with imaginary complementarizations and psychological rationalizations.

So everything tells us that there is a common core to perceptive (practical) and affective (magical) phenomena, where some are not yet differentiated from others. The common locus of these phenomena is psychological vision, crossroads of objectivations as of subjectivations, of the real as of the imaginary, a place from which they light up one another. The common process is projection-identification, but whereas affective projection-identifications let themselves be swept along by imaginary processes, objective projection-identifications carry along imaginary processes within the frameworks of practical determination: the subject projects the rationalizing structures that identify the thing not with him, but with the thing itself, that is, with a type or *genre*.

Psychological vision is at the very kernel of practical and imaginary processes. It turns just as well toward one or the other direction. In practical perception the tendencies toward ubiquity, doubling, animism, are atrophied, smothered, or diverted to the purposes of objective recognition, and we end up with objects fixed in their consistency, their homogeneity, their generality.

In affective vision the phenomena of objectivation are muddled, blurred, or charged with subjectivity, veritable batteries of soul. In magical vision they are atrophied, submerged by metamorphoses, or else fetishized. In this last case it is the object itself, complete and irreducible, that abruptly inverts its objectivity in the mirror of the imaginary: magic kidnaps the double that is within it and carries it away in its delirium.

Thus the same nascent psychological processes lead just as easily to practical, objective, rational vision as to affective, subjective, magical vision. They are polyvalent, and this polyvalence enables us to understand that practical vision can be charged with magic or participation, that magical vision can coexist with practical vision, as with archaic peoples where this coexistence determines perception itself. *We understand, then, by the same token, that the fundamental processes of the cinema, which tend to bring into play and arouse the mobility, the global nature, the ubiquity of psychological vision, correspond at the same time to phenomena of practical perception and phenomena of affective participation.*

The cinema is in the image of both and in this way provokes them both. Just as a spider envelops and sucks in its prey, the camera feels out all the angles of the cathedral, plunges in, withdraws, winds around, and penetrates it to finally nourish not only a subjective communication but a practical knowledge: the cathedral is captured in its diverse aspects, diverse angles—it is an objective document.

So the mobility of the camera and the fragmentation into shots correspond to total, affective, and practical processes. They are total because still in the nascent state, undifferentiated. Their natural tendency is to distinguish themselves, almost to the point of opposing each other: then there is a rupture between magic and science. Subjectivity and objectivity are first of all twin sisters before becoming enemies.

It is on the level of their continuity and their rupture—that is, of their dialectic—that we must follow them in the cinema.

Movement and Life

Here again we must come back to the source, to what differentiates the cinematograph from photography, and what equally differentiates the cinema from the cinematograph—real in the first case, artificial in the second—*movement*.

Movement restores the corporeality and life that photography had frozen. It brings an irresistible feeling of reality.

And it is because movement restores corporeality to what was endowed with it that it gives corporeality to what is devoid of it. We see this well when the moving camera unflattens the painted canvas, opens up depths in the two-dimensional picture, and brings out the autonomy of the characters. In the same way, through tracking, things acquire their strong contours.

The experiments cited by Michotte allow us to isolate this phenomenon in the elementary state, since they concern the thing most lacking, if not in depth, at least in substance: a geometrical figure. A parallelepiped projected onto a screen is no more detached from the screen than the same figure drawn with chalk on a blackboard is detached from the board; by contrast, once set in motion, the segregation proceeds before the spectator's eyes: the parallelepiped has its own "reality," that is, its corporeality.

More generally still, it is because movement restores life to what has it that it gives life to what does not have it. So it can give body to the incorporeal, reality to unreality, life to the inanimate. To lie, to produce illusions! That is the initial result of the prodigious truth of movement. Once set in motion by Robertson, the exhilarating impression of reality created by the magic lantern right away created an exalting of the fantastic. In the same way, the greatest unreality arises with Méliès, as a direct function of the greatest realism ever known in the image.

Caveing wrote, very rightly, that if "the essence" of the cinematograph is "to originate in a copy, this process will transform itself into prestidigitation. In fact, the more complete this copy is as a reproduction of the world, the more free it will be in relation to it. In fact, since by definition it accurately resembles the sensory world, *the sensory world will need to resemble it accurately:* thus the cinema makes an illusionist of itself . . . suppressing what it was . . . and dialectically transforming it."[12]

It is because it gives the complete *illusion* of reality that the most complete illusion has been able to appear as reality. The reality of the photo was less lively, its possibilities for unreality less great.

But let us not forget the reverse side of the dialectic. Movement has a double face: it is not only a power of corporeal realism, but also an affective power, or *kinesthesia*. It is so bound to biological experience that it brings with it the inner feeling of life as well as its external reality. Not only the body but also the soul. Not feeling alone, not reality alone: *the feeling of reality*.

In and through this feeling of reality, the soul accordingly increases life, and thus the corporeal reality of beings whose real movement is restored; their corporeal reality accordingly heightens this same life. Things themselves can henceforth be carried along, if they are transformed artificially, in this biological and animistic circuit. In the same way that movement can give body to what is without it, it can breathe soul into all that it animates. So the child gives life to all that is movement and soul to all that is life. The cinema will implement this logic: what is alive will seize death.

We see that the cinema has exalted and privileged movement. It wins every time. Movement is its *mana*.

And if it is true, as Claude Lévi-Strauss indicates, that all in all mana signifies "*truc machin*," something indeterminate, we understand that it is things and machines, illusions of movement, that give birth to the cinema.[13]

Everything begins with the metamorphosis at the Opéra, which is the prestidigitation of movement. Then comes the setting in motion of the camera, with Méliès, Promio, the Brighton filmmakers, one or another of whom discovers tracking, one of the inventions with the most claimants, because one of the most spontaneous inventions of the cinema. Then there are the shots that leap from the one to the other. Then the medium shot and, above all, the close-up allow us to capture the "imperceptible" movements of the face.

Finally montage, which completes the definitive passage from the cinematograph to the cinema, injects its rhythm, its organizing movement, where there was only a succession of scenes, shots, images. Everything is in motion, the rustling of leaves, the batting of eyelashes, or the explosion of atoms. The music itself is there to spur on the movement of the images. It enlivens images fixed in one moment with all the movements of the soul. And when suddenly music and image are immobilized, there is a moment of extreme tension in the movement. This immobility has meaning, value, gravity only as an expectation—of the door that is going to open, the gunshot that is going to go off, the word of deliverance that is going to burst out.

Through movement, and "by virtue of these secret operations of the mind thanks to which the real and the unreal merge," the cinema has become more real and more unreal than the cinematograph.[14] Movement is the soul of the cinema, its subjectivity and its objectivity. Behind the camera, navigator of time and space, the double track of life and dream spreads out into the infinite.

The cinema got rid of its starched cap, this "tograph" that was weighing it down—as moving pictures became movies—to reveal, in its shortened form, where only its pure semantic root, its essence, survives: *kinemas*.

Three-Dimensionality of Music

The realist powers of movement are exerted even where movement can seem most fluid, subjective, immaterial: music.

The musical score, which G. Van Parys says must make itself heard and not listened to, most often neither makes itself heard nor listened to, but merges with the film. The technical term, *mixing*, masticatory and digestive, betrays the destiny of a music that is amalgamated with sounds, words, and more broadly with film itself. We do not remember, after a film, whether there was music or not, when there was or was not music, except in cases where music is intentionally given star billing.

Where does this heard but unperceived music disappear to? And why, although disappearing, is its absence disagreeably felt? Why is it indispensable to the point that there is practically no film without its accompaniment?

"A silent film seen without musical accompaniment makes the spectator feel uncomfortable," says Balázs, and he adds, with his usual penetration: this is "a phenomenon which has a psycho-physical explanation. The explanation is that for the silent film the music was not merely an additional instrument for expressing a mood but to some extent a sort of third dimension added to the two dimensions of the screen. . . . As long as the spectator hears music . . . he accepts the image on the screen as a true picture of live reality. But as soon as the moving pictures really become silent, they at once appear flat, the flickering of suddenly bloodless shadows."[15]

Balázs saw very well that music is a *factor of reality*. But he did not grasp that if music makes the image on the screen be accepted "as a true picture of live reality," it is precisely because it is "an additional instrument for expressing a mood."

It is because it gives it a supplement of *subjective* life that it strengthens the *real* life, the convincing, objective, truth of the film images.[16]

Music, movement of the soul, illustrates the great law of movement. Music and movement, which are the soul of affective participation, illustrate in the same stroke the great law of participation: the soul gives flesh and body, affective participation makes objectivity blossom into objective presence.

Petrouchka

Like movement, like music, participation jointly gives soul and reality to all that it embraces. It is not just by chance that music—subjectivity itself—makes the final contribution so that the current of real life can fully irrigate the images.

"The integration of the dynamic plane of affectivity and the tendencies to the visual image contribute to creating in cinematic fiction all the dimensions of the subjective reality of the waking state," said M. Ponzo.[17] He could have added:

and of the objective reality of the waking state. At the cinema, as in life, the one does not go without the other. Subjectivity and objectivity are not crude givens, but products of man sprung from the same source. In its perpetually reborn flow, projection-identification makes subjective and objective life spring up at the same time, the one carrying along the other.

Participation has always been able to give life and soul to statuettes, marionettes, puppets, to printed signs from which the heroes of the novel are born as ectoplasms. Wooden statues are for pious crowds more real still than film stars are for us, stars who, moreover, inspire in us the same behavior, but atrophied, because our faith itself has atrophied into the aesthetic. The story of the marionette Petrouchka is the story of all the true false characters of the imaginary.

The curtain rises. The puppet moves about at the will of the strings, animated by the scraping of the violin. And suddenly seized by love, it escapes, runs among the spectators at the fair, suffers, cries, desires, and dies. But it is only straw that comes out of its burst belly. And us, who are we? For such is the ultimate question that the puppet poses for us: "If you, spectators, have believed in me, if for you I have lived with a body, a soul, and a heart, like you, and if I die as you are going to die, what more are you yourself? Are you of flesh or straw? Much less than I who am reborn with each performance, who am from another realm. . . . And you are well aware that my theater is brother to your altars, that I, a doll, am brother to your gods, that before me you are at the very sources whence your religion was born."

Some symbolic, allusive forms are enough for us to see corporeal specters, almost more real than ourselves, come to life. A statue is enough for us to see an immortal god, a puppet to see there the image of our condition.

At the very limit, participation creates its own object from all the pieces—the hallucination is the extreme subjective vision that becomes absolutely objective perception. Reality is lacking, but its objectivity is not. The double of the hallucination is even the absolute object: a being of reason eternally identified with itself because amortal. The most incorruptible body is the one that comes from the soul!

Photographic Orthodoxy

But hallucination and the double are extreme, fragile objectivations of a subjectivity that at the same time loses all contact with objective reality.

Most often, subjective participations in the waking state, left to themselves, incompletely exude objective presence. In my daydream I speak with a present but hazy interlocutor. In my reading, the objectivity of the Petrouchka of the novel appears to me in terms of an ectoplasmic secretion, always floating. To objectively concretize with more precision and ease, participation needs an external support, symbolic forms, puppets, drawings, statues, tableaux.

At the cinema, film chemically, physically, optically provides *the supports of objectivity, without error or failure*. Objectivity is brought in at the outset, like a blueprint.

The cinema shatters all the objective frameworks of the cinematograph, *except this last one*. Photography saves and holds on to the original objectivity of the cinematograph. Much more: it finally imposes it on the cinema. Like the paleontologist who pieces together the mammoth from a molar, the spectator, thanks to apparent forms that have been maintained and saved, endlessly reconstructs the objective world. Photographic orthodoxy imperturbably sets the action of consistency in motion, despite the subjective whirlwind that surrounds, breaks up, and swamps the image. Its objectivity is *the guardrail* of the imaginary. It guides perceptive restoration. And in the same way that consistency has the habit of spontaneously organizing visible movements, appearances and disappearances, leaps and metamorphoses, the microscopies and macroscopies of the retinal image, *the spectator reacts before the screen as before an external retina telelinked to his brain*: without cease, kaleidoscopic fragments, minuscule figurations, and gigantic faces are engulfed as if in a funnel to reappear at an average size, consistent, "normal." Photographic "high fidelity" makes objectivity triumph to the point that the spectator most often remains as unconscious of the strange phenomena that unfold on the screen as of those that develop on his retina.

At the same time, all participations stemming from the dissolution of the cinematographic universe, all the fluidity of the cinema, come to engulf their plasma within the corset of photographic objectivity. In this sense, they carry in themselves a supplement of soul and flesh as we have seen for music. The magical universe that cannot be freely deployed becomes subjective presence within objectivity. The reality that is reborn around forms, which, although shattered, have not lost the reality of their appearance—their character of objective reflection—is replete with presence. The joint bringing into play of consistency and participation surmounts a rupture that they themselves have provoked and makes a richer world than the cinematograph emerge into *objective presence*.

Total Cinema

Objective presence: all the attributes of objectivity are in fact present, during the first quarter of the twentieth century, in the flat, gray, silent image of the cinema.

When he saw the talkies in London for the first time, Steve Passeur exclaimed: "The silent cinema was speaking." He added, "or rather, it is you who made it speak by whispering the characters' dialogue very quickly and softly."[18] No one, in fact, "whispered the dialogue very quickly and softly," but it was the spectator who made the film speak. A process of silent audition, sonorous visuality, of which we are unconscious at the moment itself, of which we cannot not be unconscious, for any attempt to be conscious breaks the charm, that is, reminds us that it is impossible to hear what is silent.[19] A simple step backward, nevertheless, shows us that we have accumulated memories in sound. René Clair, rereading thirty years later one of his articles written in 1923, noted that "sound and dialogue could be suggested by silent images . . . and the spectators' imagination did the rest." He added: "This power of suggestion was so effective that more than once I have heard people . . . insist that a particular old film was a talkie when in fact it was silent. . . . These people . . . were convinced they *heard* the dialogue."[20] Said Pierre Scize: "I think of *Kameradschaft (Comradeship)* and suddenly realize that it is a talking film."[21] And Rivette: "You would really have to be deaf not to have your memory haunted by the lively and clear resonance of Lillian Gish."[22] Altman (on *Battleship Potemkin*): "Suddenly the tarpaulin is raised to the cry that swells each time we hear it: Brothers! Brothers! Brothers!"[23]

Effectively, the silent film spoke. Better, it was even capable of making silence; hence, with some exaggeration, Brasillach was able to say that silence was the great contribution brought by sound film. Silence is not muteness. It did not escape Balázs that silence is an experience of space. In fact, and we are paraphrasing Pascal, infinite space is infinite silence. What is lost to view is lost to hearing.

Silent cinema also knew other silences. Let us remember: transfixed gazes, close-ups of unsettling objects, that is, the sight of things questioned by the close-up. Silence is void or plenitude, terror or ecstasy, paroxysm or absence of soul. Silent cinema thus already featured silence, but sound film can translate it by noise, whereas silent cinema conveyed silence by silence. Silent cinema produced silence. The sound film gives it speech.[24] But everything was already talking from the time of the silent film, even, as little as there was of it, silence.

When, in practical life, everything is quiet, we have an impression of deafness if we doubt ourselves, of unreality if we doubt the world. The cinematograph, from its appearance, was tacitly heard. Already participation filled it with noises. Already *objective presence* went beyond the boundaries of the single *objective given:* that of apparent forms and real movement.

The problem of color is slightly different from that of sound. We are practically and perceptively much less affected by the destruction of colors than by the disappearance of sound. The psychologists of the first International Congress of Filmology (1947) showed that in general our attention accords little importance to fading colors before the "production" of the object.[25] Dreams, moreover, are only rarely in color, yet without their "reality" suffering because of this. So it was very easy for the cinema to do without color.

Where color is only a supplement, an inessential pleasure for participation as for objectivity, its absence is without doubt purely and simply ignored; it is neither present nor absent. However, the black-and-white cinema can very easily imply the presence of colors. Where the *objective and affective* quality of objects is linked to their colors, as in Bette Davis's dress in *Jezebel* (William Wyler, 1938), these colors are undoubtedly as present as sounds were in silent cinema. Thus the world of black and white is not decolorized but infracolorized and partially endowed with essential colors.

In the historical development of the cinema, color meets a weaker need than that of sound and, what is more, is still not universally imposed. A luxury of perception, it remained for a long time a luxury of "superproductions." On the other hand, the first colors, garish and false, contradicted chromatic *objectivity* and appeared less realistic than the always "natural" black and white. The most discrete, soft-hued colors were the most favorably welcomed.

Finally, black and white has been putting up its own resistance for more than twenty years. It offers possibilities that still partially exclude color. At the present stage, affective artifice, particular powers of suggestion, and a magical halo remain attached to the play of shadow and light.[26]

Color is only a luxury of perception but any luxury, taking root, becomes a need. It does not have the powers of black and white, but it develops others. Color goes hand in hand with sobriety and splendor. It is when it is able to be discrete and sumptuous at the same time that it triumphs. At the moment, it is learning how to become as natural as black and white and at the same time to gain an aesthetic effectiveness; it is already capable of sometimes effacing itself behind objects and action, and sometimes effacing objects and action behind it.

So, if color is on the way to becoming necessary to film, it needed twenty years of perfecting and insistence to begin to devitalize black and white, which had not waited for its arrival to institute a total universe.

The silent cinema speaks, black-and-white film is not without color. In the same way, depth is present on the two-dimensional screen. "It is undeniable that we see the volume of these images."[27] "In cinematic vision the flat screen disappears."[28] "The (two-dimensional) tableaux of our great artists, seen in films, acquire the characteristics of three-dimensionality."[29]

It is important not to confuse corporealization, segregation, and three-dimensionality, which converge in the same overall effect of depth. In any figurative representation, there is already the embryo of corporeality. Thus naive or archaic paintings that ignore or scorn perspective (three-dimensionality) restore a certain corporeality. It is in establishing perspective that Renaissance painting restores visible (called real) forms and dimensions and in this way suggests a three-dimensionality that increases corporeality accordingly. Photography itself automatically suggests this three-dimensionality. This is why our photographic perception, rather than being shocked by absences, relies on signs of presence and depth to see bodies in a space.

Cinematic movement accentuates corporealization to the point of effective segregation, very clearly opposing the object in motion and the motionless background. To all real movements, the cinema, mobilizing the camera, adds the infinite range of artificial movements, and in this way brings increased and new corporealizations and segregations. In the same way that the initially immobile child learns the contours of things by walking and touching them, the camera, mobilizing the spectator, may reveal to him new effects of voluminousness and emptiness that converge in a more and more vivid impression of depth or three-dimensionality. It is in regard to the cinema that the photo appears flat. And it is where movement is most efficient, that is, in tracking, that depth acquires all its muscle or invents itself from all the pieces of a flat setting, as we know from the first great success of the genre in *Cabiria* right up to the last great, aeronautical super-tracking shot of the Massif of Mont-Blanc in CinemaScope (Ichac's *Horizons nouveaux*).

What we call stereoscopic cinema, since then, is cinema that places the main stress on volumes and voids: it insists on depth, exaggerates it. Although in increasing degrees archaic painting, the photo, and cinema suggest depth, the cinema of depth hypostatizes this suggestion, but only the suggestion: the three-dimensional system plays on the depth of the screen, or on the duality of binocular vision, but the things that it shows *do not have depth*—they always remain patches of shadow and light.

There is no decisive leap between stereoscopic cinema and cinema, between cinema and cinematograph, between cinematograph and photo. In fact, in the course of one film, we pass without stopping from quasi-photographic images (fixed shots of fixed objects, an immobile chair) to cinematographic images (fixed shots of mobile objects), then to what is properly called cinema (camera mobility). We do not feel the difference between one and the other. We rarely have the impression that we are losing and regaining depth in the course of the development of the film. We fashion a perceptive medium, an average depth. Here again our

perception tends to stabilize and render things constant—
that is, objective and rational. Three-dimensionality and corporeality are the blueprints of our perception that we apply
on each favorable occasion. The cinema summons them and
brings them into play.

In the same way that beings and things wrest themselves
from the screen in their volume and depth, the image overflows the small standard screen, laterally and in height. Already the cinematographic screen, a fixed frame, was not
experienced as a prison. The cinema invented the camera's
rotation upon itself (the vertical or horizontal pan) to open
the entire space to the spectator.

The moment there was a serious crisis in cinema attendance, the search for a supplement of objective presence
brought about the extension (CinemaScope, Cinerama) and
volumization (stereoscopy) of the image. It is because they
constitute two concretizing aspects of the same tendency
toward the emancipation of the image from the screen that
the two techniques asserted themselves and fought against
each other at the same time until the most economic and
simple prevailed (CinemaScope). That is also why a sort of
confusion occurred in the first days of CinemaScope, presented to the masses as a process of depth and experienced
as such by numerous spectators.[30]

In the same way that talking film achieves implicit
speech, that stereoscopy explicitly suggests implicit depth,
that color explicitly makes blossom its range of colors, its
seeds and its buds hidden away in the underlying palette
of black and white, so CinemaScope, Cinerama, and other
processes achieve—very partially, almost symbolically—a
spatial overflow that is already *effected psychologically*.

But for thirty years, a voiceless and gray image was able
to represent the world and life in their concrete totality. In
other words, vision alone—accompanied by some sort of
music—was able to assume the function and role of the other
senses, to reconstitute a multisensorial and multidimensional

universe. Nowadays still, "who registers that the little photographic image of the film is lacking a dimension?" Who
notices that film has no smell? Nowadays still, Larousse's
primitive old definition, "animated views," remains un-
changed. This definition does not even mention that these
scenes were able to be silent, without color, limited in their
range of focus, flat. It ignores the fact that in future color,
sound, depth, and the wide screen are part of the system.
The Larousse definition remains faithful to the shared sentiment that says, "I have seen it with my own eyes," meaning, "I have also heard, colored, and given depth to it."

This total objective presence assumes a dialectic of the
senses, which "translate each other without any need of
an interpreter," and, correlatively, this symbolism in things
"which links each sensible quality to the rest."[31] It assumes,
above all, that the visual sense is the predominant sense, the
imperialist sense in modern man. Radio, attaching itself to
the image, becomes television, that is, home cinema. Cinema, taking on speech, remains visual. And if sound still
plays only a secondary and, moreover, scarcely "realist" role
(see chapter 6), it is because it is already objectively implied
in the visual image.[32] The visual dialectic of the cinema constructs a total, objective, and concrete world. Radio, through
the dialectic of hearing, reconstructs a total world as well,
but a vague, obscure one that we have a presentiment of
rather than feel. And in the same way that hallucination in
hearing is very poor in relation to that of the eye, radiophonic hallucination is vague beside that of the screen.

Hallucination is not a misplaced term here, since it renders the passivity of the spectator before his vision as well as
the fabricating work of his mind. Indeed, all perception is
hallucination correctly guided by signs. But in the cinema,
it is a question of a prodigious syncretized reconstruction
where sounds, voices, smells come to be integrated, a reconstruction that is effected from the single visual image, the
Salzburg bough that offers itself to objective crystallization.[33]

Perhaps we now have at hand the elements necessary to resolve a problem outlined in a preceding chapter. The techniques of sound, color, and the panoramic screen (and one day we will need to cite stereoscopy) were not responding to the key needs of the cinema. The spectator brought them along at the same time as his eyes, his head, and his wallet. Nevertheless, they have today become *needs*, an as-if-absolute need from now on for talking film, a need that is slowly imposing itself for color, a need that is constituting itself right before our eyes for the panoramic screen. What is this need, then, that is not one, this nonneed become need? One thing is clear at the outset, which is the relativity of human needs. Our most elementary requirements—water, gas, electricity—are the luxuries of yesterday or other places. In the same way Coca-Cola is not at all a need for those who do not know about it but becomes one for those who have become used to it, talking film, for example, has become a need out of habit. To this habit a pleasure is added, an ease unknown in silent cinema. The cinema discharges the spectator's mind of one part of its task: it speaks for him. Talking film encourages a sensory laziness by creating a new sensual pleasure. The mind is happy, it frees itself, it lets the mind-machine work in its place. It allows itself to be entranced, subjugated, possessed. To this pleasure new riches are added. We have shown this for color, we will see it for talking film. After talking film, silent cinema becomes truly silent; after color, black and white become gray; after CinemaScope, the traditional screen becomes small. From then on the mind goes on strike when we want to take it back to its original activities. This evolution is normal. It is the very evolution of the cinema: it constantly becomes a little more comfortable to the senses, without, however, the situation of the spectator of *The Robe* differing fundamentally from the one watching *Cabiria*.

In fact, no less admirable than the dialectic that transforms luxury into need is the regulating one, which brings back what is enriched to a state analogous to its original poverty, which was already wealth. In the silent film, sound, color, and depth were virtual. In the talking film, in color and in depth, they are present to the point of exaggeration. Now, here like there, a sort of regulating equivalence of perception is produced. Before the silent film, perception exaggerates, or rather, it constructs sound, color, depth, starting from nothing. In the talking film, it attenuates color and depth. Once the surprise and wonder have passed, sound, color, and depth are arranged in terms of the image. It is always vision that commands. The stabilizing mind produces a sort of equilibrium where what is acquired loses its richness, but can only be lost through the creation of deprivation.

The Failure of the Total Cinematograph

We can now explain why sound, color, and the wide screen only universally start to become widespread from 1925 onward.

We can no longer believe that it was necessary to wait for technical discoveries: these discoveries were all present since the Exposition of 1900. Let us go further: the Lumière brothers' camera, at the time of its appearance and still five years later, was only one moment in a series of perpetually evolving inventions.

Of all the devices dreamed up, projected, and even realized from 1889 to 1900, Lumière's was without doubt the most modest. Edison sought a synthesis of the phonograph and the cinematograph, that is, already, the talking film. Grimoin-Sanson, inventor of the phototachygraph, wanted a cinema more "total" still: the Cinécosmorama! His two-eyed projector achieved absolute cinematographic envelopment on the circular screen. The Cinécosmorama was not a myth. An ascent and descent in a balloon were projected to spectators who became seasick and marveled. It is said that the danger of fire condemned the first Cinécosmorama or

Cinéorama, which had no successors. But is that enough to explain this failure?

The idea of the circular screen was more than "in the air." If Colonel Moessard had launched it, the American inventor Chase had taken out a patent on a cyclorama, which was tried out in 1894, and Baron had invented a device for "circular, animated," projections in "color and sound": the Cinématorama (1896). Lumière himself had installed a giant screen twenty-five meters wide and fifteen meters high in the Galerie des machines at the Exposition of 1900. In 1898, Lauste had made biograph projections on a giant screen at the Crystal Palace in London.

In a parallel fashion, the tendencies to depth, color, and sound were materializing. On November 3, 1900, Lumière patented "a device intended to show stereoscopic images in motion." Edison had already used color in 1894 for the Kinetoscope *(Annabelle Dancing)*; the colored films projected in the years 1896–97 and afterward were numerous enough (panoramic views of Grimoin-Sanson's Cinécosmorama, films by Méliès). In 1905, Louis Lumière found a solution that could be applied to film. Something more remarkable still, not only had speech been successfully grafted onto film in the first days of the cinematograph, but it was originally connected to it, or, rather, to the Kinetograph. As Sadoul stressed, the *first film projected was a sound film*. On October 6, 1889, returning from a trip to Europe, Edison found himself welcomed by the image of Dickson, who, greeting him ceremoniously with his top hat raised, declared: "Good morning, Mr Edison, glad to see you back. Hope you like the kinetophone."[34] On July 27, 1891—that is, four years before the first Lumière presentation—Marey communicated the invention of the Phonoscope, made by Demenÿ, to the Academy of Sciences. Since then, film has never ceased to speak: it spoke at the institute in 1899 when August Baron presented his sound film; it chattered at the 1900 Exposition with the Phonorama, invented by Berthon,

Dussaud, and Janssen, next to Clément Maurice's "Phono-Cinéma-Théâtre." From 1904 to 1910, Lauste totally resolved the problem of registering sound on film beside the image.

Thus the nascent cinematograph is already talking, in color, in depth, and on the giant or circular screen.[35] It tends irresistibly toward the total cinematograph. Why, then, did the various attempts to produce the total cinematograph, already apparently equipped from top to toe from 1900, not know any tomorrow? Why are they scarcely known nowadays, the day after that? Why for thirty years did the cinema let itself be limited to the small, rectangular, silent, black-and-white screen?

Were the techniques not perfected? In fact color, originally painted onto each image, had to wait for new discoveries to be caught by the image itself, but as early as 1905, Lumière had found the process applicable to film. Depth still does not manage to do without either lenses or installation equipment that is too costly. But on the other hand, processes having to do with sound and with projection onto the panoramic or circular screen were already known, had already been tried out, from film's infancy, and were available in the years 1900–1910.

Not only technical but economic causes, then? Without a doubt, the spread of sound cinema, of the big screen, of the system of multiple projections, supposed investment costs too heavy for the nascent industry of the cinema. Ciné-cosmorama, Cinématorama, Phonorama, Phono-Cinéma-Théâtre could at the most be exhibited as marvels of the Universal Expositions. The humble fairground tours of the first years, the nickelodeons of the suburban quarters, would they have been able to take on such heavy loads?

It is true, then, that in 1900 great technical and economic difficulties opposed the generalization of a sound that was not fixed onto film, of a color that was only coloring, of a screen that enlarged itself only at the expense of the clarity of the image or with the multiplication of projectors. Sound would have prevented the constitution of the first and necessary world market. The "total" film would have weighed down and perhaps crushed the nascent cinema.

As risky as it may have been to take a chance on what was possible, these difficulties, nevertheless, would not have been insuperable for the realization of an absolute need. And whatever they may have been, these difficulties did not constitute the true obstacle.

On the contrary, proof of this is provided by the fact that not one of the developments—such as sound, depth, color, or Cinema-Scope—was due to the immediate taking advantage of an invention. The developments had to wait for financial crises. The Warner Bros. crisis was needed to definitively launch sound, the Great Depression of 1929–35 to launch superproductions in Technicolor, the fall in public attendance and the competition of television in 1947–53 to launch Cinema-Scope and other processes of the wide screen. Then, and then only, thanks to the means of publicity put into play, a new interest crystallized, stabilized, took root, became a need. It was crises of capitalism that integrated sound, color, and the wide screen into the cinema.[36]

This explanation could suffice, but it would still not totally explain the paradox. At the 1900 Exposition, it is the cinematograph, and not the cinema, that tends to become total when it tries to take on sound, color, and the wide screen. Nonetheless, these inventions only enter into practice a quarter of a century later, after the cinema has completely extricated itself from the cinematograph. Instead of being at the point of departure for this revolution, they blossom at the end of it: they follow it instead of preceding it. *So we may assume that it is this same revolution that put the brakes on and stopped in their place sound, color, depth, and the wide screen, around 1900.*

The moment the 1900 Exposition seems to indicate the beginning of the total cinematograph, already, secretly, with

Méliès, the cinema is born. It was to fix itself to the primitive and simplistic Lumière machine for twenty-five years, the time it took to realize itself. *There is undoubtedly a fundamental correlation between the rise of the cinema and the immobilization of the mechanical invention.* The cinema, in bringing its participations, in the same way brought this supplement of sound, color, space, and volume that the inventors sought to graft onto the primitive image. Its objective reality was increased by its subjective reality. The total cinematograph? It was the cinema, objective presence.

In the same stroke, technical and economic difficulties were bypassed: the cinema, son of poverty, was the total cinematograph of the poor, of bricoleurs and entertainers. The cinema saved money on sound and color for thirty to fifty years, and continues to do without the total cinema. It is music that brings depth, and for less expense!

The cinema even needed, to realize itself in all its richness, to nip the total cinematograph in the bud. It succeeded here, the techniques being still too rudimentary or costly. Edison renounced the search for the cinematographic grail, while Friese-Greene and Lumière gave up. They turned their backs on cinema and never understood it. Better, from 1895 to 1932, Louis Lumière truly invented the total cinematograph (1895, cinematograph; 1900, giant screen; 1905, color; 1932–34, depth), but no one ever cared about it. The total cinematograph remained and remains like a mummy wrapped in bandages. Now and again the cinema rips off one of its formulas. From 1896 the invention was pursued, no longer in the art of making machines, but in the art of using them. The conjurers had replaced the inventors: they had become creators.

And it was when the creation was complete that sensory improvements of sound and color came to crown the edifice.

Cinema is the product of a dialectic where the objective truth of the image and the subjective participation of the spectator confront and join each other. It enriches the latter in a first stage (1900–25) but, once the systems of participation are set up, it will enrich the former (1925–55). This genesis, which is not complete, accordingly enriches and strengthens objective presence outside of the spectator (on the screen) and within him (in his participation).

Objective presence—in the image of the real world. But the real world has its lifeblood, its substance. It does not need us to exist. Our friends and our loves live outside of us. Reality transcends our subjectivity. The objectivity of the world of the cinema needs our *personal* participation to take shape and essence. This luminous pulverulence on the screen is like powdered plasmas, which, before having water added to them, are only dust.

This world needs our substance in order to live. At the moment of participation, all the film's characters are externally determined, but internally free. They have two dimensions, but internally three: externally they are ghosts; internally, they live. That is, they are also *externally* in three dimensions, externally corporeal, externally free. They live a life that is drawn from us. They have taken our souls and our bodies, have adjusted them to their size and their passions. It is rather we who, in the dark theater, are their ghosts, their audience of ectoplasms. Provisionally dead, we watch the living.

6 The Complex of Dream and Reality

The subjective participations that fix upon the objective image give it soul and flesh: objective presence. However, between the destruction of the objective frames of the cinematograph and their reestablishment by the cinema spectator, there is an infinitesimal gap. Through this eye of the needle enters a whole caravan of magic, introducing in contraband the opium of the unreal world.

Certainly magic cannot be deployed freely: it is locked in the objective world and can only irrigate it.

But the contradiction is there, between the vision, for example, of the revolver loaded with animist menace, bigger than a piece of artillery, and the continuity that restores it to its original twenty centimeters, just as our reason imposes a Jivaresque reduction on the vision of faces of the dimensions of those of Easter Island.[1] The contradiction is absorbed or surmounted in objective presence but is not extinguished. Continuity violated by metamorphoses and rational identity violated by the double are again enclosed, but they have been violated. Moreover, for the naive spectator, the oneiric subterranean universe can suddenly submerge the objective universe: buildings vanish or sink into the ground,[2] the enormous insect in close-up is now identified as the tsetse fly, the knife that the Congolese blacksmith makes in the image of scenes filmed in close shots is larger than the real knife

(Ombredane). Extreme cases, but ones that show us that appearances are in ferment under their rational obviousness, that the magic of the cinema bubbles away beneath its perceptive rigidity. The objective universe, if it superimposes itself on the oneiric universe so far as to almost efface it, is not only subjected to its radioactivity, but does not completely nullify it. The symbiosis has not abolished the profound duality.

Thus the rotation of the earth around the sun, once it becomes evident, makes us forget without dissipating it the evidence, or rather the previous appearance, of the rotation of the sun around the earth; whence comes our double attitude in regard to a sun that *rises* and *sets*, although we know it is immobile. In the same way, objective consciousness of the immobility of things makes us forget the prodigious and unapparent appearances on the screen without dissolving them. The double sun, both satellite and star, the hidden and the obvious, shines on a universe that is at once *single and double*.

Within perception, at that infinitesimal moment of objective correction, the cinema tends to provoke a vision in the visionary sense of the term. The artificial effects of shadow and light are added to the fluidity of forms in metamorphoses. So a certain duality is maintained, and the cinema has maintained it voluntarily. At the same time, within objective presence, it makes us *perceive* (in the practical sense of the term) and *makes us see* (in the visionary sense).

So we can assimilate this spectacle just as well to oneiric vision as to practical perception, *but on condition that we do it conjointly*.

The Attributes of the Dream— the Precision of the Real

We have already noted the analogies that make films resemble dreams: the structures of the film are magical and respond to the same imaginary needs as those of the dream; the cinema screening displays parahypnotic characteristics (darkness, bewitchment by the image, "comfortable" relaxation, passivity, and physical powerlessness).

But the spectator's "relaxation" is not hypnosis: the powerlessness of the dreamer is frightening and that of the spectator happy: the latter knows that he is at an inoffensive spectacle. The dreamer believes in the absolute reality of his absolutely unreal dream.

The film, by contrast, has a reality outside of the spectator: a *materiality*, even if it is only the impression left on the film strip. But however objectively perceived, however much it is a reflection of real forms and movements, the film is recognized as unreal by the spectator, that is to say, as imaginary. The news itself loses its practical reality: the real *original* acts are in the past, absent; the spectator knows that he is seeing *an* image and dereifies his vision to experience it aesthetically. Also, in comparison to the dream or the hallucination—pure reified ectoplasms—the cinema is a *complex* of reality and unreality; it establishes a dual state, straddling the state of wakefulness and dreaming. Certainly, the spectator is not in a state of hypnosis, but the autonomous alpha rhythm from his brain picked up by electroencephalography is already more ample and steady.

Closer to the cinema is the daydream, itself at the crossroads of the waking state and the dream. There the segregation between the dreamer and his fantasy is pushed much further than in sleep: while living through loves, riches, triumphs, we continue to remain ourselves, on the other side of the dream, on the prosaic edges of everyday life. A *watch light* controls the overflow of these diurnal dreams, preventing them from being too freely, too fantastically extravagant. But like the dream, however, the daydream is a closed vision, an empty crystallization of the fantasies of one subjectivity, while the film is an *open vision*, opened onto the world, because also determined by it.

Closer to the cinema in a certain sense, the daydream differs from it in another: the diurnal surroundings dim, almost efface its images; it is much more vague and hazy than the dream, and than, of course, the film.

For at the cinema, as Paul Valéry said, all the attributes of the dream are cloaked in the precision of the real. The film universe is permanently structured by objective perception and the consciousness of being awake.

Furthermore, the practical perceptions of real life are themselves equally imbued with affective and magical participation; they regularize appearances that mark it in one way or another; they develop hallucinatory processes to give total form (gestalt) to the fragmentary signs that catch our eye.

At the cinema, however, the "hallucinatory" processes are much more developed than in practical life, since a total objective presence emerges from simple luminous streaks on the screen. Its perception is accordingly less independent of subjectivity. The latter not only seeps into but profoundly permeates things. The practical smothers vision under perception; the cinema revives vision under perception.

Cinema and Vision of the Archaic World

In this sense, the universe of the cinema can be related to that of archaic perception.

The psychological processes that are at the birth of magical vision, as of practical perception, are in fact much less differentiated among archaic peoples than among the "civilized." That does not mean that practical perception is underdeveloped there; the experiments of Ombredane, such as the one with the chicken, have shown us that it can even be much more acute than ours.[3] But the magical vision that accompanies it has at least the same force. Archaic hunters, for example, know well that it is necessary to make arrows and spears to kill game, and they practice this concrete industry and art with extreme precision. But they also cast, on the image of the animal, the preliminary spell; they practice mimetic propitiatory rites. They practice the magical hunting rites but also really hunt game. The one does not dispense with the other, but backs it up and promotes it.

The frames of practical perception are fixed but equally open to the fantastic, and, reciprocally, the fantastic has all the characteristics of objective reality. Lévy-Bruhl endlessly showed that if archaic peoples believe that a sorcerer has killed one of those close to them, they are nevertheless not ignorant of the fact that the latter was taken by a crocodile in the river. Every object, like every real event, opens a window onto the unreal; the unreal impinges on the real. The quotidian and the fantastic are the same thing with a double face.

It is we who split the contradictory unity of the practical and the magical, or rather, of that which we henceforth call practical and magical, while our tools, clothing, masks, and images exist and act on both levels.

Historical evolution has worked to decant, to dissociate the two orders, to circumscribe the dream, the hallucination, the spectacle, the image, to recognize them as such and nothing more, to localize and fix magic in religion, to clean up practical perception. At the same time, aesthetics and art, quintessential heirs of magic, the image, the dream, and religion, have sought to constitute themselves in enclosed domains; they are henceforth great reserves of the imaginary, like those regions of Africa or America where we protect primeval savage freedom from nature and men.

Nevertheless, this differentiation has never been, is not, absolute, complete, radical. It is obvious that the frames of practical perception are not absent from imaginary vision; the real remains present even in the extravagance of the dream. Even in *Alice in Wonderland*, consistency and the principle of contradiction are respected to the essential extent that they allow the narrative, the discourse.

Conversely, as we have seen, practical perception still implies imaginary processes in atrophied form and is partly

determined by them. Moreover, and it is to deceive ourselves not to recognize it, the great forest of magic still
reclaims the domains of sex and death. Our whole practical
world is surrounded with rites, superstitions;[4] the imaginary
is still latent in symbols and reigns in the aesthetic; hallucinations are always possible at each lapse of perception.
Emotions suddenly blur differences and confound the two
realities. Our friends, our loyalties, our goods, our happiness, our ills, once again mix up the two orders.

New magico-affective-practical syncretisms are formed
as they are in love. As they are in the cinema.

The cinema effects a kind of resurrection of the archaic
vision of the world in rediscovering the almost exact superimposition of practical perception and magical vision—
their syncretic conjunction. It summons, allows, tolerates
the fantastic and inscribes it in the real. It *renews*, as Epstein
says so accurately, the spectacle of nature, and "man finds
once again something of his spiritual infancy, of the ancient
freshness of his sensibility and thought, primitive shocks of
surprise that have provoked and directed his comprehension of the world. . . . [T]he explanation that first imposes
itself on the spectator belongs to the old animistic and mystical order."[5]

The object, that is, the very product of the processes of
abstraction through which man extracts fragments of nature
from anthropo-cosmomorphic subjectivity to transform them
into things, that is, into *utilities*, is reintroduced into the
great viscosity of participation *without losing itself.*

In *Le cinématographe vu de l'Etna*, Epstein, in a curious
detour, rediscovers in the objects of the cinema the same
condensation of soul as in magical and sacred objects. "Those
lives it creates, by summoning objects out of the shadows of
indifference into the light of dramatic concern . . . are like
the life in charms and amulets, the ominous, tabooed objects of certain primitive religions. If we wish to understand
how an animal, a plant, or a stone can inspire respect, fear,

or horror, those three most sacred sentiments, I think we must watch them on the screen."[6]

The very strong analogies between the cinema and the archaic vision of the world cannot, nevertheless, be pursued to the point of identification. For the archaic person, magic is reified. At the cinema, as we have endlessly repeated, it is liquefied, transmuted into sentiment. Conversely, the perception of archaic peoples is practical: it infringes on the real, submits to it and concretely transforms it. Film perception occurs within a consciousness that knows that the image is not practical life; the mechanisms of objective perception are in motion, but they are not connected to the transmission. They run, in neutral, not on empty, but transform their energy into affective warmth. *What finally prevents the objective truth of film from being integrated into what is serious in practical life is aesthetic consciousness.*

The Aesthetic, as Watch Light and Dreamer

Aesthetic vision is that of divided consciousness, participating and skeptical at the same time. The aesthetic attitude defines itself precisely by the conjunction of rational knowledge and subjective participation. It is the key to the vault of the spectatorial situation, which affectively mixes up the subject and the spectacle but dissociates them practically.

As a watch light, the aesthetic dereifies (subjectivizes) the magic of the cinema and at the same time differentiates the cinema from the dream as from archaic vision. *As a dreamer*, it turns wakened perception away from the practical, toward the imaginary and affective participation. At once dreamer and watcher, the aesthetic is what unites dream and reality—thus what differentiates the cinema from the dream and from reality.

Oneiric vision is the prisoner of diurnal perception, but the latter is emasculated by a consciousness of unreality. Objectivity is in its turn prisoner of affective participation.

It is caught between magical vision and aesthetic vision. So the spectator, who *realizes* the film, confers all the rationalizations of perception on it; at the same time he derealizes this reality that he has just fabricated, he situates it extraempirically, he lives it affectively and not practically, and internalizes his responses instead of externalizing them in acts.

This unreality does not destroy reality: "Observable reality . . . is not at all weakened or altered in any way whatsoever by the knowledge that it is only an illusion."[7] This reality does not dissipate unreality. Better still: this reality is fabricated as much by the powers of illusion as these powers of illusion are born from the image of reality.

An incessant dialectic within an extraordinary complex of the real and unreal. The magico-affective unreal is absorbed in a perceptive reality itself derealized in aesthetic vision.

The Complex of the Real and the Unreal

Subjectivity and objectivity are not only superimposed but endlessly reborn, the one from the other, in a ceaseless round of objectivizing subjectivity and subjectivizing objectivity. The real is bathed, bordered on, crossed, swept along by the unreal. The unreal is molded, determined, rationalized, internalized by the real.

The cinematograph, a two-faced Janus, presented the real and the unreal in the same undifferentiated unity. The objective image was a mirror of subjectivity. It was not of the real *and* the marvelous *(photogénie)*, but of the marvelous *because* real, of the real *because* marvelous. An illusion of reality. A reality of illusion. The cinema has retained and exalted this virtue, which gives "the paroxysms of existence a supernatural character."

But the revolutionary originality of the cinema is to have dissociated and opposed the unreal and the real like two electrodes. Méliès made the original split. A magical universe entered into contradiction with the objective universe. The fantastic was opposed to the documentary. Fantastic and documentary, diverging and deriving the one from the other, discovered an intermediate register allowing all possible combinations.

On March 16, 1902, the first program in the first cinema properly speaking, the Electric Theater of Los Angeles, already embraced the whole field, going from the real to the unreal: "*Course de taureaux—Le président Diaz à Mexico— Gulliver—Voyage dans la lune (A Trip to the Moon)—Le royaume des fées (The Kingdom of the Fairies)*."[8] Since that time, programs present news, documentary, cartoon, and fiction film at the same time.

Not only does each program cover the whole expanse of the complex of the real and unreal, but each film is polarized on the one hand by the realism of objects and forms and on the other hand by the unrealism of the music. Between these two poles, the *fiction film*, which is the classic product of the cinema, its universal secretion, opens up a domain where the true, the seemingly true, the idealized, the fanciful, the incredible, are mixed up and combined. It is not just a middle term between the fantastic and the documentary, but a great complex within which multiple complexes are developed, constituted, and destroyed. Many pieces of unreality and reality are juxtaposed in the fiction film to create a puzzle, heterogeneous in its parts, curiously homogeneous in its totality. *Everything unfolds as if the requirement of reality were not uniform for everything that makes up the one film.*

Objects and Forms

It is not our intention to describe and analyze the fiction film in itself, but to use it as an example of the dialectical syncretism of the unreal and the real that characterizes the cinema.

At one pole of this syncretism are the objective forms. Except in relation to animation,[9] which as a result is clearly fantastic, the cinema has until now remained intransigent about respecting "real" appearances. It is the magician of the unreal, Méliès himself, who put forward without equivocation the golden rule of the truth of things: "*All is needed to give an appearance of truth to entirely artificial things. . . .* [I]n *material* matters, the cinematograph must do better than the theater and it must not accept conventional practices."[10] Whereas the theater can (must, we maintain) be satisfied with backdrops and conventional signs, the cinema needs *objects* and an environment that appear to be authentic. Its demand *for corporeal exactitude is fundamental*. While film accepts a postsynchronized voice, an extravagant plot, an orchestra at the bottom of a mine, and a face of a star invulnerable to the grime of the coal, it would not accept a skip that does not have the material form of a skip, a pickax that does not have the material form of a pickax.

The object cannot sustain any attack on its objectivity. The great influence of *Caligari* was not able to prevent the total failure of subjective decor. The expressionist lesson was retained for photography but refused for the object itself. The camera can freely play with forms, but the set designer cannot.

The camera can and must be subjective, not the object. The cinema can and must distort our point of view on things, but not the things. So there is an absolute, universal demand for "real" decor, whence comes the false paradox, gigantic studios whose job is to fabricate the appearance of this reality without respite.

The scenery, the objects, the costumes, if they must be much more convincing than in the theater, can be much less truthful—the word is Bilinsky's. The cinema uses contrivances and tricks that are much more artificial than those of the theater but that *deceive the eye* much more effectively. We can dream with this "realism" founded on the deceptions of some apparent forms; what the spectator thinks he sees objectively, corporeally, is precisely effects and fakery. Such is the strange destiny of the cinema: to fabricate illusion with beings of real flesh, to fabricate reality out of papier-mâché illusion.

The requirement of objective reality has determined a general tendency toward the "natural" that has infected the theater itself. The performance of the actor that still resonated with sacred possession, tragic excess, his made-up face that was still a mask, his costumes of pomp and grandeur, entered into the naturalist circuit.[11] Gestures, movements, dialogue tend to contribute to the truth of the object, that is, to resemble the gestures and movements of everyday life. There are very few films in verse, very few film operas, and most are transcribed from the stage *(Hamlet, The Medium);* there are even fewer *Alexander Nevsky*s.

The objectivity of apparent forms thus makes the natural exert its influence over the whole universe of fiction film. Formal realism is sovereign, total, and only loosens its grip to triumph all the more. Thus, in dream depictions, scenery can again become expressionist, symbolic, filled with unknown or simply incongruous objects; *but at the same time film differentiates its universe from that of the dream: it shows us indisputably that its universe is that of the waking state, and what marks the difference between the two worlds is the objectivity, the corporeality, the rationality of things.*

Nevertheless, the sovereign object is gnawed away from within and circumscribed from the outside. It is worked on from the inside by its own objectivity. The demand for rationality and identity that is at the basis of objective vision often goes so far as to reduce its forms to a standard recognizable model. "It is not the costume in the latest fashion that would make the film old-fashioned, but a costume that borrows what is essential from the contemporary figure. This stylization, what is more, is necessary for rapid shots, for a maximum of suggestion in a minimum of time."[12] The typical object is the object that is superobjectified in some way. But the essence of the real can transform a form into a conventional sign and finally turn itself against the real: typical landscapes, typical costumes, typical dwellings, and so on, lose all truthfulness.

Furthermore, the flow of participation that carries the forms along, if it cannot directly erode them, at least has at its disposal the *choice* of objects to idealize or make reality wretched: stars' dresses are obviously real dresses, but worn as a function of the myth that is proper to the star, and of the scene to be interpreted. Pleasant, luxurious, or squalid objects will be chosen to give atmosphere. Objects and scenery thus chosen, opulent residences or bohemian caravans, will be able to inflect realism toward unrealism much more surely than will the musical score.

Not being able to determine their forms, the unreal can control the choice of objects; it can envelop them in a halo, paint them with an impalpable unguent. The objectivity of beings and things is surrounded by the incessant subjectivity of shadows and lighting. The realist taboo brusquely disappears at the border of the object and ceases to make itself respected thanks to the play of shadow and light. Night at the cinema—it was sometimes blue in silent films—is a conventional night, an aesthetic night, where we can always obscurely see the light and clearly see the dark. The lighting of a candle illuminates a room. Shadows and light, each of them exaggerated, stylized, are so many assaults on empirical truth, but they are accepted. Moreover, to accentuate or bring out the subjective quality of the image, the mise-en-scène frequently plays with doubling to the power of two, by means of a mirror or the placement of windows between the spectator and things. What Lotte Eisner says of the German film applies more generally. She notes the perpetual gleaming of objects or persons on a glass surface, the "smooth surfaces of windows, . . . car windows, the glazed leaves of the revolving door. . . , wet pavements and . . . reflections . . . in . . . lavatory mirrors."[13]

Endlessly, then, shadows and light transfigure faces and

scenery. Endlessly, reflective effects are interposed. Bearers of the latent fantastic, they are the ordinary paraphernalia of the "realist" film. They surround the fortress of objectivity with a ghostly dance, to the accompaniment of winds and storms.

And, of course, it is to the very heart of these objective forms that the great anthropo-cosmic participation penetrates. Objects perform, take on soul and life. In the midst of realism flourishes an animism.

Thus a complex of reality and unreality crystallizes around objective forms. The latter imperturbably turn toward the pole of the real. The force of the influence of this objective realism is spread by the demand for "naturalness" in the fiction film as a whole. A power of reality emanates from the screen, as Balázs says. But at the same time, artificial choices determine the presence of the object. The latter can be reduced to its *nucleus* or prototype. Around it dance the will-o'-the-wisps, shadows and lights; before and behind it gleams the image of its own image. The supernatural surrounds the natural like a halo. A ceaseless dialectic links these different states of reality and unreality, to the point of complete reversibility, where the object becomes soul.

Sound and Music

In the domain of sound, the complex of reality and unreality is first of all composed around musical unreality. Real life is obviously lacking in symphonic exhalations. Nevertheless, music, already accompanying the silent film, became integrated in the sound track. This demand for musicality is at the opposite pole from the demand for objectivity. An extraordinary contradiction between the eye and hearing, the latter gently relishing what the former could not allow.

What is more, the sound track is teeming with attacks on this apparent reality that is so fiercely protected in the representation of objects. Speech does not come from the mouths of characters at all, but from a microphone external to the screen. The correspondence of their words to the movement of their lips is broken by postsynchronization and dubbing. The dubbed film's voices without conviction belie a "naturalness" still essential elsewhere. Characters even go so far as to change voice and language, according to whether they sing or speak.

But if the eye is intransigent, hearing is tolerant. Eighty percent of French spectators prefer dubbed films to the original versions.[14] Charles Ford says that "in Italy, up until 1940, dubbed films were in fact asynchronous without it bothering the public."[15] Dubbing has perhaps improved slightly, but the asynchronism remains. Numerous sequences, and even numerous films, such as *La Strada*, are shot silent and synchronized later. The awkward result does not bother the spectator.

Jesus, Nero, and Ali Baba, in costumes and scenery that strive to be historically faithful, nevertheless speak French, American, or Russian. Of course intelligibility comes before objectivity. But the arbitrariness of linguistic convention is not felt at all. In the same way, film music flies off the hinges of reality without this betrayal doing violence to the impression of reality. Better—in conjunction with the dialectic that turns the objectivity of things into subjectivity, the subjectivity of music consolidates and increases this objectivity.

A complex of the unreal and the real surrounds the very axis of unreality, music. So from the object to music, two complexes oppose but resemble each other, each nourished by the ceaseless transfers, transmutations, reconversions that the development of the film sets in motion.

Fiction

This development goes by way of fiction for the overwhelming majority of great films. The fiction film is the classic product of universal cinema. Let us repeat it, as if to unsettle the obviousness of this truth and make it appear in its strangeness: the European, American, even Soviet cinemas, the Japanese, Hindu, South American, Egyptian, and very soon Black African cinemas, have developed, develop, and are going to develop with fiction films.

Fiction, as the name indicates, is not reality, or rather its fictive reality is nothing other than imaginary reality. The imaginary layer can be very slim, translucent, scarcely a pretext around the objective image. It can, conversely, envelop it in a fantastic coating. For as many types of fiction (or genres of film) as there are, there are so many degrees of unreality and reality. Each type of fiction can be defined according to the freedom and the virulence of imaginary projection-identifications in relation to reality, according to the resistance or the intransigence of the real in relation to the imaginary—that is, in the end, according to its complex system of credibility and participation. In other words, affective needs and rational needs interlock architecturally to constitute complexes of fiction. These needs are diversely determined according to the stages of life and the society, social class, and so on. At the same time, the dominant tendencies of fiction appear as so many cultural lines of force. We pass imperceptibly from the anthropological to the historical and sociological plane.

Thus the fantastic, which flourishes in the childhoods of humanity as in the childhoods of art, responds, within our bourgeois civilization, to the needs of a mental age prior to twelve years (Zazzo). Before twelve and already more or less detached from fixations on animals, children's preferences go to cartoons, puppets, legendary settings, and extravagant actions. A survey by Kathleen Woolf and Marjorie Fiske in relation to comics shows us that after the animal stage and before adventures lies the stage of the fantastic (ghosts).[16] It also seems that among the three film genres preferred by boys and girls less than twelve years of age, the only one in common is the ghost film.[17]

There comes the age where the fantastic falls into disrepute; we cease believing in it, we despise it. From ten or twelve years old, as B. Zazzo and R. Zazzo have shown, a need for rationalization and objectivation asserts itself. From then on, the maximum efficiency and optimum euphoria of participation are framed by plots said to be "realist" although far-fetched. Boys lose interest in the fantastic as in the dream and prefer actors and real environments to cartoons, puppets, and mythic settings. "It is too childish," say these innocents, who do not know and perhaps will never know that realism hides adult childishness.

Finally comes, or can come, the age of going beyond stages, that is, of their joint preservation, where the power of accommodation of a projection-identification, without prejudices or constraints, is supple enough to adapt itself to all genres, to savor the fantastic like realism, naïveté like subtlety.

The birth of the cinema took place within a civilization where the fantastic was already relegated to "Children's Corner." Nevertheless, the history of the cinema does not miss the opportunity to renew its imaginary phylogenesis: its first moment is that of the fantastic. But this moment is hurried and incomplete, like an embryogenetic process. We can at once track the multiple and convergent processes that break up, internalize, and rationalize the fantastic to transform it into *fantasy* or the novelistic.

We can see all of Méliès's magic *tricks* become the key techniques of the ciné-novel (superimpositions, fades, dissolves, tracking shots, masking, close-ups, and so on), the fantastic play of the shadow and the double transformed themselves into techniques generically called "photography." We see the contents of films slide from the supernatural to the amazing.

Feuillade's *Fantomas* (1913) symbolizes well the passage from the fantastic to fantasy: *Fantomas* bears the name of a ghost, but is not one; curtains quiver, shadows stir, doors open mysteriously, but in the end all of that is explained *naturally*. *Les mystères de New-York* (Gasnier, 1915–16),[18] in their turn, are an expression of this same passage from the mythic to the mysterious. The films of Douglas Fairbanks, acrobatic extravaganzas, border on the fantastic—and sometimes even return to it anew *(The Thief of Bagdad)*. Each upsurge in the fantastic is followed by a recuperation of fantasy. The successor to *Nosferatu* the vampire (Murnau, 1922) is the vampire of the news items (Fritz Lang's *M*, 1931).

Armed to the teeth in fantasy, the fantastic can be accepted only under the justifying cover of the dream, of hallucination, of madness, of the comic. Then it enters into the circuit of the rational. Horror becomes a vision of horror, and *Caligari* itself must be "explained" as a madman's dream. Magic becomes the hallucination of *The Lost Weekend* or the dream in *Spellbound*. The invisible voice, cavernous or whispered, is no longer that of the double but the voice of conscience; blurred and cloudy images, shrill and haunting music that made us enter into the kingdom of ghosts and death henceforth introduce us into the subjectivity of the dream. The "it was only a dream" is one of the most commonly used formulas to make the film pliable to the spectator's rational participation and vice versa *(François Premier [Francis the First], O.K. Nerone [O.K. Nero], A Connecticut Yankee in King Arthur's Court)*. Outbreaks of the fantastic, such as those inaugurated by *The Ghost Goes West* and the *Topper* films, are often now accompanied by an indispensable humor adapted to a projection-identification that can find its ancient pleasure only in the midst of skepticism.

The essential characteristic of fantasy is the *rationalization* of the fantastic. There are multiple possible and different rationalizations according to the genre of films, comic or tragic, adventure, detective, and so on. Thus, for example, the classic detective mystery comes within the province of the fantastic so long as the detective does not apply his rationality to it: there appeared to be ghostliness, ubiquity, sorcery, until the reestablishment of identity (destruction of the alibi) and the triumph of rational causality (discovery of the motive). The fantastic is equally rationalized in the adventure film. At a first stage, chance, coincidence, mysteries of birth, predictions that are realized, twins (doubles), and the invulnerability of the hero still verge on the fantastic. At a second stage, no more than a magic halo emanates from the somewhat superhuman exploits of the heroes and somewhat providential coincidences of the film.

The greater the rationalization, the more realist the film. The magic has become subterranean, has concealed and covered itself, indeed, has dissolved. Myth is more or less profoundly, more or less cleverly, brought back to the norms of objectivity or wrapped in verisimilitude. Now magic is effectively destroyed, now it is only camouflaged behind a thousand small Stendhalian touches of objectivity and rationality. Most often there is destruction and camouflage at the same time.

Realism, this refusal of falsity to better adhere to fiction, is the security provided to a consciousness that is ashamed to be engaged in magic, and *that can no longer freely dream in the waking state*. In the waking state, one needs a certain verisimilitude to let oneself be taken in a dream. Projection-identification must ceaselessly be encouraged by a timid "that could happen (to me)." It needs guarantees of authenticity. The modern doubting Thomases of the cinemas can no longer believe with the candor of the innocents.

Fantasy rationalizes and objectifies magic, but it keeps its subjective nucleus. Realism is the objective appearance of fantasy, but fiction is its subjective structure. Fantasy must have the appearance of objectivity and the structures of subjectivity. Its distinctive characteristic is to create a magical climate within a framework of rational (realist) explanations.

Within realist fantasy, the meeting and blending of magic and rationalization, the soul complex blossoms: the life and adventures of the soul, love in all its splendor, shine forth on the screen.

Fantasy, then, is the preponderant fiction of the cinema. It constitutes a veritable complex of the real and the imaginary, a sort of protein of soul where affective and rational needs have found a certain molecular equilibrium. This complex is maintained by the mass support of the spectators, backed up by mass desertions when the equilibrium is broken. Any attack on its "realism," like the opposite, any excess of reality, the one suspending adherence to the rational, the other drying up affective participation, and they discredit themselves: the hesitations, unease, protestations, disaffection, form a statistical barrier to a genuine expansion of the full-length documentary as of the fantastic film.

Within these boundaries, the complex of fantasy is multiple, heterogeneous. The characters in a given film, for example, do not all have the same quality of reality: a strange process of decantation distinguishes the primary and secondary roles. The latter, rationalized according to an average type or genre, veritable "stereotypes," are "bit parts," reduced to the rank of objects endowed with vague subjectivity. By contrast, the norms and servitudes of real life tend to evaporate in contact with heroes. The latter constitute the archetypes of a glorified humanity. As François Ricci said, "True men, but stronger, more clever, more enticing—true women, but more beautiful, with eyebrows more arched, more shapely legs."[19] The cinema often demands what the theater often disregards, the beauty of bodies and faces. The same with the beauty of souls. The Star System makes these idealizations blossom into divinations.

Complex of the real and the unreal, fantasy is integrated in this polymorphous complex of the real and the unreal that is film. There is not an "either/or" of film realism and unrealism, but a dialectical totality with multiple forms. The truthful, the seemingly truthful, the incredible, the possible, the idealized, the stylized, defined objects, undefined music, combine in a mixture with infinite possibilities.

These infinite possibilities settle and crystallize in systems of fiction that vary, evolve from the origins of the cinema, and multiply according to the needs in question. Their *crystallization* allows us, beyond the ceaseless Brownian movement of the real and the unreal, to grasp the sociological determination of the film. Let us repeat it: every system of fiction is, *in itself*, a historical and socially determined product. The two apparently intangible arches between which flows the combined stream of filmic reality and unreality—photographic objectivity and musical subjectivity—are themselves historically determined; a new age, a new art of cinema is possible that would ignore music or exaggerate it, that would deobjectify or desubjectify objects. Moreover, filmic crystallizations are ceaselessly in motion because they are precisely sensitive to the transformations of the real world; the latter act as radioactive emissions that unbalance and find a new equilibrium for the system through chemical mutations or formations of isotopes.

If the important thing, from the sociological point of view, is the determination of systems—the object of our subsequent study[20]—the essential thing, from the anthropological point of view, is the infinite possibility of the dialectic of the unreal and the real.

When the cinema differentiated itself from the cinematograph in welcoming dream and wakefulness with open arms, in this rupture and this very opposition it opened out a field of strange complementarities, of endless mutations, irresistible reversibilities: faces became landscapes, landscapes faces, objects were charged with soul, music gave body to things. The spectator began to sail in an infinite ocean, subjected to contradictory and changing winds that drew him irresistibly toward the screen to make him affectively adhere to its vision and distance him from it to reestablish objective distance. In these transmutations and whirlwinds where dream and reality are mixed up, the one bringing the other back to life, is *the specificity of the cinema* whose exquisite essence is so ardently sought, while its essence is nonessence, that is, dialectical movement. *The cinematograph was the undifferentiated or nascent unity of the unreal and the real. The cinema is the dialectical unity of the real and the unreal.*

Mother Vision

Here again, the anthropological purity of the cinema appears. It covers the whole field of the real world, which it places within arm's reach, and the whole field of the imaginary world, since it participates just as well in dream vision as in perception in the waking state. The anthropological field, which goes from the objective me (the double) to the subjective me (feeling of self, soul), from the subjective world (anthropo-cosmomorphism) to the objective world (practical perception), is virtually within the "field" of the camera.

Holding together this magical quality and this objective quality, bearer of all possible magico-affective developments, the cinema is like a kind of great archetypal womb that contains in embryogenetic potential all visions of the world. Whence its analogy with the mother vision of humanity (the archaic conception of the world).

But, contrary to this, the vision of the cinema is turned away from the practical. It is engulfed in the aesthetic. It also corresponds to the great *aesthetic mother,* who covers all spectacles of nature and the whole field of the imaginary, all dreams and all thoughts. *If the aesthetic is the distinctive characteristic of the cinema, the cinema is the distinctive characteristic of the aesthetic: the cinema is the broadest aesthetic ever possible.* This does not mean that film is superior to any other form of art, but that, the aesthetic field of the cinema being broader, it tolerates the greatest number of possible artistic forms and allows, ideally, the richest works possible.

Among all the possible aesthetics and visions of the world, films take up and establish those that are established for them by actual human needs. A dominant vision, a preponderant complex of the unreal and the real, emerges. Anthropology once again brings us back, imperceptibly, to history.

7 Birth of a Reason, Blossoming of a Language

The image is only an abstraction: some visual forms. These few forms are nevertheless sufficient for us to recognize the thing photographed. They are *signs*. But they are symbols more than signs. The image *represents*—the word is right—it restores a *presence*.

In fact, everything that suggests, contains, or reveals another thing or more than itself is symbolic. The symbol is at once abstract sign, almost always more impoverished than what it symbolizes, and concrete presence, since it is able to restore its richness. The symbol is, in a way, the abstraction made concrete. Symbolic abstraction begins with a fragment or a feature detached from its whole, such as a horse's mane, a handkerchief, or a perfume; it goes as far as analogical representation (the image in every sense of the term) and the conventional sign (such as the political or religious symbol). These meaningful abstractions are symbolic precisely because the horse's mane, handkerchief, perfume, photo, metaphor, cross, and so on, communicate not only the idea but the presence of that of which they are only fragments or signs.

Every thing, according to the perspective in which it is considered, can, at a given moment, become a symbol. The image itself is symbolic by nature, by function.

From Symbol to Language

The cinematograph, with its single image, consisted of only one single symbol. In the same way that the original molecule of hydrogen burst open and became differentiated to give birth to all combinations of matter, the single and elementary shot of the cinematograph burst open to give birth to all possible symbolic combinations. Each shot became a particular symbol. New symbolisms were superimposed on that of the image: that of the fragment (close-up, medium shot, reverse shot), the feature (anthropomorphized objects, cosmomorphized faces), the analogy (waves breaking on the rocks symbolizing the embrace or the storm beneath a skull), music, noises, and so on.

The cinema shot henceforth carries a high-tension symbolic force that increases tenfold the affective power as well as the expressive power of the image.

This energizing power in the same stroke allows the increase and filling in of discontinuities, gaping holes from shot to shot. The shot increases its concrete and abstract characteristics by being inserted in a chain of symbols that establishes a veritable narration. Each shot takes its meaning in relation to the preceding one and directs the meaning of the following one. The movement of the whole gives the meaning of the detail, and the detail feeds into the sense of the movement of the whole.[1] *The succession of shots tends to create a discourse within which the particular shot plays the role of intelligible sign.* In other words, the cinema develops a system of abstraction, of discursiveness, of ideation. It exudes a language, that is, a logic and an order—a reason.

Ultimate marvel: *the cinema allows us to see the birth of a reason, from the very system of participation from which a magic and a soul is born.*

They are *the same techniques* of the camera and montage, the same shots charged with affectivity that tend toward the sign and rational intelligibility. We can even follow, in certain cases (the fade, dissolve, superimposition), the perfect cycle, the integral development that goes from fantastic metamorphosis to grammatical sign.

Méliès's metamorphosis gives birth to the dissolve, as disappearance does to the fade. Stripped of its magic, the dissolve becomes poetic effect or dream. These effects are progressively weakened; the dissolve (like the fade, which tends to be reabsorbed into the lap dissolve) is reduced to a purely syntactic function: it is the sign of an essential connection between two shots.

Thus magic not only atrophied in order to make room for affective participation, but the latter, through usage and wear, progressively hardened into abstraction: the magic trick transformed itself into a sign of intelligence. Nevertheless, metamorphosis can come back to life in the fantastic or comic genre, and Charlie Chaplin in *The Gold Rush* symbolically becomes a chicken.

In the same way, superimposition, a magical effect at the outset (ghosts, doubling) becomes symbolico-affective (memory, dream),[2] then purely indicative. The superimposition of a newspaper seller on the streets of New York tells us that the press is spreading throughout the city the news of the event presented in the preceding images.

Beyond the fade, the dissolve, and the superimposition, we could draw up a catalog of symbols hardened into signs under the abrasive effect of repetition: the withering bouquet, leaves flying off the calendar, the hands of a watch spinning around, the accumulation of cigarette butts in an ashtray: all these images that compress time have become symbols, then signs of time passing. The same for the train speeding into the countryside, the plane in the sky (a sign that the film's heroes are traveling), and so on.

The process is the same as in our verbal language, where marvelous metaphors have slackened and ossified into "clichés." In the same way, cinema "stereotypes" are symbols whose affective sap has turned wooden. They accordingly better assert their signifying role and even initiate conceptualization: they are not adjectival qualities but quasi-ideas (the idea of time passing, the idea of the journey, the idea of love, like the idea of the dream, the idea of memory) that appear at the end of an authentic intellectual ontogenesis.

Consequently, we can grasp the continuity that goes from the symbol to the sign. Of course, we cannot absolutely differentiate these two notions, for there is sign in the symbol, as there is symbolism in the sign. Symbolism is an unstable complex where affective presence can ultimately become magical, where intellectual signification can ultimately take on a purely abstract character. The cinema shows how certain images tend to constitute themselves as grammatical instruments (the fade, the dissolve, the superimposition) or rhetorics (the same, plus ellipses, metaphors, even the periphrases cited above). This veritable grammatical specialization is the extreme result, upon some privileged images, of a general tropism that directs the other image-symbols toward discursive signification.

At an intermediary level, we see "stereotypes" crystallize: typical objects, typical characters, typical gestures. The screen universe is thus Aristotelianized: objects, characters, and stereotyped gestures make their intelligible essence appear: they are entities of reason.

Without destroying the affective qualities of the image, and therefore its symbolic ambivalence, all the techniques of the cinema activate and solicit processes of abstraction and rationalization that go on to contribute to the constitution of an intellectual system.

From Participation to Understanding

The camera mobility that we have successively examined from the point of view of ubiquity, then of kinesthesia and affective participation, then finally of processes of objective perception, continues (tracking and so on) and discontinues (succession of shots), pursues and activates the work of rational decoding of this perception by imitating our attention; the latter is nothing other, in fact, than the implementation of our faculty of choice and elimination, that is, of abstraction.

Every detail shot (insert) is properly an abstraction: it eliminates from the field a more or less great part of the represented scene. Moreover, the close-up and even the medium shot deliberately efface the depth of field: soft focus behind objects, faces, and bodies brought closer cloud perspective. The camera, then, makes a selection on the surface as well as in depth in order to eliminate everything that is not meaningfully linked to the action. The mise-en-scène is the unity of these operations of abstraction (establishment of shots). But *the art* of the mise-en-scène consists in struggling against the impoverishment that the necessary abstraction involves. Thus, for example, the director will be able to concentrate on deschematizing attention through a game of hide-and-seek that excites it in pretending to deceive it at the same time as he provides a viewing field: he will show, in the first shot, a chosen fake object (a cannon ready to fire, for example), while what is essential is situated in the background (a regiment marching or a general giving his orders). There are innumerable games of filmic trompe l'oeil, unknown in the theater, that invert the places of setting and actors in the visual field. Welles and Wyler themselves have used depth of field to simultaneously show two objects worthy of attention without determining the spectator's choice in advance, as in the scenes of the telephone and the marriage in *The Best Years of Our Lives*, admirably analyzed by Bazin.[3] This is at once a reaction against an excess of abstraction and an excess of affective adherence to the image. It tends to situate the film at a higher level of participation and intelligibility. So it is possible, particularly thanks to CinemaScope, that the use of breadth and depth allows the development of a cinema that is less abstract but more "intelligent," less immediately affective but more moving in the end, that will one day relegate to the rank of hoaxes and tricks the present-day formulas of the excessively selective camera.

Each shot, at the same time as it establishes the field of attention, is a guide to a field of meaning. In addition to the stereotypes and grammatical tools already signaled, certain shots, such as the high-angle shot and the low-angle shot, accentuate the indicative value implied in their symbolic quality: the high-angle shot shriveling things and the low-angle shot making them gigantic have the function of communicating more than sentiment—still not completely the idea, but the sentiment-idea of decline or grandeur. In a way that is complex, because polyvalent and fluid, the movements and positions of the camera suppose and give rise to a potentially ideogrammatic language, where each shot-symbol carries its share of abstraction, more or less great, more or less codified, where certain shots play the role of tonic stress, of dieresis or silence, and where the movement of the whole constitutes a veritable narration.

It is because every cinema shot contains a germ of abstraction that the camera, passing from one to the other, can be called a pen, as Astruc put it.

The cinematograph was only a spectacle, like the theater. The cinema has grafted a narrativity onto it analagous to that of the novel. In a way it has synthesized the structures of the theater and the novel.[4]

The Language of Sounds

The cinema frees itself, then, from the cinematograph to constitute itself in an intelligible system. All its techniques rise from the obscure roots of magic to the rational surface of discourse.

All its techniques: here again, the example of music is enlightening.

The first expressive commentaries, called incidentals, were *already also* signs of intelligence; this role has been increased in the sound film, where the music announces what the image still does not show or would not show on its own. The musical scores of films are composed of extremely stereotyped and therefore more eloquent accompaniments than the signs of Elizabethan theater. A close-up of an immobile face, tumultuous music, and there is no doubt: it is a storm inside a skull. A door opens, but the melody has become disturbing, shrill, or is replaced by a solemn percussion: a sign of menace or danger, like the drumroll for the grand leap of the acrobat. Music plays a very precise role as subtitles. It gives us the meaning of the image: meditation, memory, sleep, dream, spirituality, desire. Ombredane did a simple but exhaustive experiment in projecting the fighting of grubs in *Assassins d'eau douce* (Painlevé) with two successive sound tracks. With the first sound track, jazz music, the Congolese natives interpreted the sequence as a pleasant frolic, a game. With the second one, in which their own head cutters' ritual chant swelled, they saw murder and destruction, even suggesting—and this is the power of music's projection-identification—that the victorious grubs would return home carrying their victims' severed heads. The meaning of *The Living Desert* (Walt Disney, 1954) is entirely fabricated by the music: the film shows images of aggression, of struggle for life without mercy, of hunger and desolation, but what accompanies, or, better, what guides the movements of the creatures is ballet music, a droll rhythm belonging to animation; life in the living desert becomes, through the absurd grace of the musical score, a great amusing game, a naturalistic *Silly Symphony*, a lighthearted gambol. The music engages the spectator in a pleasant and playful participation and at the same time betrays the truth of the images to submit them to an anodyne philosophy.

In fact, most often, we see music signifying the image and at the same time the image signifying the music in a sort of contest of intelligence. This analogical complementarity is, moreover, the result of the marriage between music and cinema. Film music, an ineffable language of feeling, translates itself into an intelligible language of signs. It explains, as Jaubert says.

Unlike music, and despite the fact that the latter is only one aspect of it, sound is potentially realist. The sounds and voices that are laid down on film are, from the outset, real sounds and voices. Sound is not an *image*—it is reproduced, but it is neither shadow nor reflection of its original: it is its *recording*. In this sense, sounds and words have directed film toward an increased realism. We have already noted the role of sounds in the neorealist film; more broadly, the whole of the cinema has gone beyond a neorealist stage with sound. Voices have become social, bringing their accents, their guttural speech, a thousand truths of everyday life.

Despite its realist nature, talking film began with the "magic" of singing voices: *The Jazz Singer*. It burst in with the trumpets of a first judgment, mercilessly eliminating the majority of silent actors. And why? Their voices were not "phonogenic." "We call a voice phonogenic that, going through the microphone, not only maintains its qualities, but acquires new ones."[5] The phonogenic voice "charms" or "bewitches" us. As Parker Tyler analyzed it, the "talkies" created stars possessed by their voices much more than possessing them, such as Marlene Dietrich or Lauren Bacall.

Sound film, moreover, gives a reality to the myth of the internal voice. The "to be or not to be" is not spoken by the mouth of Hamlet but by an other self (the *Hamlet* of Laurence Olivier). The interior monologue dissociates itself in tête-à-tête with an invisible double. Cavernous, whispering, disembodied voices haunt the cinema. A narrating voice commands the performance, a ghost that tells a story, a voice from the beyond, a wandering subjectivity, an invisible presence. It is murmuring, confidential, as if it were doing a "reading for a shadow," in Pizella's beautiful words.[6]

Narrating voices perform on a triple register. They more easily render stories in the past, manipulations of time, and their mixing in the same imaginary temporality. What is more, economizing linkages and transitions, they allow the rhythm of images to accelerate and so precipitate the dynamism of participation. Finally, verbal discourse can henceforth add and even substitute its own logic for the discourse of images. The two systems tend more and more to interpenetrate and structure each other. Since *The Power and the Glory*, and particularly since *Citizen Kane*, the narrating voice tends to drive the film. In the same way, the succession of shots, the heterogeneous mosaic of images, becomes more and more discontinuous, elliptical, and abstract. Words, sounds, and music act as linkages. They tend to replace the bird flying, the ball continuing to roll, the gestural retort. Conceptual language tends to become the *cement* of montage.

The cinema annexes conceptual language: speech can henceforth structure the film as a discourse, crown it with a discourse *(The Great Dictator)*, or express ideas in the film *(Limelight*, a "thinking" film in the manner of Shakespeare, where the heroes in their particular predicament evoke in words the problems of life and death).

Finally, the *selection* of sound is, as we have seen elsewhere, much more urgent than visual selection. The abstracting processes of attention are literally at work in perfecting true close-ups and resonant soft focus. Film eliminates or attenuates sounds of secondary importance, selects essential sounds and exaggerates them—the ticktock of the clock at the fateful moment of the attack on Pearl Harbor *(From Here to Eternity)* or the bombing of Hiroshima *(Children of Hiroshima)*. The sound operator precisely plays the psychological role of understanding related to the ear—the microphone. Let a conversation begin in a music hall, in a forge, or in the provincial countryside and the sound of cicadas, hammers, the parade, is smothered, muffled, dimmed.[7]

Sound, unlike the majority of cinematic techniques, does

not take part in the genetic elaboration of the years 1896–1910. It appears only when the cinema has already been established. But inscribing itself in film, it becomes in its turn a total phenomenon, covering all registers, from magic to the logos.[8]

Film tends toward reason. It tends there from its intimate and ultimate genetic movement. This tendency is expressed diversely, and on different levels. Every image, symbolic by nature, tends to draw out a meaning at the same time as an affective participation. Certain images, certain objects within the image, tend more particularly toward becoming *stereotypes*. In some cases, stereotyping ends up in the crystallization of veritable grammatical tools. The film, a *narrative system*, can by virtue of its internal construction—script, cutting, and plot—become a true logical and demonstrative *discourse*.

Consequently, it has often and very well been observed that beneath the language of film appear the laws and rhythms of ideation (Zazzo), the eloquence of discourse (Cohen-Séat), a logical system (Francastel), the very movement of conceptual thought (Bergson). Film fulfills itself and blossoms into rationality.

But let us not forget that this rationality crowns a continuous, unique, and contradictory movement. And we find ourselves not "at the bottom of the problem," as theological minds say, but *in its living source and its concrete totality*.

Participation and Logos

Zazzo says, and we come back to a quotation to complete it, "Filmic language rediscovers beneath classical discourse the laws and rhythms of our ideation, just as others have maintained that it is identified with oneiric thought." But, let us repeat it, we cannot limit ourselves to posing the simple, even peaceful, coexistence of the oneiric and the intellectual.

The opposing tendencies of psychology have taken sides—dream for some, logic for others. Each one sings its score through specialized journals and amiably, eclectically, accepts being contradicted. None wants to confront the contradiction that is at the heart of the cinema.

The partitions and distinctions within the human sciences prevent us from grasping the profound continuity between magic, sentiment, and reason, although this contradictory unity is the Gordian knot of all anthropology. If cinema becomes magic, sentiment, and reason in the same movement, there is clearly a profound unity between sentiment, magic, and reason.

This same unity of the psyche in the nascent state does not know the compartmentalizations of the psychology books. The technical and magic, objectivity and subjectivity, sentiment and reason are born in the same movement. If, at a certain stage, magic and sentiment are contradicted by reason, they are originally linked.

That is why the germ of abstraction is already in participation. The child who moves the object and brings it to his mouth starts upon the process of knowledge that abstracts this object from the environment and will establish its consistency and its identity. Reciprocally, participation underlies all intellection. To explain is to identify, said Emile Meyerson. We must complete this sentence: to identify with what has been projected. The intelligence proceeds by the projection of abstract "patterns" and identification with these patterns. It is a practical participation that, alienating and reifying its own processes, extends perception. The words of a language are only man's own substance—*his speech, his signs*—become tools. Here again, this *utilitarian reification* cannot be opposed absolutely to magical reification: depending on whether they are turned toward the practical or toward affectivity, poetry and reason are the *same movements*.

We can now see, then, that *participation* equally constructs magic and reason, that the latter reciprocally construct and destroy one another; that finally, magic, sentiment, and reason can be syncretically associated with one another. There is no pure magic, no pure sentiment, no pure reason. In other words, magic, sentiment, and reason are not distinct qualities or faculties of the human mind, but three fundamental polarizations of the same total phenomenon. They are not essences. Magic and sentiment are also means of knowing. And our rational concepts are themselves still imbued with magic, as Mauss observed.[9] All that is human serves as a vehicle for the whole human in a measure that is particular to him. Which does not at all prevent the fact that at the extreme, magic, feelings, and reason distinguish and oppose themselves absolutely, in a repulsive magnetization.

It is because every film image is symbolic that the cinema carries within it all the riches of the human mind in its nascent state. The distinctive feature of the symbol is to unite within it magic, sentiment, and abstraction. The symbol is "realistically" linked, in the scholastic, that is, magical sense of the term, to the thing that is symbolized. It fixes its affective presence there. It is finally an abstract sign, a means of recognition and of knowledge. The symbol is at the origin of all languages, which are nothing other than a series of symbols effecting communication, that is, the evocation of a total reality by fragments, conventions, summaries, or attributes.

That is why the supports and the tools of the cinema are at the outset those of emotional tone and rational deciphering and construct an imaginary and a discourse at the same time. The ubiquity of the camera is the unique foundation of the magic and reason, the sentiment and intelligence of the cinema. The fantastic and fictional cinema share the same techniques as the educational cinema.

The cinema unveils and opens up the intellectual structures of participation, the participative structures of intelligence, and thus, as well as the theory of magic and affectivity, it illuminates the "theory of the formation of ideas and their development."[10] Its natural and fundamental movement is none other than the natural and fundamental movement of the human mind at its source, that is, in its first totality. *It is because all participation at the same time leads to a subjectivity and an objectivity, a rationality and an affectivity, that a circular dialectic carries the film along as an objective-subjective, rational-affective system.*

The cinema is both a kinesthesia, a brute force driving affective participations, and the development of a logos. Movement becomes rhythm, and rhythm becomes language. From movement to kinesthesia and to discourse. From the image to the feeling and the idea!

Such is the very genetic process of the cinema. In the same movement that it disengages from the cinematograph, in the same movement that it engages in magico-affective participation, it extracts itself from the empirical succession of images to construct itself according to the "laws and rhythms of ideation."

In the same movement, but not at the same time. It was naturally, genetically necessary to commence with Méliès's "little magic formulas" before arriving at "the syntax of a language," to pass by way of the preliminary flowering of the stage of the soul (Griffith) before reaching, with Eisenstein, the stage of dialectical totality.

It is in fact at the moment when Eisenstein discovers and puts into practice his conception of images that provoke feelings that provoke ideas that the transformation from the cinematograph into the cinema is completed. The latter, certainly, will still evolve. But it is shaped from that time on: *it is a coherent system where the deepening and utilization of the affective power of images culminates in a logos.*

Eisenstein describes the cinema as the only concrete and dynamic art that enables the activation of the operations of thought, the only one capable of restoring to the intelligence its vital concrete and emotional sources; it demonstrates experimentally that feeling is not irrational fantasy, but a moment of knowledge. He does not oppose magic (which he has not named as such, but whose analogical, anthropo-cosmomorphic nature he has recognized and defined in the theory of "attractions") to the rational. He does not so much take the part of the one or the other, but he wants to grasp them at their common source, he wants to produce symbols bursting with all their riches, objects charged with soul, souls charged with ideas. The creative renewal of the idea will be brought about from anthropo-cosmomorphic participation, and it is anthropo-cosmomorphism that conveys, that will give birth to, the idea on the surface of daily life.

The greatest idea in the world—progress—takes shape at the same time as a drop of milk on a separator *(The General Line)*. In a chunk of putrid meat the idea of revolution ferments *(Battleship Potemkin)*.

The General Line, like *Battleship Potemkin* and Dovzhenko's *Earth*, is constructed in discourse, but nothing speaks. The affective system secretes a logos. The images are parables and symbols of an ideology that is created and takes shape.

The ideology is not tacked onto the film. It is not external to it, and the images are not pretexts. It seems to be born and reborn without cease in the spectator, whose generosity and love are obliged to take on their intellectual responsibilities. The cinema has become pedagogy through its language of images and images alone.[11]

At the apex of the cinema, from *Battleship Potemkin* to *La Strada*, the "magic" of images is not fetishized, but tends to enrich a participation that does not decline into complacencies of the soul, but concentrates all its sap into the blossoming of an idea.

Obviously, films that achieve this plenitude are rare. Most of the time, the dialectical unity is shattered, broken up, or incomplete. The fiction film does not go beyond the stage of the soul, and the eventual "ideas" there are badly amalgamated, introduced in contraband, where they are only pretexts to excite affective participation (thus a film claims to denounce prostitution in order to better show the prostitute); we are often dealing with a regressive movement that goes from the idea to sentiment and from sentiment to magic (the myth of love). Ideas are put into play to provoke feelings that must culminate in certain images (negligees, kisses, chases, fights), while what are called propaganda films rarely avoid long-winded preaching, abstract pedagogy. In spite of all this, within these films, the Eisensteinian law is at work, intermittently, most often blocked, atrophied, distorted, or diverted.

On the other hand, and necessarily, each of the three perspectives (magic, sentiment, idea) has established its genre: the fantasy film, the fiction film, the educational film. But while the educational genre is opposed to the fantasy film, it uses the same *language*. It is this same language implied in Méliès's magic spells that allows P. M. Schuhl to envisage an abstract cinema, not in Hans Richter's sense, but as an instrument of philosophical thought.

This *language* realizes the unity of contraries in the Eisensteinian synthesis but equally allows the differentiation and the fixation of contraries: it is a *total and polyfunctional language*.

Conceptual Language, Musical Language, the Language of the Film

It is under this heading that the cinema can rightly be compared to the very vehicle of all human communications: language itself.

"Language does not have a particularly cognitive role and is tied just as well to . . . affectivity as to . . . knowledge. . . . The prime function of language is not to designate objects and to reason about them, while attributing it a secondary affective power."[12] Sommerfield already noted that "the Aranta language, more archaic than any other he knows . . .

has as a characteristic to express only actions and states, but not objects (nor qualities objectively represented)."[13] Language is not only a system of arbitrary signs; word-signs are also, through their contents, symbols rich in affective presence. Between the language of poetry and scientific language, there is apparently an infinity that separates the magical from the technical, and yet it is the same language. Larousse's definition, "communication of thought, expression of feelings," only juxtaposes the two consubstantial and contradictory qualities.

In reality, words are from the outset still not simple labels, as in the nominalist conception, but total symbols loaded with the named presence. They are anthropo-cosmomorphic intermediaries, human projections condensing fragments of the cosmos. The archaic sentence, anthropo-cosmomorphic by nature, always designates the idea by way of *analogy*, that is, image and metaphor. What is more, poetic language has almost completely conserved this first "magic."

The language of the cinema comes from the same genesis, knows the same dialectical continuity as the language of words, but it is much less differentiated. That is why it resembles archaic language. One expresses itself through images (analogical metaphors), and the other is made from images. Both ceaselessly bring anthropo-cosmomorphic processes into play in a particularly vivid way.

Archaic language is profoundly determined by rhythmical schemata that are weakened in our own: at the slightest opportunity, the slightest elation, it becomes *song*. Narrative capacities, which have not yet reached the stage of abstract discourse, develop in sequences, each one commencing with an "I saw," with partial reiterations and evocations like so many flashbacks, or leitmotifs. In the same way, film is rhythmico-musical, as Ombredane puts it. It is enveloped in music and organized in rhythm. It is linked by sequences and uses the flashback like the cutback. To the extent that poets rediscover or re-create a language in the nascent state, the same analogies can be discerned. Eisenstein's analyses of the poems of Pushkin, Hugo, and Shelley are exemplary in this regard. "This mystical and concrete mentality which has almost been eliminated[14] from our great common languages, will it not become powerful enough to remake our languages in its image and impose its ways on them?" asked Vendryes. It has, in fact, happened: in the cinema.

But here, still, we must not neglect differences.

The cinema does not practically have conventional vocabulary at its disposal. Its signs are nothing other than stereotyped symbols, metamorphoses and disappearances transformed into commas and periods (the dissolve, the fade). If the cinema tends toward the concept, it is deprived of *concepts* in the nominalist sense of the term. Archaic language is already a tool kit of concepts, the words are just as much *arbitrary reifications*. The language of film knows very little of reifications: it remains fluid. The stock of signs that it has built up for itself remains very limited and is not absolutely indispensable to it: we can even do without lap dissolves.[15]

The fluidity that differentiates the cinema from the language of words brings it close to music, since both can do without words to discourse and since their effects remain "ineffable." Everything that makes the cinema closer to archaic language than ordinary language is basically what renders archaic language closer to music: rhythm, leitmotifs, repetitions. And more: fluidity, intensity, simultaneity.

But music cannot achieve objectivity: it does not represent objects. The cinema starts from objects and goes to the soul. Music starts from the soul, but even though descriptive, does not arrive at things. Objectivity dissolves the music, which melts into the film image, while the image does not melt into it.

The object is what differentiates the cinema from music, but also from the language of words, which has only purely conventional signs to designate it.

Starting from objects, the cinema can construct pictograms or ideograms, but much more concrete than those of any verbal language. Too concrete still, however, to become concepts, they remain in the state of preconcepts. Film never congeals into a purely conventional system, and, because of this, it cannot rise to a certain degree of abstraction. In one sense, the cinema is richer than the language of words. "One can say almost everything with image and sound; one can say almost nothing with speech," said Flaherty.[16] In one sense it is poorer: Flaherty could only express this idea through speech.

So the language of cinema is situated between that of words and that of music: that is why it succeeded in attracting them and joining them in an expressive polyphony that uses the disembodied song of the soul (music) as the vehicle for intellectual communication (words). It summons all languages because it is itself a potential syncretism of all languages: these function as a counterpoint, depend on one another, constitute a language orchestra. But if it communicates with music and speech, if it uses the one and the other, it keeps its originality. Certainly there was an understandable apprehension when talking pictures appeared. This language, "more candid and uninhibited than in any spoken soliloquy,"[17] was it not going to be driven away like good money by bad, according to Gresham's fatal law? In fact, talking film has been destructive—particularly to comic expression. But in thirty years of silence, the cinema had had time to develop its language. Sound has not lessened the "specificity" of the cinema and has even developed it in certain areas, opening up the possibilities of counterpoint indicated by Eisenstein and Pudovkin.[18] As Cohen-Séat said, "Film has not ceased to be silent because speech was given to man."[19] That is, film has not lost its own language.

The cinema respects so-called objective forms: in this way it is intelligible. Words are arbitrary conventions.[20] The cinema was not founded on arbitrary conventions: in this way it is universally intelligible. There are languages of words, there is *only one* language of cinema. What has no name in any language finds it has precisely the same name in all languages, as Lucien Sève put it. The language of cinema, in its entirety, is founded not on particular reifications, but on universal processes of participation. Its elementary signs are capsules of universal magic (metamorphoses, doublings). These signs remain universal because they are founded on and mixed with universal—objective—givens of perception: forms reproduced by the photographic image.

The double universality, that of the object and that of magic, undifferentiated in its nascent state, constitutes a natural Esperanto of sentiment and reason, and creates a kind of Weberian *comprehension*, provided we not oppose absolutely, as Max Weber did, comprehension and explanation.

A Natural Esperanto

The Lumière cinematograph, despite the monocular eye of the camera, the two-dimensionality of the screen, the absence of sound, color, and so on, was immediately intelligible, and its immediate spread throughout the world in the years 1895–97 proved its universality. The cinema is more universal still than the cinematograph, *to the essential extent* that it is supported by nascent anthropological structures.

The immediate comprehension, let us say, rather, participation-comprehension of this language by children as by archaic peoples is the very test of this universality.

It is within the most remote populations, in the middle of the bush, with native groups who have never seen films, that the universality of the language of cinema appears striking, that participation in film is manifested in its purity. "The illiterate African is often passionately attracted by the cinema."[21] Following numerous projections of educational cinema in East Africa, Julian Huxley could even affirm that the intelligibility of the cinema is superior to that

IMAGE	MAGICAL VISION	FEELING	OBJECTIVE PERCEPTION	IDEA
Movements and positions of the camera	Ubiquity	Kinesthesia / Affective presence	Envelopments / Perceptive leaps	Selectivity (abstraction) / Narrativity
Close-up	Macroscopic animism	Affective intensity	(Restoration through continuity)	Selectivity (abstraction)
High-angle shot	Shriveling	Symbolic abasement	(Restoration through continuity)	Sign of failure
Low-angle shot	Gigantism	Symbolic exaltation	(Restoration through continuity)	Sign of grandeur
Music	Unreal	Affective participation	Factor of reality	Factor of intelligibility
Words	Disincarnated "voices," whistling of the wind, unsettling voices	Allow the rhythm of the film to accelerate, and	Reality	Selection of sounds,
Sounds			Objective reality	narrativity of voices,

			thus intensify participation		architecture of the film Conceptualization
Dissolve	Metamorphosis		"Poetic" effect	" "	Grammatical sign
Superimposition	Phantom		Daydream, dream, presence of memory	" "	Grammatical sign
Object	Anthropomorphized		Charged with "soul"	Objective reality	Stereotyping Sign Idea
Contents and forms of the image	Anthropo-cosmomorphism		Affective projection-identification	Objectivation	Symbolism and sign in a discursive continuity
IMAGE **MOVEMENT**	⟶ ⟷		**FEELING** **KINESTHESIA**	⟷ ⟷	**IDEA** **DISCOURSE**

Figure 5. Film language.

of photography (1929): "All those who have noticed how the primitive native has difficulty recognizing a fixed image, are amazed at the facility with which he understands animated images, cinema."

Among all the experiments with films shown in the bush, Ombredane's most recent one on the Congolese who had never seen film seems decisive to us, because of the meticulousness and precision of the techniques employed and the clarity of the results.[22] The spectators' accounts did not reveal "any difficulty with the apprehension of moving images as such" in films composed of the visual techniques of the cinema (close-up, reverse shot, camera movements, and so on).

In the same way, film is intelligible to children in a decisive measure since it interests them. It is natural to them. They rarely feel so present, *at home*. (We know well that children enter into the universe of film quite naturally since we bemoan the childishness of films.) The succession of different shots does not disconcert the small child or destroy his impression of reality. From four to seven years of age, children follow the articulations of the filmic story within sequences. The first superimposition, the first dissolve, often establishes (we will come back to this "often") an immediate comprehension.

The experiments of René and Bianca Zazzo are all the more significant since they are concerned with abnormal or retarded children.[23] After the projection of a sequence of *The Path to Life*, Zazzo and Zazzo were able to note an amazing comprehension of the dynamism of the action (thirty-seven out of forty-two abnormal children), a real capacity to follow this action in space, a great number of correct interpretations (sixteen out of forty-two) of "shot reverse shots,"[24] a certain number of coherent accounts of the sequence. The film raises this same "slightly imbecilic" child (who has not been able to understand a drawing) to a level of interpretation that he will never reach in other domains.[25]

For his part, A. Marzi had noted that the mentally weak could understand the cinema.[26] Numerous examples equally show us that explanation through film is more effective for archaic peoples than educational or religious sermons.

Certainly, there have been parallel reports of the difficulties of comprehension among Africans (Van Bever), and with children (Heuyer). What are they, and where do these incomprehensions come from?

Certain sporadic difficulties of visual adaptability call into question not the language, but the defective quality of an image, which can then provoke misunderstandings: thus the Congolese see rain fall where we recognize streaks on the film.

If optical difficulties are eliminated, it is also necessary, to clarify the problem, to take sociological difficulties into account. Everything in a film cannot be universal, of course, since every film is a socially determined product. The values, customs, and objects that are unknown for a given social group remain, of course, strange in the film. So every film is diversely intelligible, incompletely intelligible.

As Ombredane demonstrated, the Congolese man still living within his traditional system cannot comprehend current themes of Western film like *the lure of profit*. Only being interested in his immediate needs, what matters to him is not wealth, but prestige. In the same way, he cannot understand the act of begging, the tradition of his clan making mutual help obligatory. All that is sociologically strange to him is mentally strange. That is why, brought up in the school of fraternity, he remains deaf to the message of the Good Samaritan teaching him the virtue of the selfish: Christian charity. In the same way, the meaning of leaves flying off calendars or cigarette butts heaped in an ashtray cannot reach the man who knows neither calendar nor ashtray.

Frequently, techniques and contents are not easily separable. To the extent that its content is incomprehensible, the story's technique becomes so. Certain childish or primitive trepidations are analagous to our own before the "different" films of Isidore Isou.

More subtle to analyze are the difficulties that arise when the language of film properly speaking is situated at a level of abstraction that the spectator has not yet reached.

In the same way that children of the mental age of ten to twelve cannot construct a verbal discourse, they cannot grasp the general discourse of a film: they only apprehend isolated sequences that they connect by a "then, he did . . ." (Heuyer). The successions of shots, image-signs, lap dissolves, superimpositions, which most of the time are immediately understood, disturb or shatter the understanding of a film to the extent that they are drained of their natural symbolism. The sign is the most abstract, the most belated product of the cinema: it can be assimilated only after a certain amount of use and a certain evolution. That is why children who immediately grasp the ghostly or oneiric sense of superimposition can only later grasp its syntactic uses.[27]

As a general rule, everything that comes from the development of the cinema in the sense of a more and more abstract, eliptical, or sophisticated use of techniques risks being out of the reach of new audiences, for reasons that have nothing to do with the native essence of film language, but with historical and social conditions that have been able to transform some of its elements into shorthand notations or refined effects.

The speed of the rhythm is itself the product of a sociological evolution; fifty years of cinema have accelerated the internal movement of films. Not only must the new public adapt to this speed, but certain publics accustomed to the cinema still have difficulty keeping up. It is not only Sellers and the Colonial Film Unit who ask for slow films, but also the Service cinématographique du ministère de l'agriculture in France.[28] The (relative) excess of speed, the eliptical multiplications and concentrations are connected. The underlying thing is the phenomenon of acceleration. The film breaks down, then, for those who have trouble following at the very spot where an ellipse established continuity. Yet fifty years' lateness can easily be recuperated by children, country folk, or archaic peoples. Wherever the cinema sets up its screen, an accelerated filmic "acculturation" takes place, which confirms that the difficulty was not in the language but in its delivery.

Conversely, if the objects exhibited are immobile, if the camera is itself immobile, there is no longer a film but a rough and spasmodic succession of postcards. There are numerous documentaries and educational films, precisely but naively intended for children and archaic peoples, where nothing ever moves in the image and where the camera is restricted to tirelessly repeating a dreary panoramic shot. The film drags along languidly. The succession of images is abstract. It bores or shocks. The camera changes place and perspective in an awkward fashion. The universe has lost its viscosity, objects their anthropo-cosmomorphic qualities. The spectator's participation fails to link the scenes. Each change of shot is felt like a nervous jolt. Although truer, the documentary sometimes seems less real than the action film. That is why it is not only steeped in music, but the external continuity of a piquant commentary intended to prevent us from dozing off is added to it.

We understand that the stasis that disenchants the universe of the cinema renders its language unintelligible to the child or the archaic person. The dissolves that link three static or quasi-static shots, one of the beach, another of the sea, the third of seaweed (a Zazzo experiment), will not be understood in their descriptive articulation. Immobility is the death sentence of intelligibility. On the other hand, the same dissolve will effectively fulfill its function within an action and a movement.

Like a phonograph record turned too quickly, a record turned too slowly loses all meaning. In the same way for the cinema, excessive slowing down, like excessive acceleration, equally creates unintelligibility. *These two opposing unintelligibilities are basically identical. Too fast or too slow, the language of film detaches itself from affective participation and becomes, in both cases, abstract.*

Stasis tends to dessicate and destroy intelligibility, deprived of the lifeblood of participation. The loss of movement is in a vital sense the loss of the cinema's breath.

Thus we understand that certain experiments carried out with documentaries have led to erroneous conclusions about the intelligibility of the fade, the dissolve, and so on. As if the problem of language's *intellection in itself* could be posed in its most abstract framework, which, paradoxically, can seem the most concrete to the experimenter who naively believes the film with still images is simpler, easier, than the film with moving images.

A medium shot or a close-up can pass unnoticed, that is, be "understood" by a new spectator if no strangeness or heterogeneity comes to disrupt the movement of the film, if this movement is actual and not a quasi-juxtaposition of inanimate photos, if this movement is not too accelerated, *if, when all is said and done, the language of film is not separated from its fluid and dynamic source: participation in its nascent state.* On the other hand, if these elementary conditions are not fulfilled (the same as in our language of words—too fast a delivery, hermetic language, or a juxtaposition of nouns without a verb are unintelligible), all the strange things disrupt the movement of the film, the inadequate movement intrudes on the meaning of the images. Then the girl from the Siberian kolkhoz, as Balázs reports, exclaims: "It was horrible. . . . Human beings were torn to pieces and the heads thrown one way and the bodies the other and the hands somewhere else again";[29] the African sees houses vanish into thin air or sink back into the soil, or an elephant-fly;[30] the child is amazed at the strange metamorphosis of a bus into a hearse. Their incomprehension is nothing other than a regressive comprehension: the sign explodes, is pulverized, and only its original magic remains (metamorphosis, ubiquity, the ghost), but isolated, incomprehensible. Scratch the universality of film: what remains is Méliès and magic.

Difficulties of comprehension, then, are real and considerable, but we must *understand* this incomprehension: a UNESCO survey carried out in forty-three countries concluded that "the fact of being illiterate is a serious obstacle to the understanding of cinematographic language." And certainly the illiterate person understands less easily than the literate one. But there is not, at the cinema, this insuperable gap that separates the illiterate person from writing. It is not the principle of the intelligibility of language that must be questioned, but that of the degree of abstraction that the illiterate person can attain. He easily reaches the stage of *abstraction that involves his understanding of signs and narrativity when the latter and the former remain in the nascent movement of participation, of the symbol, of the idea.*

The language of cinema offers us this understanding of things and the world anterior to abstract intelligence but that prepares for it, leads to it, and is the primary shared locus of the human mind. Thirty years ago, Moussinac predicted that the cinema would speak human unity. Has it not already done so? *Is it not the natural Esperanto, the original universal language?*

The universal intelligibility of this language is the indissociable extension of the universal participation that the cinema elicits. What is important is not only that Africans or children understand film, but that they love it. What is important is that the cinema has awakened, reawakened, or attracted to it a need.

Whence the effective and affective universality of the cinema all over the world. As our own research, following on from others, has shown us,[31] the need for cinema, if it is most intense among adolescents, nevertheless affects people of all ages. This appeal makes itself felt with almost the same force whatever the sex, social class, or circumstances, and it is geographic and economic determinations (dispersed habitat, operating difficulties) that curb the development of this need. Born of the great urban centers, of machine civilizations, the cinema very early extended beyond the zone of the technical environment that produced it. Of the big cities, it won over the countryside. Of the great industrial nations, it spread across all continents. Fifteen billion annual admissions across the whole of the globe. Wherever it has spread, it has acclimated itself. It is worthy of note that at the moment the second-biggest film-producing country is India, which has scarcely developed industrially, and that Egypt produces almost as many films as France.[32]

Children all over the world play cowboys.[33] Adults all over the world go to see cowboys. "High society" and those excluded from society have the same participation. To all those who are amazed at this affective and mental communion between the literate and the illiterate, the emperor and the Negro, Rimbaud responded in advance. "Emperor, you are black." And it is without a doubt the sole human virtue of the emperor. *Our negritude is our profound humanity*.

Starting from this universality, other universalities are grafted and blossom, that of a new language, of signs this time. If it is not true, as Balázs believed,[34] that the silent film revived a perfect sign language, abandoned by man since prehistory,[35] for the very good reason that gestures, the smile, even tears have distinct meanings according to civilizations, it is nevertheless true that the American film has spread across the globe a veritable new sign language, a gestural Esperanto that is easy to learn and whose universe, under the sway of the cinema, from then on knows the vocabulary. There is a "degree zero of sign language," in Mario Roques's words, but thanks to the cinema. We will come back to this elsewhere.

Universal themes, a cosmopolitan creation, universal influences and role are the fruits of the original anthropological universality. And, without getting into problems to be taken up later, let us note that Charlie Chaplin is the exemplary test of all these universalities. Chaplin is the first creator of all time who wagered on universality—on the child. His films, which he presented in preview to kids in suburban neighborhoods, still and always will reign over the childlike universe of the "Pathé-Babies." They have been welcomed and accepted just as well by adults, blacks, whites, the literate, and the illiterate. The nomads of Iran, the children of China join Élie Faure and Louis Delluc in a participation and an understanding that is, if not the same, at least common.

That is the cinema. What it is concerned with and what interests it is the mind in its infancy, which carries within it, still indistinct and muddled, human totality.

Hegel explained why poetry is the supreme art. "Like music, it contains the immediate perception of the soul by itself, which is missing in architecture, sculpture and painting. On the other hand it develops in the field of the imagination and the latter creates a whole world of objects not completely lacking in the fixed character of painting and sculpture. Finally, more than any art, it is capable of presenting an event."

Cinema, like music, contains the immediate perception of the soul as it perceives itself. Like poetry, it develops in the field of the imaginary. But more than poetry, more than painting and sculpture, it works by and through a world of objects endowed with practical determination and narratively presents a chain of events. It lacks the concept, but *it produces it*, and in this way, if it does not express them all—at least, perhaps, not yet—it puts in ferment all the potentialities of the human mind.

8 *The Semi-imaginary*
Reality of Man

The world was reflected in the mirror of the cinematograph. The cinema offers us the reflection no longer only of the world but of the human mind.

The cinema is psychic, Epstein has said. Its rooms are veritable mental laboratories where a collective mind materializes from a beam of light. The mind of the spectator performs tremendous, nonstop work, without which a film would be nothing but a Brownian movement on the screen, or at the most a fluttering of twenty-four images per second. Starting from this whirl of lights, two dynamisms, two systems of participation, that of the screen and that of the spectator, are exchanged, flow into one another, complete each other and join in a single dynamism. The film is that moment where two psyches, that incorporated in the film and that of the spectator, unite. "The screen is that place where active thought and spectatorial thought meet and take on the material appearance of being an action" (Epstein).

This symbiosis is possible only because it unites two currents of the same nature. "The mind of the spectator is as active as that of the filmmaker," says Francastel; in other words, it is a question of the same activity. And the spectator, who is all, is also nothing. The participation that creates the film is created by it. The nascent kernel of the system of projection-identification that radiates through the room is in the film.

Nascent mind, total mind, the cinema is so to speak a sort of mind-machine or machine for thinking, "mimic and rival brother of the intelligence" (Cohen-Séat), a quasi-robot. It has no legs, no body, no head, but the moment the beam of light flickers on the screen, a human machine is put into action. It sees in our place in the sense that "to see, is to . . . extract, read and select, transform," and, effectively, we see again on the screen "what the cinema has already seen." "The new gaze of the screen forces itself on our passive gaze."[1] Like a blender, the cinema processes perceptual work. It imitates mechanically—let us understand this word in its literal sense—what are no less appropriately called the psychic mechanisms of approach and assimilation. "An essential trait of the cinema is that it works for and on behalf of the spectator. It substitutes its investigation for ours."[2]

The psyche of the cinema not only elaborates our perception of the real, it also secretes the imaginary. Veritable robot of the imaginary, the cinema "imagines for me, imagines in my place and at the same time outside me, with an imagination that is more intense and precise."[3] It develops a dream that is conscious in many respects and organized in all respects.

Film represents and at the same time signifies. It remixes the real, the unreal, the present, real life, memory, and dream on the same shared mental level. Like the human mind, it is also as much lying as truthful, as mythomaniacal as lucid. It was only one moment—the moment of the cinematograph—this great open eye, "without prejudices, without morals, free from influence," that sees all, evades nothing in its field, that Epstein was speaking about.[4] The cinema, by contrast, is montage, that is, choice, distortion, special effects. "Images alone are nothing, only montage converts them into truth or falsehood." There are historical images, but cinema is not the reflection of history, it is at the very most historian: it tells stories that we take for History. It is impossible to recognize its faked documents, Constantine's false donation,[5] its Apocrypha. In its early days, the Passion Play of the villagers of Oberammergau was filmed on a New York skyscraper, the naval battle of Cuba in a bathtub, and the Boer War in a Brooklyn garden.

The field of the cinema has enlarged and shrunken to the dimensions of the mental field.

It is not pure chance if the language of psychology and that of the cinema often coincide in terms of projection, representation, field, and images. Film is constructed in the likeness of our total psyche.

To draw the whole truth from this proposition, we must turn it inside out, like a pocket; if the cinema is in the image of our psyche, our psyche is in the image of the cinema. The inventors of the cinema have empirically and unconsciously projected into the open air the structures of the imaginary, the tremendous mobility of psychological assimilation, the processes of our intelligence. Everything that can be said of the cinema goes for the human mind itself, its power at once conserving, animating, and creative of animated images. The cinema makes us understand not only theater, poetry, and music, but also the internal theater of the mind: dreams, imaginings, representations: *this little cinema that we have in our head*.

This little cinema that we have in our head is this time alienated into the world. We can see the human psyche in action in the real universe, that is, reciprocally, "reality seen through a brain and a heart" (Walter Ruttman).

In fact, the cinema indissolubly unites the objective reality of the world, as photography reflects it, and the subjective vision of this world, as painting called primitive or naive represents it. Naive painting orders and transforms the world according to psychic participation; it denies optical appearance; one minute it gives the same average size to characters situated at different distances, the next, it substitutes a psychological appearance for optical appearance. It exaggerates or diminishes the dimensions of objects or beings to give them those of love, deference, contempt (and in that very way translates the sociological values attached to these representations); it ignores or transgresses the constraints of time and space, showing successive or geographically distant actions in the same space. Naive painting is thus guided by an immediate spirit that effects a humanization of vision on the picture itself. In the photograph, by contrast, things are left to their apparent dimensions and forms, lost in space, and enclosed in the uniqueness of the moment.

The cinema participates in two universes, that of photography and that of nonrealist painting, or, rather, it unites them syncretically. It respects the reality, if we can put it this way, of the optical illusion; it shows things separated and isolated by time and space, and that was how it initially appeared as the cinematograph, that is, animated photography. But it ceaselessly corrects the optical illusion with the processes of naive painting: medium shots, close-ups. It ceaselessly reestablishes values in terms of care and expression, or else, like realist painting when it seeks to rediscover the meanings of primitive painting, it uses high-angle shots and low-angle shots. Most cinema techniques are responding to the same expressive needs as so-called primitive painting, but within the photographic universe.

The cinema, then, is the world, but half assimilated by the human mind. It is the human mind, but actively projected into the world in its work of elaboration and transformation, of exchange and assimilation. Its double and syncretic nature, objective and subjective, reveals its secret essence; that is, the function and the functioning of the human mind in the world.

The cinema allows us to see the process of the penetration of man in the world and the inseparable process of the penetration of the world in man. This process is first of all one of exploration; it begins with the cinematograph, which places the unknown world within arm's reach, or, rather, within reach of the eye. The cinema pursues and develops the exploratory work of the cinematograph. Perched on the horse's saddle, the airplane's engine, the buoy in the storm, the camera has become the omnipresent eye. It sweeps across the ocean depths and the stellar night equally well. Much more: this new remote-controlled gaze, endowed with all the powers of the machine, goes beyond the optical wall that the physical eye could not cross. Even before the cinematograph, Marey and Muybridge, succeeding in breaking down movement, were the first to bring about this surpassing of the visual sense. Since then, the cinema has extended this new empire in all directions. Beyond the optical wall, the eye sees the movement of things that are apparently immobile (accelerated motion), the detail of things that are too fast (slow motion), and, above all, swept into microscopic and macroscopic infinity, it finally perceives the infrasensitive and the suprasensitive. Behind the telephoto lens, at the tip of the guided missile, the eye patrols, explores. Before man even broke away from the stratosphere, the telepathic eye made its way to the furthermost bounds of interplanetary no-man's-land. It is already impatient for the shores of the macrocosm, ready to take off, to be first on the moon. The cinema will precede us on the planets. But in the exploration of infinitely small worlds, it has already irresistibly and irreversibly left us behind.

Research of the microscopic world is mixed with scientific research itself:[6] microcinematography is truly ahead of the human mind.

So through all films, and through a veritable "supplement to the sense of sight," a "documentary deciphering of the visible world" is carried out. "Today, every fifteen-year-old child, in all classes of society, has a great many times seen the skyscrapers of New York, the ports of the Extreme-Orient, the glaciers of Greenland. . . . Filmed novels have rendered familiar to all children all the eternal emptiness that troubles the human soul, all the painful mysteries of life, of love and death."[7]

At the same time as it was beginning to collect materials for learning, the Lumière cinematograph was already imbuing them with Raymond Lulle's alchemical powder of projection and sympathy: cinematographic doubling was already a catalyst for subjectivity. The cinema goes further: all the things that it projects are already selected, impregnated, blended, semiassimilated in a mental fluid where time and space are no longer obstacles but are mixed up in one plasma. All the diastases of the mind are already in action in the world on the screen. They are projected into the universe and bring back identifiable substances from it. *The cinema reflects the mental commerce of man with the world.*

This commerce is a psychological-practical assimilation of knowledge or of consciousness. The genetic study of the cinema, in revealing to us that *magic* and, more broadly, *magical participation* inaugurate this active commerce with the world, at the same time teaches us that the penetration of the human mind in the world is inseparable from an imaginary efflorescence.

The spectrum analysis of the cinema completes the genetic analysis. It reveals to us the original and profound unity of knowledge and myth, of intelligence and feeling.

The secretion of the imaginary and the comprehension of the real, born from the same psyche in its nascent state, are complementarily connected in the midst of concrete psychological activity, that is, of mental commerce with the world.

Effectively, everything enters us, is retained, anticipated, communicates by way of images more or less inflated by the imaginary. This imaginary complex, which assures and disturbs participation at the same time, constitutes a placental secretion that envelops and nourishes us. Even in the state of wakefulness and even outside of any spectacle, man walks, solitary, surrounded by a cloud of images, his "fantasies." And not only in these daydreams: the loves that he believes to be of flesh and tears are animated postcards, delirious representations. Images slide between his perception and himself, they make him see what he wants to see. The substance of the imaginary is mixed up with our life of the soul, our affective reality.

The permanent source of the imaginary is participation. What can seem most unreal is born from what is most real. Participation is the concrete presence of man in the world: his life. Certainly, imaginary projection-identifications are apparently only its epiphenomena or deliriums. They carry all the impossible dreams, all the lies that man makes up for himself, all the illusions that he deceives himself with (spectacles, arts). Myths and religions are there to testify to their incredible unreality. Our feelings distort things, deceive us about events and beings. It is not by chance that sentiment signifies naïveté or weakness, that magic signifies error, helplessness, dupery.

But it is not only in the capacity of the reality of error or foolishness that we are envisaging the reality of the imaginary. We also want to remind ourselves that its myths are founded *in reality;* they even express the vital first reality of man. Magic, myth of all myths, is not only a myth. The analogy of the human microcosm to the macrocosm is also a biological truth; man is freed from the specializations and constraints that weigh upon the other animal species: he is the summation and battlefield of the forces that animate all living species; he is open to all the solicitations of the world that surrounds him, whence the infinite range of his mimicry and participation. Correlatively, human individuality is affirmed at the expense of specific instincts that atrophy, and the *double* is the spontaneous expression of this fundamental biological affirmation. It is, then, the biological reality of man, self-determined individual and indeterminate microcosm, that produces the magical vision of the world, that is, the system of affective participation.

Without a doubt, individuality does not *practically* possess the powers of the double and does not practically embrace cosmic totality. *But the unreality of this myth, founded in reality, reveals to us the reality of the need that cannot be realized.*

This contradiction between the real being and his real need is unified by the concrete man, united not statically but in work. What can diversely be called human "personality," "consciousness," "nature," stems not only from practical exchanges between man and nature and social exchanges between men, but also from endless exchanges between the individual and his imaginary double, and from these anthropo-cosmomorphic exchanges, again imaginary, with things or beings in nature that man feels, sympathetically, participate in his own life. In the course of this ceaseless shuttle between the "I" that is another and the others that are in the "I," between the subjective consciousness of the world and the objective consciousness of the self, between the outside and the inside, the immediately objective self (double) is internalized, the internalized double atrophies and is spiritualized into soul; the immediately subjective macrocosm is objectivized to constitute the objective world subjected to laws.

Genetically, man is enriched in the course of all these imaginary transfers; the imaginary is the ferment of the work of the self on the self and on nature through which the reality of man is constructed and developed.

Thus the imaginary cannot be dissociated from "human nature"—from material man. It is an integral and vital part of him. It contributes to his practical formation. It constitutes a veritable scaffolding of projection-identifications from which, at the same time as he masks himself, man knows and constructs himself. Man does not exist totally, but this semi-existence is his existence. Imaginary man and practical man *(Homo faber)* are two faces of one "being of need," as D. Mascolo puts it. Let us say it another way, with Gorky: the reality of man is semi-imaginary.

Certainly the dream is opposed to the tool. The richness and proliferation of our dreams respond to our state of extreme practical indigence, sleep. At the moment of extreme insertion of the practical in the real, the technical appears and phantasms disappear to make way for the rational. But this contradiction is born of the unity of need: deprivation is the *need* itself from which compensating images spring up. Work is the need that drives away images and fixes itself on the tool.

The dream and the tool, which seem to contradict and despise one another, work along the same lines. The technical is used practically to give human form to nature and cosmic power to man. To the anthropo-cosmomorphism of the imaginary corresponds the anthropo-cosmomorphism of the practical, to the alienation and projection of human substance in dreams corresponds the alienation and projection in tools and work, that is, this long, uninterrupted effort to give reality to the fundamental need: to make man the subject of the world.

In fact, we cannot genetically dissociate imaginary participations with animals and plants from the domestication of animals and plants, the oneiric fascination of fire from the conquest of fire. In the same way, we cannot dissociate hunting or fertility rites from hunting or culture. The imaginary and the technical rely on one another, help each other. They always meet not only as negatives of each other but as mutual fermenting agents.

Thus, in the vanguard of the practical, *technical invention* only crowns an obsessive dream. All great inventions are preceded by mythical aspirations, and their novelty seems so unreal that trickery, sorcery, or madness are seen in them.

This is because, even in its extreme unreality, the dream is itself ahead of reality. The imaginary blends in the same osmosis the unreal and the real, fact and need, not only to attribute to reality the charms of the imaginary, but also to confer on the imaginary the capacities of reality. Every dream is an unreal fulfillment, but one that aspires to practical fulfillment. That is why social utopias foreshadow future societies, alchemy foreshadows chemistry, the wings of Icarus foreshadow those of the airplane.

We think we have sent the dream away into the night and reserved work for the day, but we cannot separate technology, the effective pilot of evolution, from the imaginary that precedes it, ahead of the world, in the oneiric fulfillment of our needs.

Thus the fantastic transformation and the material transformation of nature and man intersect and replace one another. Dream and tool meet and fertilize one another. Our dreams prepare for our technologies: a machine among machines, the airplane is born of a dream. Our technologies maintain our dreams: a machine among machines, the cinema has been taken over by the imaginary.

The cinema testifies to the opposition of the imaginary and the practical as to their unity.

Their opposition: like all fantasizing, films are proliferations of expectation, ectoplasms to keep the soul warm. That is what cinema is first of all: the disturbed image, given over to impotent desires and neurotic fears, its cancerous burgeoning, its morbid plethora. True life is absent, and it is only a substitute that keeps us company waiting for Godot. The world within arm's reach, man the subject of the world—it is only a program of illusion. Man the subject of the world is still only and will perhaps never be anything other than a representation, a spectacle—of the cinema.[8]

But at the same time, and in a contradictory way (and it is this concrete contradiction that we will have to analyze in the future), like every imaginary, the cinema is actual commerce with the world. Its kernel, which is imaginary projection-identification, is rich in all the riches of participation. It is the very kernel of our affective life, and the latter, at the kernel of the semi-imaginary and semipractical reality of man, is rich in its turn in human totality—*that is, in the work of production of man by man, by the humanization of the world and the cosmosization of man.*

The cinema is in its essence indeterminate, open, like man himself. This anthropological characteristic could seem to enable him to escape history and social determination. But anthropology, as we understand it, does not oppose eternal man to the contingency of the moment or historical reality to abstract man.

It is on the contrary in human evolution—that is, the history of societies—that we have wanted to grasp what there is too much of a tendency to consider as noumenal essences. So, we have envisaged the aesthetic essence of the cinema, not as something transcendentally obvious, but in relation to magic. Reciprocally, the magical essence of the cinema appeared to us in relation to the aesthetic. This means that it is not the original magic that comes back to life in the cinema, but a reduced, atrophied magic, submerged in the higher affective-rational syncretism that is the aesthetic; it means the aesthetic is not an original human given—there was no Picasso of the caves exhibiting his prehistoric works to amateurs, and they are magical shadows that the Javanese Wayang made dance on the rock faces—but the evolutionary product of the decline of magic and religion. That means, in a word, that the very nature of the aesthetic, double consciousness, participating and skeptical at the same time, is historical.

Likewise, we have seen that the visual character of the cinema had to be considered in its historicity. The genesis of a language of the silent image, accompanied solely by music, has been able to be effected with ease and effectiveness only within a civilization where the preeminence of the eye has been progressively affirmed at the expense of the other senses, as much for the real as for the imaginary. While the sixteenth century is a time before seeing "hears and scents, inhales breaths and captures sounds," as L. Febvre showed in his *Rabelais*, the cinema reveals the decline of hearing (the inadequacy of the sound source in relation to visual sources, the approximations involved in dubbing, the schematization of sound mixing, and so on) at the same time as it establishes its empire from the concrete and analytic powers of the eye.[9] To connect the genesis of the cinema to the progress of the eye is by the same token to connect it to the general development of civilization and technology, to place it in that very moment that seems indifferent to it.

Much more directly, much more clearly still, the anthropology of the cinema places us at the very heart of historical actuality.

It is in fact because it is an anthropological mirror that the cinema necessarily reflects practical and imaginary realities, that is, also, the needs, communications, and problems of the human individuality of its century. So the various complexes of magic, affectivity, and reason, of the unreal and the real that constitute the molecular structure of films, take us back to contemporary social complexes and their components, to the progressions of reason in the world, to the civilization of the soul, to the magics of the twentieth century, legacies of archaic magic and the fetishistic fixations of our individual and collective life. We have already been able to observe the predominance of fiction or realist fantasy to the detriment of the fantastic and the documentary, the hypertrophy of the soul complex. In a later study, we will need to extend the analysis of, on the one hand, general trends and, on the other hand, differential, cultural, social, and national trends that are expressed in the cinema.

The anthropology of the imaginary, then, leads us to the heart of contemporary problems. But let us remember that that is where it started. The cinema is a mirror—the screen—but it is at the same time a *machine*, a device for filming and projection. It is the product of a machine era. It is even in the vanguard of mechanization. In fact the machine, which seemed to be limited to replacing human labor, is now spread throughout all sectors of life. It takes over from mental work—machines for calculating, thinking. It inserts itself into the heart of nonwork, that is, of leisure. Omnipresent, it tends to constitute, as Georges Freidmann's analyses have shown, not only a set of tools, but a *new environment*, which from then on conditions the whole of civilization—that is, the human personality.[10] We are at a moment in history where man's inner essence is introduced into the machine, where, reciprocally, the machine envelops and determines the essence of man—better still, realizes it.

The cinema poses one of the key human problems of industrial mechanization, to take up another of Georges Friedmann's expressions. It is one of those modern technologies—electricity, radio, telephone, record player, airplane—that reconstitute, but in a practical way, the magical universe where remote-controlled action, ubiquity, presence-absence, and metamorphosis reign. The cinema is not content with providing the biological eye with a mechanical extension that allows it to see more clearly and further; it does not only play the role of a machine to set intellectual operations in motion. It is the mother-machine, genetrix of the imaginary, and, reciprocally, the imaginary determined by the machine. The latter has installed itself at the heart of the aesthetic that we thought reserved for individual artisanal creations: the division of labor, rationalization, and standardization command the production of films. This very word *production* has replaced that of creation.

This machine, dedicated not to the fabrication of material goods but to the satisfaction of imaginary needs, has created a dream industry. As a result, all the determinations of the capitalist system have presided over the birth and flourishing of the economy of the cinema. The accelerated genesis of the art of film cannot be explained apart from the fierce competition of the years 1900–1914; the subsequent improvements in sound and color were brought about by the difficulties of the Hollywood monopolies. More broadly, affective needs entered into the circuit of *industrial merchandise*. At the same time, we can foresee the object of our impending studies: the dream factory is a soul factory, a personality factory.

The cinema cannot be dissociated from the revolutionary movement—and the contradictions at the heart of this movement—that is sweeping civilization along. This movement tends toward universality: the powers of technology and the economy are deployed across the world market, and the theater of the universal movement of the accession of the masses to individuality is worldwide. The cinema industry is a typical industry, the merchandise that is film is typical merchandise of the world market. Its universal language and its universal art are the products of a universal gestation and diffusion. These multiple universalities converge on a fundamental contradiction between the needs of the masses and the needs of capitalist industry. This contradiction is at the heart of the content of films. But the result of this is that it returns us to the very heart of genetic anthropology, since the latter studies man, who realizes and transforms himself in society, man that *is* society and history.

Anthropology, history, sociology are contained, refer to one another, in the same total vision or genetic anthropology. The anthropology of the cinema is necessarily articulated upon its sociology and its history, on the one hand because, mirror of participation and human realities, the cinema is necessarily a mirror of the participation and realities of this century, and on the other hand because we have studied the genesis of the cinema as an ontophylogenetic complex. In the same way that the newborn recommences the historical development of the species modified by the particularity of its social environment—which is itself only one moment in the development of the species—so the development of the cinema recommences that of the history of the human mind, but subject from the outset to the particularities of the environment, that is, what is inherited from the phylum.

Genetic anthropology, which grasps the cinema at its ontophylogenetic kernel, allows us just as much to illuminate its own ontogenesis by phylogenesis as the phylogenesis by its ontogenesis. Its effectiveness is double. We are present at the efflorescence of an art, the seventh by name, but at the same time we better understand the structures common to all art and this formidable unconscious reality within art that produces art. In return, it is this phylogenetic reality that allows us to better understand the seventh art.

Before our eyes, a veritable visitation of the virgin film by the human mind was brought about: the machine to reflect the world effected its own metamorphosis into a machine to imitate the mind. We have been able to see the irruption of the spirit into the crude world, Hegelian negativity at work, and the negation of this negation: the instant flourishing of magic, original humanity; then, through a shortcut blurred by the phylogenetic situation, all the psychic powers—feeling, soul, idea, reason—are incarnated in the cinematographic image. The world is humanized before our eyes. This humanization illuminates the cinema, but it is also man himself, in his semi-imaginary nature, that the cinema illuminates.

This is possible only because the *cinema* is a privileged subject for analysis. Its birth came about almost before our eyes: we can seize the very movement of its formation and its development as if under a laboratory lens. Its genesis has been quasi-natural: the cinema arose from the cinematograph outside of any conscious decision-making process, just as the cinematograph became fixed into spectacle outside of any conscious decision-making process. "The miracle of the cinema is that the progress of the revelations it offers us follows the automatic process of its development. Its discoveries educate us."[11] We have thus been able to be witness to an extraordinary unconscious product, nourished by an in-depth anthropo-historical (ontophylogenetic) process.

It is precisely these unconscious depths that offer themselves to our consciousness. It is because it is alienated in the cinema that the unconscious activity of man offers itself up to analysis. But the latter can apprehend these prodigious riches only if it captures the *movement* of this alienation.

Movement. This is the key word of our method: it is in *history* that we have considered the cinema; it is in its *genesis* that we have studied it; it is in relation to the psychic *processes* involved that we have analyzed it. We have brought everything back to movement. But we have also wanted to avoid considering movement as an abstract principle, an immovable key word; we have wanted to bring it back to man. At the same time, we have wanted to avoid considering humanity as a mystical virtue for humanists. We have also seen the magic of the cinema, the humanity of this magic, the soul of this humanity, the humanity of this soul in the *concrete processes* of *participation*.

Projection-identification allows us to bring fixed things and conceptual essences back to their human processes. All mass comes back to energy. Must we not Einsteinize in their turn the sciences of man, can we not explore those social *things* of which Durkheim spoke by applying to them an equivalent of the formula $E = MC^2$? To consider the sociological masses in terms of the energy that produces and structures them is at the same time to show how energy becomes social matter. This is the genetic road already traced by Hegel and Marx. Participation is precisely the common site, at once biological, affective, and intellectual, of the first human energies. Doubling, a magical or spiritualist notion, appears to us as an elementary process of projection. Anthropo-cosmomorphism is not a kind of special faculty, proper to children and backward people, but the spontaneous movement of projection-identification. The latter is extended, refined, pursued in works of reason and technology, just as it is alienated in reifications and fetishes. The beginnings precisely allow us to see the processes of projection-identification in their real and observable productive work. They allow us to plunge, without getting lost, into the fundamental contradictions that define the cinema. They situate us at the crossroads of forces, at the live and active proton where individual and collective mental powers are involved; history, society, economy, laws, pleasures, spectacle, communication, action.

And in the same way that the physicochemical sciences go by way of the energizing unity of matter to find the atomic and molecular complex proper to each body, so, finally, it is by returning to original energizing human sources *that this total complex can take shape, a complex whose particular constellations in the end give us this specificity of the cinema so searched for in the platonic sky of essences.*

This investigation is not finished, so our conclusion can only be an introduction to the study of what is to follow. Before envisaging the social role of the cinema, we must consider the contents of films in their triple reality that is anthropological, historical, and social, and always in the light of the processes of projection-identification. Once more, filmic material is privileged, precisely because it is at the limit of materiality, semifluid, in motion.

The time has come when sociological "extraspection" replaces and complements psychological introspection. The secret messages, the innermost depths of the soul are there, alienated, tapped in this imaginary that expresses universal needs as well as those of the twentieth century.

Of course from the time he appeared on earth, man has alienated his images, fixing them in bone, in ivory, or on the walls of caves. Certainly the cinema belongs to the same family as the cave drawings of Les Eyzies, of Altamira and Lascaux, the scribblings of children, the frescoes of Michelangelo, sacred and profane representations, myths, legends, and literature. *But never so incarnated in the world itself, never so much grappling with natural reality.* That is why we had to wait for the cinema for imaginary processes to be externalized so originally and totally. We can at last "visualize our dreams" because they have cast themselves onto real material.[12]

At last, for the first time, by means of the machine, in their own likeness, our dreams are projected and objectified. They are industrially fabricated, collectively shared.

They come back upon our waking life to mold it, to teach us how to live or not to live. We reabsorb them, socialized, useful, or else they lose themselves in us, we lose ourselves in them. There they are, stored ectoplasms, astral bodies that feed off our persons and feed us, archives of soul. We must try to question them—that is, to reintegrate the imaginary in the reality of man.

Author's Preface to the 1978 Edition

This book is a meteorite. It speaks of the cinema, but neither of cinematic art nor industry. It describes itself as an essay in anthropology, but it does not spring up from the space of what is recognized as anthropological science. It did not "open up a field," "show a way." In principle, from the very outset, it is not of concern to any category of readers, and it has only had the few readers it has had through misunderstanding. I hope that this new preface will not manage to dissipate all these misunderstandings.

At first sight, I could consider this book, with its satellite, *Les stars*, written directly afterward (1957),[1] as marginal, almost external to the main themes that, from *L'an zéro de l'Allemagne* (1946) and *L'homme et la mort* (1951), have made me oscillate for twenty-five years between investigation in the ever-changing present and reflection on anthropo-sociology. In fact, in 1950–51, when I was entering the Centre national de la recherche scientifique as a researcher in the Sociology Section, no internal necessity drove me to choose the cinema as a theme for study. On the contrary, I would have liked to work on the themes that obsessed me, themes related to communism. But I was then in the depth of the dustbins of history (I am still there, but on the surface); I had doubly excluded myself, and was consequently doubly excluded, from both the "bourgeois" world and the Stalinist world. To dare then to battle on two fronts, at the very heart of the institution I had just entered as a neophyte, was to risk being crushed between two grindstones. I lacked the courage to broach a sociologically virulent, directly politicizable subject, that is, to attack in the same stroke academicism, acephalous empiricism, and arrogant doctrinairism.

So I wanted to find a refuge subject. On the other hand, I wanted a subject that pleased my patron, Georges Friedmann, whose influence played a decisive role in my admission to the CNRS. Friedmann saw and thought "machine." I thought first of all of the aesthetic (a politically defused subject) of the machine in contemporary society. The subject suited Friedmann, but very rapidly, even before any preliminary investigation, it bored me. I chose the cinema. Of course, the cinema is a machine, a machine art, an artindustry. Of course, I was inspired by the idea, already complex and recursive, of understanding society with the help of the cinema while understanding the cinema with the help of society. But I was also driven by something very personal, the fascination of my adolescence and my adult feeling that the cinema is much more beautiful, moving, extraordinary than any other representation.

Yes, I am from one of the first generations whose formation is inseparable from the cinema. Certainly, there have been novels, also consuming. But the possession was not as physical. I remember films that made an impact on me, sometimes with a hallucinatory intensity, between the ages of eleven and eighteen years (1932–39). In 1932, I think, *City Girl*, an American film,[2] a family of farmers, agricultural machines, harvest, a son brings back a wife from the town, brothers who are rivals, rustic and savage desires, as in Zola— I no longer really know what happens, but I remember my desire. Then Brigitte Helm, the Antinéa of *L'Atlantide*, for whom I kill Mo.hange. The mouth and gaze of woman, Gina Manès, *La voie sans disque*. Insane bewitchments. But also—

was I fifteen years old?—this film, *The Threepenny Opera;* why do this music, this history, this revelation of poverty and derision, of which I understood nothing and everything, possess me forever, and, each time I see or hear them again, why do they tear me apart? And, in 1936 or 1938, I no longer know, but before it closes, the Bellevilloise cinema shows *The Path to Life*, and it is one of the most violent shocks of my existence, which suddenly opened me to a radiance, of the kind we receive in mystical tableaux, overwhelming light, although it came from a star already dead.[3]

The cinema? A marginal, epiphenomenal subject for a "sociologist," a subject far removed from life while we were at the height of the cold war, in the final years of Stalinism— a subject, neverthless, that brought me back to *my own life*.

I begin my "research" by sifting through surveys, studies on film, its audiences, its "contents," its "influence," but I am irresistibly taken by the problem of the "magic" of the cinema. The ideas that had emerged from my previous book, *L'homme et la mort*, inform and direct my examination. What had ceaselessly compelled me while working on *L'homme et la mort* was astonishment before this formidable imaginary universe of myths, gods, spirits, a universe not only superimposed on real life, but part of this anthropo-social real life. It was, in short, astonishment that the imaginary is a constitutive part of human reality. Now, in its way, the incredible feeling of reality emanating from images artificially reproduced and produced on the screen posed the same problem as if in reverse. In *L'homme et la mort*, it had seemed to me that there were two and only two sources (that could be combined in various ways) for universal beliefs in the afterlife: one being belief in, or, better, experience of the *double*, the *alter ego*, the *ego alter*, another self, recognized in the reflection, the shadow, liberated in dreams; the other being the belief in the metamorphosis of one form of life into another. And I started from this question: In what sense and in what new way does the modern cinematic universe revive the archaic universe of doubles? Why did the cinematograph, originally a technique for the reproduction of movement whose use seemed to have to be practical, indeed, scientific, veer since its birth into cinema, that is, into imaginary spectacle and, first of all with Méliès's films, into a magical spectacle of *metamorphoses*? There was somewhere, I felt, a profound link between the kingdom of the dead and that of the cinema; it was the kingdom of shadows, the one, of course, of Plato's cave.

Thus, before even broaching the problem of the cinema as a historico-sociological phenomenon, I had to envisage this "anthropological" problem linked to something very fundamental and archaic in the human mind.

For me, the cinema revived this key question of all philosophy and all anthropology: What is this thing that we call mind if we think of its activity, that we call brain if we conceive it as a machine-organ? What is its relation to external reality, given that what characterizes *Homo* is not so much that he is *faber*, maker of tools, *sapiens*, rational and "realistic," but that he is also *demens*, producer of fantasies, myths, ideologies, magics? This book began with the double mystery, that of the imaginary reality of the cinema and the imaginary reality of man. My goal could not only be to consider the cinema in the light of anthropology; it was also to consider *anthropos* in the light of the cinema, while these two lights were, are, both flickering and uncertain. So it was necessary to illuminate the one with the other in an uninterrupted spiral-type process. Thus I did at the same time the anthropology of the cinema and the cinematographology of the *anthropos*, in a looping movement: the human mind sheds light on the cinema which sheds light on

I did not know then that this procedure was in fact a method; it took me twenty years to formulate theoretically and paradigmatically what in fact I practiced spontaneously. (Of course to my detriment, since such a procedure could only be strange, bizarre, uninteresting, confusing for the good cinephile, the good anthropologist, the good sociologist.)

The problem was fascinating: the brain————the mind

(I cannot dissociate these two terms, which perpetually come back to one another) does not directly know external reality. It is enclosed, in a cerebral black box, and only receives, via the sensory receptors and neural networks (*which are themselves cerebral representations*), excitations (themselves *represented* in the form of undulating/corpuscular pathways), which it transforms into *representations*, that is, into images. One can even say that the mind is a representation of the brain, but that the brain is itself a representation of the mind: in other words, *the only reality of which we are certain is the representation, that is, the image, that is, nonreality*, since the image refers to an unknown reality. Of course, these images are articulated, organized, not only according to external stimuli, but also according to our logic, our ideology, that is to say also, our culture. All that is perceived as real thus passes through the image form. Then it is reborn as memory, that is, an image of an image. Therefore, the cinema, like all visual representation (painting, drawing), is one image of an image, but, like the photo, it is an image of the perceptive image, and, better than the photo, it is an animated—that is—living image. It is as representation of living representation that cinema invites us to reflect on the imaginary of reality and the reality of the imaginary.

So the reader will follow this first vein of investigation: the image. In a sense, everything revolves around the image, because *the image is not only the nexus between the real and the imaginary, but the radical and simultaneous constitutive act of the real and the imaginary*. From then on we can perceive the paradoxical character of the image-reflection, or "double," which carries on the one hand a potential for objectivation (distinguishing and isolating "objects," allowing a retreat and distanciation) and on the other hand, simultaneously, a potential for subjectivation (the transfiguring power of the double, the "charm" of the image, *photogénie*).

Hence it is necessary to conceive of not only the distinction but also the confusion between real and imaginary; not only their opposition and competition, but also their complex unity and their complementarity. We must conceive of communications, transformations, and real ⟶ imaginary permutation. And yet that is what is very difficult to conceive. I did not then see where the nub of the difficulty was, and I see it now: it is because our thought has been commanded/controlled since the Cartesian era by a paradigm of disjunction/reduction/simplification that leads us to shatter and mutilate the complexity of phenomena. What we lack, then, is a paradigm that allows us to see the complex unity and complementarity of what is equally heterogeneous or antagonistic.

Thus, as far as the cinema is concerned, the very mode of prevailing thought conceals the complex unity and complementarity of the real and the imaginary, one of these notions necessarily excluding the other. In the same way, this mode of thinking breaks up, under the form of disjunctive alternatives, what makes for the very originality of the cinema, that is, the fact that it is at the same time art and industry, at once social phenomenon and aesthetic phenomenon, a phenomenon that takes us back simultaneously to the modernity of our century and the archaism of our minds.

And here we have a second vein of investigation: the relation between modernity and archaism. It links up with an exploration uninterrupted from *L'homme et la mort* until today. I have never undertaken any research that did not involve the recognition not only of a latency but also of a rebirth of archaism in the very development of our modernity. There, in, for, through the cinema, was the wonder of the archaic universe of doubles, ghosts, on screens, possessing us, bewitching us, living in us, for us, our unlived life, nourishing our lived life of dreams, desires, aspirations, norms—and all this archaism coming back to life through the totally modern action of mechanized technology, of the cinematic industry, *and in a modern aesthetic situation*.

Although cinema is considered an art, numbered the seventh, the aesthetic situation experienced by every spectator was obscured once it was envisaged as mass medium and sociological phenomenon. What is then obscured is what is essential: you, us, me, while intensely bewitched, possessed, eroticized, excited, terrified, loving, suffering, playing, hating—we do not stop knowing that we are in a seat contemplating an imaginary spectacle: *we experience the cinema in a state of double consciousness*. Now, this state of double consciousness, although obvious, is not perceived, is not analyzed, because the paradigm of disjunction does not allow us to conceive of the unity of two antinomic consciousnesses in one being. What we must precisely examine is this astonishing phenomenon *where the illusion of reality is inseparable from the awareness that it is really an illusion*, without, however, this awareness killing the feeling of reality.

The Cinema, or The Imaginary Man presented itself as the first "anthropological" volume of a work in two volumes; the second, "historico-sociological" one was to insert the cinema in its cultural/social problematic. This second volume was prepared, but not written; I realized that to immerse myself culturally/socially, I could not dissociate the cinema from a cultural industry linked to a distinctive communication technology (the mass media) that produced a mass culture. So I enlarged my project, which resulted in *L'esprit du temps* (1961). Nevertheless, straight after *The Cinema*, I had written *The Stars*. This little book well illustrates my sociological purpose, which is to consider the cinema as a multidimensional or, to employ my present-day language, complex phenomenon. In fact, *The Cinema*, like each of my books, is built upon a refusal of disjunctive thinking and is part of a battle against reductive thought. Here, I refuse the glorious alternatives: the cinema is on the one hand an industry, which excludes art, and on the other hand an art, which excludes industry. On the contrary, what is astonishing is that industry and art are combined in a relation that is not only antagonistic and competing, but also complementary. As I have tried to demonstrate, the cinema, like mass culture, thrives on the paradox that (industrial, capitalist, state-controlled) production needs at once to exclude creation (which is deviance, anomic marginality, destandardization) but also to include it (because it is invention, innovation, originality, and because any work needs a minimum of singularity); and everything is played out, humanly, randomly, statistically, culturally, in the game of creation/production. The problem is not to decree that there can be no original creation in the Hollywood-type capitalist system, as the indolent Zhdanov of our movie theaters did, but rather to ask ourselves how production so standardized, so subjugated to the final product, has been able to continuously produce a minority of admirable films.

There remains the problem of socially situating the cinema. A disjunctive alternative still rules there. Either the cinema closes in on itself and becomes a hermetic entity that is concerned only with its own laws and rules, or else the cinema is as if dissolved in order to become pure and simple reflection or product of society. In fact the cinema is a relatively autonomous phenomenon, but one that, like any autonomous phenomenon, can only be autonomized thanks to the sociocultural ecology that co-organizes it. The problem is to try to conceive of the type of articulation and the circuit that operates between the open system that is the cinema and the cultural, social system, which is itself multidimensional. It is this principle of complex sociocultural articulation that is lacking in my book, since it is orphaned of its second volume. Nevertheless, I do indicate that this articulation is possible only if we know how to integrate the production and the productivity of the imaginary into social reality, if we know that anthropo-social reality is made of transmutations, circulations, blendings of the real and the imaginary. Let us add: the real emerges into reality only when it is woven with the imaginary, which solidifies it, gives it consistency and thickness—in other words, *reifies* it.

Since this book first appeared, there have been theoretically important essays, many analyses, many subtleties, much logomachy, much that is bizarre, much arrogance, and the latest event is the birth and the rapid rise of the semiology of the cinema. It is certainly the absent, ignored, unknown point of view here. Effectively, the cinema is a mine teeming with semiotic problems, since film is also trace, sign, symbol, *analogon*. But to be honest, if I feel retrospectively that I would have liked to reflect and work on these semiotic ventures, I can see that in principle my purpose is different. If it stops where semiotics begins, I think it begins where semiotics stops: it begins with the "double" and *mimesis;* it begins with the problematic of the human mind, which secretes the "double" and effects *mimesis* through projections/identifications. In the same way that generative linguistics begins where structural linguistics stops, because it takes into consideration the human mind———— brain,

my project is concerned with a generative anthropo-sociology. ("Language, after all, has no existence outside of mental representation. . . . Whatever its properties may be, they must be furnished by the mental processes of the organism that invented it," says Chomsky in *Le langage et la pensée*.)[4]

All this in order to say that the study of the cinema is not an interlude, a diversion in my bibliography, although it corresponds to a period of withdrawal. Daughter of chance, my need latched onto it. In studying the cinema, I not only studied the cinema, but I continued to study the imaginary man. So I consider the cinema as an object, not peripheral, of secondary importance, indeed ridiculous (my colleagues doubled up with laughter when I said I was going to "work" on the cinema), but as a privileged object for a serious anthropo-sociology, because it poses a Gordian knot of fundamental questionings. In this book, I believe I maintained throughout the examination, what I want to call amazement, surprise, wonder: I did not hasten to find the cinema obvious, normal, banal, functional. On the contrary, right to the end, I experienced what the spectators of the first Lumière spectacles and Méliès's first films experienced. And it is not only the marvelous machine to capture and project images that astonishes me, but also our fabulous mental machine, that great mystery, that unknown continent of our science. My work today is quite different. But this work is at the same time the same, in its obsession and in its method, which at that time had not yet taken the form of a method.[5]

Edgar Morin
December 1977

Notes

Translator's Introduction

1. Edgar Morin, *Le cinéma ou l'homme imaginaire: Essai d'anthropologie sociologique* (Paris: Les Éditions de Minuit, 1985). This book was originally published in 1956 with the subtitle *Essai d'anthropologie*. All quotes from this work presented in this introduction come from this translation, *The Cinema, or The Imaginary Man*.

2. See Morin's discussion in *Pour sortir du vingtième siècle* (Paris: Fernand Nathan, 1981), 91–109.

3. Edgar Morin, *Mes démons* (Paris: Éditions Stock, 1994), 22; my translation. All subsequent translations of quotations from books that have not yet appeared in English translation are my own.

4. Ibid., 217. Edgar Morin, *L'esprit du temps: Essai sur la culture de masse* (Paris: La Galerie de Grasset, 1962).

5. See Chapter 7, this volume. In France, Charlie Chaplin was known as Charlot. Throughout this book I have translated the latter as either Chaplin or Charlie Chaplin.

6. See the author's preface to the 1978 edition at the end of this volume.

7. See Edgar Morin, *Introduction à la pensée complexe* (Paris: ESF, 1990), 111. Morin is now president of the Association pour la pensée complexe, an organization with global reach, including links to UNESCO, dedicated to reconnecting and reforming fields of knowledge. See also the *French Cultural Studies* special issue on Morin, vol. 8, pt. 3, 24 (October 1997), edited by Michael Kelly; and Myron Kaufman's *Edgar Morin: From Big Brother to Fraternity* (London: Pluto, 1996).

8. Edgar Morin, *L'an zéro de l'Allemagne* (Paris: Éditions de la Cité Universelle, 1946).

9. Morin's six volumes on method were written over a twenty-seven year period, between 1977 and 2004. See *La methode*, vol. 1, *La nature de la nature* (Paris: Le Seuil, 1981); vol. 2, *La vie de la vie* (Paris: Le Seuil, 1985); vol. 3, *La connaissance de la connaissance* (Paris: Le Seuil, 1990); vol. 4, *Les idées: Leur habitat, leur vie, leurs moeurs, leur organisation* (Paris: Le Seuil, 1991); vol. 5, *L'humanité de l'humanité* (Paris: Le Seuil, 2001); vol. 6, *L'éthique complexe* (Paris: Le Seuil, 2004). Only the first volume has so far been translated into English. See *Method: Towards a Study of Humankind*, vol. 1, *The Nature of Nature*, trans. J. L. Roland Bélanger (New York: Peter Lang, 1992).

10. Morin, *Mes démons*, 280, 95; see also Morin, *Pour sortir du vingtième siècle*, 301. Edgar Morin, *Autocritique* (1959; repr., Paris: Éditions du Seuil, 1994).

11. See Morin, *Mes démons*, 131–32, 202–4.

12. See Morin, *Pour sortir du vingtième siècle*, 78.

13. See, for example, Morin, *Introduction à la pensée complexe*, 132.

14. Morin, *Mes démons*, 17.

15. See Karl Marx, "Manifesto of the Communist Party," in *The Marx-Engels Reader*, ed. R. Tucker (New York: Norton, 1972). Morin himself also stresses the importance of the notion of the "dereification of matter." See *Introduction à la pensée complexe*, 27.

16. Morin, *Introduction à la pensée complexe*, 27.

17. The original title was *L'homme et la mort dans l'histoire* (Paris: Corrêa, 1951). The title was shortened in later editions. The edition cited here was published by Éditions du Seuil in 1977.

18. Morin, *L'homme et la mort*, 349.

19. Morin, *L'esprit du temps*, 213; Edgar Morin, *The Stars*, trans. Richard Howard (New York: Grove, 1960), 121. *Les stars* was originally published by Éditions du Seuil in 1957.

20. Morin, *L'homme et la mort*, 18.

21. See, for example, Morin, *Mes démons*, 34–35, 240–41.

22. See ibid., 42.

23. Morin, *Introduction à la pensée complexe*, 131.

24. Morin and his collaborators on the journal *Arguments* were instrumental in translating and disseminating the works of Frankfurt school writers.

25. See Morin, *Introduction à la pensée complexe*, 155–56.

26. Morin, *Pour sortir du vingtième siècle*, 282.

27. See Morin, *Mes démons*, 27; *Introduction à la pensée complexe*, 77; *Pour sortir du vingtième siècle*, 249.

28. See Morin, *Mes démons*, 244–45.

29. In *Introduction à la pensée complexe*, Morin draws attention to the problematic evolutionist nature of Lévy-Bruhl's conception of the "primitive," associated with the "prelogical," noting that we more correctly call "primitive" societies "hunter-gatherer" societies today. Lévy-Bruhl, he says, did not pose for himself the question that Wittgenstein asked when reading Frazer's *Golden Bough:* "How did it happen that all these savages, who spend their time performing rites of sorcery, propitiation rites, casting spells and doing drawings, not forget to make real arrows with real bows, and have real strategies?" (96). There is an evolutionist ring to Morin's own writing on "les archaïques" in *The Cinema, or The Imaginary Man* that he would take pains to avoid today, but *The Cinema*'s argument is predicated on his convictions about the fallacious nature of "civilized" belief in linear evolutionism, and already here he had noted that Lévy-Bruhl himself discussed the coexistence of the practical and the magical, the mix of the quotidian and the fantastic in "primitive" societies. Lévy-Bruhl, in fact, evolved in his thinking, responding to criticisms of his "primitive mentality" thesis. In *The Notebooks on Primitive Mentality*, trans. P. Rivière (Oxford: Basil Blackwell, 1975), he said, for example, "There is a mystical mentality which is more marked and more easily observable among 'primitive' peoples than in our own societies, but it is present in every human mind" (101).

30. Morin, *L'homme et la mort*, 100.

31. Ibid., 105.

32. Morin, *The Stars*, 31.

33. Morin, *L'homme et la mort*, 258.

34. Ibid., 261.

35. Ibid., 371.

36. Morin, *The Stars*, 129.

37. Ibid.

38. Ibid.

39. My translation of the 1978 preface appears at the end of this volume.

40. See the author's preface to the 1978 edition.

41. Ibid.

42. See chapter 8, this volume. For all further quotes from this volume, chapter information appears in the text.

43. In this instance he is citing Léon Moussinac and Henri Wallon; see chapter 2.

44. Unfortunately, it is not possible to discuss here the "magic" at work in the "high cretinization" of much official high culture, which includes intellectual elites. But researchers (heretics) who attempted to question orthodoxies during the reign of structuralism will find recognition and little exaggeration in Morin's discussions in *Pour sortir du vingtième siècle* and *Mes démons*.

45. Morin, *The Stars*, 102.

46. Ibid., 177.

47. Edgar Morin, *Les stars* (Paris: Éditions du Seuil, 1972), 180, 177. The piece on Gardner is an appendix in the 1972 edition. Gardner was also a favorite of Cornelius Castoriadis. At a conference on "reason and imagination" in Melbourne, Castoriadis once commented that you could not get Ava Gardner in Immanuel Kant's body. I do not remember the exact context, and, alas, I will never be able to ask him about it now, but the offhand utterance is suggestive of so much to do with physicality, embodiment, theory, and gender.

48. Morin is quoting René Clair and then R. C. Oldfield; see chapter 4.

49. See Siegfried Kracauer, *Theory of Film: The Redemption of Physical Reality* (New York: Oxford University Press, 1960), particularly chap. 9, "The Spectator," and chap. 16, "Film in Our Time."

50. Pauline Kael, "Is There a Cure for Film Criticism? Or, Some Unhappy Thoughts on Siegfried Kracauer's *Theory of Film: The Redemption of Physical Reality*," in *I Lost It at the Movies* (Boston: Little, Brown, 1965).

51. Edgar Morin, with A. B. Kern, *Terre-Patrie* (Paris: Éditions du Seuil, 1996), 65–66; my translation. I prefer this translation to the one found in *Homeland Earth: A Manifesto for the New Millennium*, trans. S. M. Kelly and R. LaPointe (Cresskill, NJ: Hampton, 1999), 39.

52. Kael, "Is There a Cure for Film Criticism?" 27.

53. See, for example, Morin, "The Spirit of the Valley," in *Method*, vol. 1, *The Nature of Nature*.

54. See my discussion in Lorraine Mortimer, "Sweet Finitude: Relative Utopias with Live Inhabitants," *French Cultural Studies* 8, pt. 2, 23 (June 1997). In that article, I neglect to note, however, that in the early 1950s, Morin was closer to Barthes on the belief in progress and the attempt to conquer death than the rest of my argument might imply. Barthes and Morin were associates in the 1950s, and after Barthes's appointment in 1956, both were employed at CNRS. With Jean Duvignaud, in 1957, they founded the journal *Arguments*.

55. Roland Barthes, *Mythologies*, trans. Annette Lavers (Herts: Paladin, 1973), 9. *Mythologies* was originally published by Éditions du Seuil in 1957.

56. Ibid., 159.

57. Barthes's final book, *La chambre claire*, appeared in 1980, the year of his death. Well-known in the English-speaking world, its translation by Richard Howard, *Camera Lucida: Reflections on Photography* (London: Vintage, 2000), first appeared in 1981. Written in full acknowledgment of the love for and loss of his now deceased mother (arguably, *enabled* methodologically and expressively by them), despite Barthes's own belief, much of what he says about the phenomenological reality of photography can also apply to cinema. (He most likely related to cinema in a very different way from the way in which he related to photography.) *Camera Lucida* is written "in homage to" Sartre's *L'imaginaire*, which Morin also draws on in *The Cinema, or The Imaginary Man*, and it shares much terrain with the latter. However, although Barthes's book refers to Morin's *L'homme et la mort*, it strangely makes no reference to *The Cinema*. Morin has suggested to me (in a personal communication) that Barthes had probably read *The Cinema* when it appeared but was most likely by that time engaged with his development of semiology and probably never returned to it before writing *Camera Lucida*.

58. Morin, *Pour sortir du vingtième siècle*, 255; see also 282–83.

59. Ibid., 145.

60. Morin, *L'esprit du temps*, 157.

61. See Morin, *Pour sortir du vintième siècle*, 17–25; *Mes démons*, 293. Morin also discusses the hallucinations involved in his own early Stalinism in *Mes démons*.

62. See *Introduction à la pensée complexe*, 127–28.

63. Brian Rigby, "The Notion of 'the Anthropological' in Morin's Cultural Analysis," *French Cultural Studies* 8, pt. 3, 24 (October 1997): 337.

64. Morin, *Pour sortir du vingtième siècle*, 375.

65. Morin, *Terre-Patrie*, 208; my translation. See *Homeland Earth*, 139.

66. Václav Havel, "The Search for Meaning in a Global Civilization," in *The Fontana Postmodern Reader*, ed. Walter Truett Anderson (London: Fontana, 1996), 210–11.

67. Morin, *Terre-Patrie*, 207; my translation. See *Homeland Earth*, 139.

68. See Edgar Morin, "Chronicle of a Film," in Jean Rouch, *Ciné-Ethnography*, ed. and trans. Steven Feld (Minneapolis: University of Minnesota Press, 2003), 257.

69. Ibid., 262.

70. Béla Balázs, *Theory of the Film: Character and Growth of a New Art*, trans. E. Bone (New York: Dover, 1970), 42.

71. Morin, "Chronicle of a Film," 232.

72. Ibid., 231.

73. See ibid., 234, 248.

74. One of the "optimistic" lessons Morin himself drew from the film was "an increased faith in adolescent virtues: denial, struggle and seeking." Some of the young participants, he concluded, inspired him to resist the bourgeois life. See ibid., 262.

75. See Edgar Morin, "Avant et après la diaspora," in *L'unité de l'homme: Invariants biologiques et universaux culturels*, ed. Edgar Morin and Massimo Piattelli-Palmarini (Paris: Éditions du Seuil, 1974), 820. The "Unity of Man" colloquium was held at the Centre Royaumont pour une science de l'homme in September 1972. There is no place here for discussion of Morin's thinking in relation to woman/mother as metaphor and the relative lack of women as agents in his work overall. One of my reasons for using the generic *man* throughout this book is that I have attempted to render faithfully his *homme*, which I regard as usually tied to the masculine, despite Morin's good intentions here and in other places. (I take seriously his claim not to be a messiah delivering the truth! See Edgar Morin, "Messie, mais non," in *Arguments pour une méthode: Autour d'Edgar Morin*, ed. Daniel Bougnoux, Jean-Louis Le Moigne, and Serge Proulx [Paris: Éditions du Seuil, 1990].) It is up to us to

complexify complex thought further in relation to the "woman" problem or to put it more aptly, the "man" problem.

76. Morin, "Avant et après la diaspora," 816. The film to which Morin refers was shown by Irenaüs Eibl-Eibesfeldt. In his remarks, Morin is referring to L. L. Cavalli-Sforza's discussion of dispersion and unity.

Prologue

1. Jean Epstein, "On Certain Characteristics of *Photogénie*," trans. T. Milne, in *French Film Theory and Criticism*, vol. 1, *1907–1929*, ed. Richard Abel (Princeton, NJ: Princeton University Press, 1988), 315. [Morin's reference is to Epstein in *Le cinématographe vu de l'Etna* (Paris: Écrivains Réunies, 1926), 25, where the latter wrote of the cinema: "C'est un jeune énigme. Est-ce un art? ou moins? ou une langue d'images pareille aux hiéroglyphes de l'ancienne Égypte, dont nous méconnaissons le mystère, dont nous ignorons même tout ce que nous en ignorons?" Morin's text reads: "C'est pourquoi, comme dit Jean Epstein 'nous ignorons tout ce que nous ignorons du cinéma,'" slightly altering Epstein's words but not his sense. Morin is often less than exact in quoting sources while never, to my knowledge, betraying their sense. Throughout this translation, where I have had access to original sources, I have placed in quotation marks only what appeared in the original source. I have also, as in this instance, used existing English translations where available. Epstein's work was of fundamental importance to Morin in his writing of *Le cinéma ou l'homme imaginaire*. His collected writings can now be found in the two volumes of *Écrits sur le cinéma, 1921–1953* (Paris: Éditions Seghers, 1974). Where possible, I give page references to the works as they appear in these volumes.—Trans.]

2. A second volume will follow, which we will devote to the problems posed by the contents of films and the role of the cinema in contemporary society. [See Morin's discussion of why this volume never appeared in the author's preface to the 1978 edition, which appears at the end of this volume.—Trans.]

1. The Cinema, the Airplane

1. [*Objectif* in French means "lens" as well as "objective."—Trans.]

2. See the works listed in the bibliography section headed

"History of the Cinema," subsection "The Origins and Beginnings of the Cinematograph," particularly those by E.-J. Marey and G. Demenÿ.

3. [PTT refers to les Postes, télécommunications et télédiffusion, the French post office and telephone service.—Trans.]

4. G. Cohen-Séat, *Essai sur les principes d'une philosophie du cinéma* (Paris: PUF, 1946*)*, 26.

5. The first scientific films themselves, those of Dr. Comandon, were made under the instigation of Pathé, who, in search of the extraordinary, suddenly discovered science.

6. See Jacques Schiltz, *Le cinéma au service de l'industrie* (Paris: SDAC, 1938). Note also that the efforts of Painlevé often remained isolated.

7. "The very nature of the cinema . . . directs it toward the representation of unreal or supernatural events." Raoul Ergmann, "Le règne du fantastique," in *Cinéma d'aujourd'hui* (Congrès international du cinéma à Bâle) (Geneva: Trois Collines, 1946), 37. See the same kind of reflections in Jean Epstein, *Bonjour cinéma* (Paris: La Sirène, 1921), 43–44ff.

8. Riciotto Canudo, "Reflections on the Seventh Art," trans. C. Gorbman, in *French Film Theory and Criticism*, vol. 1, *1907–1929*, ed. Richard Abel (Princeton, NJ: Princeton University Press, 1988), 299.

9. P.-F. Quesnoy, "Le cinéma," *Le Rouge et le Noir* (July 1928): 103.

10. J.-F. Laglenne, "Cinéma et peinture," *Cahiers du Mois*, nos. 16–17 (1925): 106.

11. See Epstein, *Bonjour cinéma*, 112–13; Michel Dard, article in *Le Rouge et le Noir* (July 1928): 117; Théo Varlet, article in *Le Rouge et le Noir* (July 1928): 78; Paul Valéry, article in *Cahiers de l'IDHEC* 1 (1944); Maurice Henry, "Défense du cinéma américain," *Le Rouge et le Noir* (July 1928): 146; Jean Tédesco, "Cinéma expression," *Cahiers du Mois*, nos. 16–17 (1925): 25.

12. Étienne Souriau, "Filmologie et esthétique comparées," *Revue Internationale de Filmologie* 3, no. 10 (April-June 1952): 149.

13. Élie Faure, in *Encyclopédie française*, 16/64/19.

14. See Léon Moussinac, Naissance du cinéma (1920–24), in *L'âge ingrat du cinéma* (Paris: Sagittaire, 1946); and Henri Wallon, "De quelques problèmes psycho-physiologiques que pose le cinéma," *Revue Internationale de Filmologie* 1, no. 1 (1947): 16.

15. Élie Faure, "The Art of Cineplastics," trans. W. Pach, in *French Film Theory and Criticism*, vol. 1 (see note 8), 263.

16. [See Villiers de l'Isle Adam, *Tomorrow's Eve*, trans. R. M. Adams (Urbana: University of Illinois Press, 1982).—Trans.]

17. André Bazin, "The Myth of Total Cinema," in *What Is Cinema?* vol. 1, trans. H. Gray (Berkeley: University of California Press, 1967), 22.

18. [The Concours Lépine is an annual exposition of inventions at which prizes are given to encourage French artisans and inventors. It was first organized in 1903 after an earlier exposition inaugurated by Louis Lépine.—Trans.]

19. Particularly the mystery of the synchronicity of great inventions across cultures. An invention is never born alone. We see it spring up simultaneously, in diverse parts of the globe, as if its inventors were only the dispersed mediums of one same subterranean genius. Edison in the United States, William Friese-Greene in England, Dr. Anschütz and Skladanovsky in Germany, and other researchers in Russia, Demenÿ and Grimoin-Sanson in France, all work at the same time on the device that Lumière will be the first to perfect.

20. Marcel Lapierre, *Anthologie du cinéma* (Paris: Éditions Bernard Grasset, 1948), 13.

21. Martin Quigley Jr., *Magic Shadows: The Story of the Origin of Motion Pictures* (Washington, DC: Georgetown University Press, 1948).

22. [Étienne Gaspar Robert, who went by the name of Robertson, staged the sophisticated magic lantern show known as the Phantasmagoria, which premiered in Paris in 1798 and later toured Europe. Robertson projected skeletons, ghosts, and other frightening figures in lifelike motion. Although I have used the general word "showmen" to translate Morin's *montreurs*, this word could also be translated as the more specialized term "monstrators." As Barrett Hodsdon notes, *monstrator* was a term for "the purveyor of conscious display." The role of monstrator continued to be paramount in early cinema. See Hodsdon's *The Dawn of Cinema 1894–1915* (Sydney: Museum of Contemporary Art, 1996), 18–19. The scholar-priest Athanasius Kircher was known as the "Doctor of a Hundred Arts." His *Ars magna lucis et umbrae (The Great Art of Light and Shadow)*, which was first published in Rome in 1646,

included discussion of his own work on magic lanterns and observations on the "art-science" of magic shadows. While enjoying great distinction, in his lifetime Kircher was also charged with using the "black arts," being in league with the devil for producing images and shadows as if from nowhere. By the time of his death, magic lanterns were widely used in Europe. See Quigley, *Magic Shadows*, particularly chaps. 6–7.—Trans.]

23. Jean Przylinsky, communication at the Congrès international d'ésthetique, Paris, 1937.

24. A. Valentin, "Introduction à la magie blanche et noire," *Art Cinématographique* 4 (1927): 109.

2. The Charm of the Image

1. Marcel L'Herbier, *Intelligence du cinématographe* (Paris: Corrêa, 1946), 25.

2. The introduction of film into regions where it is unknown always provokes the same phenomenon. Lieutenant F. Dumont notes the reactions of Moroccan Berbers: "The sight of the blacksmith shoeing a donkey, of the potter moulding clay, of a man eating roasted grasshoppers, of a donkey passing by, of a camel standing up with its load, unleashes a general enthusiasm: joyous and stunned exclamations spring up all over the place." F. Dumont, "L'utilisation des auxiliaires visuels au Maroc," in *Les auxiliaires visuels et l'éducation de base* (Paris: UNESCO, 1952), 320ff.

3. [I follow Stuart Liebman and Alan Williams here in translating *féerie* as "fairy play." Says Williams: "The fairy play was an outgrowth of melodrama, which embellished the genre's extravagant visual effects with sudden transformations, disappearances, instantaneous voyages in time or space, and the like. Severed heads and disembodied bodies were common, as were appearances by the devil himself." Alan Williams, *Republic of Images: A History of French Filmmaking* (Cambridge, MA: Harvard University Press, 1992), 37ff. See also Stuart Liebman's translation of Méliès's "Les vues cinématographiques," "Cinematographic Views," in *French Film Theory and Criticism*, vol. 1, *1907–1929*, ed. Richard Abel (Princeton, NJ: Princeton University Press, 1988), 35–46; and Katherine Singer Kovacs, "George Méliès and the *Féerie*," in *Film before Griffith*, ed. J. Fell (Berkeley: University of California Press, 1983).—Trans.]

4. See Jean Epstein, "On Certain Characteristics of *Photogénie*," trans. T. Milne, in *French Film Theory and Criticism*, vol. 1 (see note 3), 315. [The emphasis is Morin's.—Trans.]

5. Jean Epstein, "Magnification," trans. Stuart Liebman, in *French Film Theory and Criticism*, vol. 1 (see note 3), 238.

6. Jean Epstein, *Bonjour cinéma* (Paris: La Sirène, 1921), 10.

7. H. Agel, *Le cinéma, a-t-il une âme?* (Paris: Collection 7e art, 1952), 64–65.

8. A. Valentin, "Introduction à la magie blanche et noire," *Art Cinématographique* 4 (1927). [Morin is probably mistaken about his source here. René Clair said: "The camera lens confers an air of legend to everything it approaches; it transposes everything that falls within its field of vision into a world of shadows, deception and illusion." See his *Reflections on the Cinema*, trans. V. Traill (London: William Kimber, 1953), 19.—Trans.]

9. Léon Moussinac, *L'âge ingrat du cinéma* (Paris: Sagittaire, 1946).

10. Georges Sadoul, *Histoire générale du cinéma*, vol. 1, *L'invention du cinéma (1832–1897)* (Paris: Denoël, 1946), 27.

11. The photographed dead are frozen, stiff, grotesque, these unknown great-aunts and great-uncles that we never knew. But those whom we love are tender and loving; we show them to others who pretend to participate in this mystical reanimation of presence, because they practice the same cult and the same rites.

12. [*Souvenir* in French is both "memory" and "souvenir."—Trans.]

13. Théophile Pathé, *Le cinéma* (Paris: Corrêa, 1942), 119–20.

14. See Charles Lancelin, *Méthode de dédoublement personnel* (Paris: H. Durville, n.d.), photos, particularly the ghost of Madame Léontine, the double of the future wife of Dr. Volpi, the ghost of Madame Lambert, and Dr. Baraduc's mental ball. [The last item, I think, is a reference to Dr. Baraduc's invention the "biometer."—Trans.]

15. Georges Sadoul, *Histoire générale du cinéma*, vol. 2, *Les pionniers du cinéma (1897–1909)* (Paris: Denoël, 1947), 54; see also the article Sadoul cites by H. Fournier, in *La nature*, January 15, 1894.

16. The study of the industry and commerce of the photo reveals the formidable need it satisfies. As early as 1862, in France, more than forty thousand families were earning a living from the photographic industry. Mayer and Poirson, *La photographie, histoire*

de sa découverte (Paris, 1862), cited in Sadoul, *Histoire générale du cinéma*, vol. 1, 41.

17. [*Esprit* in French is both "mind" and "spirit."—Trans.]

18. Jean-Paul Sartre, *The Psychology of Imagination* (New York: Citadel, 1961), 134.

19. Ibid., 52–53. Sartre is quoting E. Leroy, *Les visions du demi-sommeil* (Paris: Alcan, 1926), 28. [The emphasis is Morin's.—Trans.]

20. P. Quercy, *Les hallucinations* (Paris: PUF, 1936), 174.

21. Edgar Morin, *L'homme et la mort dans l'histoire* (Paris: Corrêa, 1951), 82–98, 124–68.

22. Dr. L'Hermitte, *L'image de notre corps* (Paris: Nouvelle Revue Critique, 1939).

23. Dr. Fretet, *La folie parmi nous* (Paris: Gallimard, 1952), 195.

24. Cited by R. Canudo, "Morceaux choisis," *Revue du Cinéma* (new series) 3, no. 13 (May 1948): 5.

25. This is one of Claude Mauriac's dominant themes in *L'amour du cinéma* (Paris: Albin Michel, 1954), where this author *senses* and feels the magic of the double in the art of film, without, however, setting out to go as far as its anthropological foundations.

26. Martin Quigley Jr., *Magic Shadows: The Story of the Origin of Motion Pictures* (Washington, DC: Georgetown University Press, 1948), 13.

27. A. Michotte van den Berck, "Le caractère de 'réalité' des projections cinématographiques," *Revue Internationale de Filmologie* 1, nos. 3–4 (October 1948): 254.

28. From its birth, photography immediately posed itself as art, but this art aimed to borrow the formulas of a school of painting: that is, to *compose* a tableau. It is spontaneously, outside the realm of "artists" recognized as such, that an art of photography develops, founded above all on the opposition of shadow and light.

29. [André Bazin, "The Ontology of the Photographic Image," in "*What Is Cinema?* vol. 1, trans. H. Gray (Berkeley: University of California Press, 1967)—Trans.]

30. See L. Page, "Le chef opérateur du son," in *Le cinéma par ceux qui le font*, ed. D. Marion (Paris: Fayard, 1949).

31. Béla Balázs, *Theory of the Film: Character and Growth of a New Art*, trans. E. Bone (New York: Dover, 1970), 110.

32. See *The Bad and the Beautiful* (Vincente Minnelli, 1952),

which brings the early period of horror films back to life, particularly the stroke of inspiration that consists of totally substituting the shadow for the actor.

33. Jean Epstein, *L'intelligence d'une machine*, in *Écrits sur le cinéma*, vol. 1, *1921–1947* (Paris: Éditions Seghers, 1974), 256.

34. Ibid., 304. The whole page titled "The Machine for the Confession of Souls" could be cited.

35. Jean Epstein, *Cinéma du diable*, in *Écrits sur le cinéma*, vol. 1 (see note 33), 392.

36. See Leo Rosten, *Hollywood: The Movie Colony, the Movie Makers* (New York: Arno, 1970).

37. René Clair, *Star Turn*, trans. J. Marks (London: Chatto & Windus, 1936), 37–38. [In fact, it is not the hero, Cecil Adams, who says this, "but a voice which Cecil Adams did not hear, for it was the voice of the author of [the] book" (34–35) who warns that actor Adams's own created characters are stronger than him.—Trans.]

38. Ramón Gomez de la Serna, *Movieland*, trans. A. Flores (New York: Macaulay, 1930), 70, 136, 139.

39. "This faculty criticizes life. . . . I no longer want to live, for it is only a semblance." Paul Valéry, article in *Cahiers de l'IDHEC* 1 (1944).

40. René Clair, in *Crapouillot*, special issue on the cinema (March 1927).

41. Cited by J. G. Auriol, "Formes et manières," *Revue du Cinéma* (new series) 3, no. 18 (October 1948).

42. R. Barjavel, *Cinéma total: Essai sur les formes futures du cinéma* (Paris: Denoël, 1944), 59. [The roc is a huge bird in Arabian mythology.—Trans.]

43. Cited in R. Mandion, *Cinéma, reflet du monde: Tableau d'un art nouveau* (Paris: Publications photographiques et cinématographiques P. Montel, 1944), 195.

44. Barjavel, *Cinéma total*, 9.

45. A. Bioy Casares, *The Invention of Morel and Other Stories (from La Trama Celeste)*, trans. R. L. C. Simms (Austin: University of Texas Press, 1964); Ray Bradbury, "The Veldt," in *The Vintage Bradbury* (New York: Vintage, 1990).

46. [See Villiers de l'Isle Adam, *Tomorrow's Eve*, trans. R. M. Adams (Urbana: University of Illinois Press, 1982).—Trans.]

47. Reported by Louis Guilloux, *Absent de Paris* (Paris: Gallimard, 1952), 182–83.

48. Barjavel, *Cinéma total*, 62. [Morin's reference is most likely to Pierre Bayard (ca.1473–1524), who was known as *le chevalier sans peur et sans reproch*, "the knight without fear and without reproach." Hippolyte Bayard (1801–87), however, was a little-known inventor of photography who received none of the glory that went to the historically acclaimed Daguerre.—Trans.]

49. See Gomez de la Serna, *Movieland*, chap. 25 ("Experimental Movies"), particularly pp. 150, 152.

50. "My abuse consists of having photographed you without your permission. Of course, it is not like an ordinary photograph; this is my latest invention. We shall live in this photograph forever. . . . We shall live for eternity." Bioy Casares, *The Invention of Morel*, 58. Here we come back once again to the magical theme of the photo that "sucks in" the living.

51. G. Cohen-Séat, *Essai sur les principes d'une philosophie du cinéma* (Paris: PUF, 1946), 24.

3. Metamorphosis of the Cinematograph into Cinema

1. We will come back later to the question of the economic and technical possibilities of the sound cinematograph, which were available in color and on the big screen in 1900.

2. "There is more difference between the Lumière machine and the way it was used than there was between all the preceding inventions and the illustrious brothers' box." R. M. Arlaud, *Cinéma bouffe (le cinéma et ses gens)* (Paris: J. Melot, 1945), 28.

3. Georges Sadoul, *Histoire générale du cinéma*, vol. 2, *Les pionniers du cinéma (1897–1909)* (Paris: Denoël, 1947), 164.

4. [Although it does not detract from Morin's general point, the "absolute" nature of the two categories is of course questionable. See, for example, Elizabeth Ezra, *Georges Méliès: The Birth of the Auteur* (Manchester, Eng.: Manchester University Press, 2000), 81, for the suggestion that this dialectic should be rethought, that the dialectic between *réalisme* and *irréalisme* is in fact contained in its entirety within Méliès's work. Ezra also mentions that in Godard's *La chinoise*, Jean-Pierre Léaud's character lectures his revolutionary comrades on the fallacy of the dichotomy between Lumière and Méliès!—Trans.]

5. [Méliès's original text, "Les vues cinématographiques," was written in 1906 and published in the *Annuaire général et international de la photographie* (Paris: Plon, 1907). Stuart Liebman's translation, "Cinematographic Views," is a slightly cut version of the original text. See *French Film Theory and Criticism*, vol. 1, *1907–1929*, ed. Richard Abel (Princeton, NJ: Princeton University Press, 1988), 35–46.—Trans.]

6. Richelet's *Philosophical Dictionary*, cited in Georges Sadoul, *Histoire générale du cinéma*, vol. 1, *L'invention du cinéma (1832–1897)* (Paris: Denoël, 1946), 201.

7. Subsequently, in the years 1914–24, shadows, halos, lights, let us say the latent magic of the double, also played a genetic and structural role in bringing to the cinema that collection of techniques that we call photography.

8. The role of the fantastic in the development of film does not stop with the downfall of Méliès's Star Film. With *Caligari*, *La charrette fantôme (The Phantom Carriage)*, and *Le brasier ardent (The Fiery Furnace)*, we witness a revival of the cinema that is enriched in substance, techniques (photography), and atmosphere. A ceaseless dialectic is at work that makes film pass from realist documentary to the fantastic and then reintegrates the fantastic processes as "means of expression that allow the cinema to translate the reality of life." With Méliès, this dialectic is only at its first stage. If, in fact, after Méliès, the fantastic decreases its terrain and role, it nevertheless experiences sudden expansions, after which it endlessly renews the *realist* art of images.

9. Edgar Morin, *L'homme et la mort dans l'histoire* (Paris: Corrêa, 1951), 99–123.

10. Méliès, "Cinematographic Views," 44.

11. Georges Sadoul, *Histoire d'un art: Le cinéma des origines à nos jours*, 3rd ed. (Paris: Flammarion, 1953), 31.

12. Abel Gance, "Le temps de l'image est venu," *Art Cinématographique* 3 (1926–27): 97.

13. See the section of the bibliography headed "Technique and Vocabulary," subsection "Techniques."

14. Blaise Cendrars, "The Modern: A New Art, the Cinema," trans. Richard Abel, in *French Film Theory and Criticism* vol. 1 (see note 5), 183.

15. Jean Epstein, *L'intelligence d'une machine*, in *Écrits sur le*

cinéma, vol. 1, *1921–1947* (Paris: Éditions Seghers, 1974), 287–88, 292.

16. Béla Balázs, *Theory of the Film: Character and Growth of a New Art*, trans. E. Bone (New York: Dover, 1970), 145.

17. Occasionally there has been a desire to represent memories completely in soft focus, notably in the films of the French avant-garde, which, being too Cartesian, no doubt, wanted to show the qualitative difference that separates the real present from the unreal past. But the evolution of film shows that the past could and should be shown exactly like the present. Soft focus was retained only residually as a transition device.

18. Following the cinema's initiative, the theater in its turn tried to fully resuscitate the past *(L'inconnue d'Arras)*, which until then it had only visualized by way of Théramène's stories or spectral visions.

19. Étienne Souriau, "Les grands caractères de l'univers filmique," in Étienne Souriau et al., *L'univers filmique* (Paris: Bibliothèque d'Esthétique, Flammarion, 1952), 17.

20. See T. L. Sherred, "E for Effort," in *The Astounding Science Fiction Anthology* (New York: Simon & Schuster, 1952); and Élie Faure, "The Art of Cineplastics," trans. W. Pach, in *French Film Theory and Criticism*, vol. 1 (see note 5), 265. Compare the same myth in its popular form, in R. M. Nizerolle, *Les aventuriers du ciel, voyages extraordinaires d'un petit parisien dans la stratosphère, la lune et les planètes*, nos. 40–41 (1936), where the hero, on the planet Jupiter, discovers the "image seeker" invented by the Jovians, which allows them to capture the images of past history on earth: the taking of the Bastille, and so on.

21. Epstein, *L'intelligence d'une machine*, 283.

22. [The limping or lame devil, Asmodée, is the main character in Alain-René Lesage's novel *Le diable boîteux*, published in 1707. He is a demon who lifts the roofs off of houses in Madrid, revealing all the secrets of the families within. *Le diable boîteux (The Lame Devil)* was also a French film released in 1948.—Trans.]

23. H. Agel, *Le cinéma, a-t-il une âme?* (Paris: Collection 7e art, 1952), 7.

24. Quoted in S. Maddison, "Le cinéma et l'information mentale des peuples primitifs," *Revue Internationale de Filmologie* 1, nos. 3–4 (October 1948): 305–10.

25. Balázs, *Theory of the Film*, 148.

26. Ibid., 147.

27. Jean Epstein, "The Senses 1 (b)," trans. T. Milne, in *French Film Theory and Criticism*, vol. 1 (see note 5), 243.

28. I. Panofsky, cited by J. C. Bouman in *Psychologie sociale du cinéma* (unpublished).

29. Faure, "The Art of Cineplastics," 265.

30. Epstein, *L'intelligence d'une machine*, 323. [The emphases are Morin's.—Trans.]

31. G. Cohen-Séat, *Essai sur les principes d'une philosophie du cinéma* (Paris: PUF, 1946), 122.

32. Balázs, *Theory of the Film*, 56.

33. René Clair, "*Coeur fidèle*," trans. S. Appelbaum, in *French Film Theory and Criticism*, vol. 1 (see note 5), 305.

34. See A. Barsacq, "*Le décor*," in *Le cinéma par ceux qui le font*, ed. D. Marion (Paris: Fayard, 1949), 192; R. Mallet-Stevens, "Le cinéma et les arts, l'architecture," *Cahiers du Mois*, nos. 16–17 (1925); L. Landry, "La formation de la sensibilité: Le rôle du sujet," *Cahiers du Mois*, nos. 16–17 (1925): 49; Balázs, *Theory of the Film*, 24–25.

35. V. Pudovkin, *Film Technique and Film Acting*, trans. I. Montagu (London: Vision, 1968), 58.

36. B. Bilinsky, "Le costume," *Art Cinématographique* 6 (1929).

37. Jean Epstein, *Cinéma du diable*, in *Écrits sur le cinéma*, vol. 1 (see note 15), 390.

38. E. Monseur, "L'âme pupilline," *Revue de l'Histoire des Religions* (January-February 1905): 1–23; E. Monseur, "L'âme poucet," *Revue de l'Histoire des Religions* (May-June 1905): 361–75.

39. Epstein, *L'intelligence d'une machine*, 256.

40. F. Léger, "A propos du cinéma," *Plans* 1 (January 1931): 80–84.

41. Epstein, *L'intelligence d'une machine*, 256.

42. Étienne Souriau, "Filmologie et esthétique comparées," *Revue Internationale de Filmologie* 3, no. 10 (April-June 1952): 120.

43. Bilinsky, "Le costume," 56.

44. Cohen-Séat, *Essai sur les principes d'une philosophie du cinéma*, 100.

45. Balázs, *Theory of the Film*, 92.

46. Ibid., 168.

47. Agel, *Le cinéma, a-t-il une âme?* 6.

48. F. Léger, "Peinture et cinéma," *Cahiers du Mois*, nos. 16–17 (1925): 107.

49. J. Manuel, "D. W. Griffith," *Revue du Cinéma* (new series) 1, no. 2 (November 1946): 31.

50. [This volume never appeared. See the author's preface to the 1978 edition.—Trans.]

51. [Maurice Leenhardt, *Do Kamo: Person and Myth in the Melanesian World*, trans. B. M. Gulati (Chicago: University of Chicago Press, 1979).—Trans.]

52. S. Lebovici, "Psychanalyse et cinéma," *Revue Internationale de Filmologie* 2, no. 5 (1949): 53. Compare E. Leroy, *Les visions de demi-sommeil* (Paris: Alcan, 1926); C. Musatti, "Le cinéma et la psychanalyse," *Revue Internationale de Filmologie* 2, no. 6 (1950): 190. [In the bibliography, Morin shows the Musatti article as appearing in vol. 2, issue no. 1 of this journal.—Trans.]

53. Conference at the Institute of Filmology, 1952.

54. R. Desoille, "Le rêve éveillé et la filmologie," in *Revue Internationale de Filmologie* 1, no. 2 (1947): 197ff.

55. Lebovici, "Psychanalyse et cinéma." Furthermore, an interesting similarity is suggested by certain contemporary psychoanalytic research. Psychoanalysts (such as B. D. Lewin in particular) have observed in their patients that "every dream appears to be a projection on a screen." This phenomenon has been described through the introduction of the new concept of the "dream screen" (verbal communication with J. P. Valabrega).

56. Epstein, *L'intelligence d'une machine*, 315.

57. Jacques Poisson, "Cinéma et psychanalyse," *Cahiers du Mois*, nos. 16–17 (1925): 176.

58. See Souriau's remarks on this subject in "Les grands caractères de l'univers filmique": "We should not, without risking serious errors, forget that the spectator who reacts in a certain way to the image is a spectator at the same time subjected to the effect of certain music. . . . Regrettably, one often reads filmological studies marred and vitiated by this omission and . . . as useless . . . as a scientific notebook where barometric observations are systematically neglected" (22–24).

59. For example, Saint Saens's score for *L'assassinat du duc de Guise*.

60. See G. Van Parys, "Le musicien," in *Le cinéma par ceux qui le font* (see note 34), particularly 263–64. See also H. Shothart, "La

musique d'écran," in *La technique du film* (Paris: Payot, 1939), 138–42. Shothart explains how he did the music for *Mutiny on the Bounty*, a symphonic score: "The same theme accompanies each appearance of the *Bounty* in the fashion of a Wagner leitmotif."

61. [*Le chemin du paradis* was the French title for UFA's musical comedy *Die Drei von der Tankstelle*.—Trans.]

62. See Landry on this subject in "La formation de la sensibilité," 40 ff.

63. Cohen-Séat, *Essai sur les principes d'une philosophie du cinéma*, 130.

4. The Soul of the Cinema

1. On this subject, see J. Norton Cru, *Du témoignage* (Paris: Gallimard, 1930); and R. Pagès, "Psychologie dite 'projective' et aperception d'autrui," *Bulletin de Psychologie* 6, no. 7 (1953): 407–19.

2. E. Fulchignoni, "Examen d'un test filmique," *Revue Internationale de Filmologie* 2, no. 6 (1950): 172.

3. P. G. Cressey, "The Motion Picture Experience as Modified by Social Background and Personality," *American Sociological Review* 3, no. 4 (August 1938): 520.

4. [Monsieur Jourdain is the main character in Molière's *Le bourgeois gentilhomme*. Nouveau riche, he can suddenly buy everything he wants and copy bourgeois manners. As he learns step by step, each new thing discovered is a revelation.—Trans.]

5. Pudovkin describes the experiment: spectators "pointed out the heavy pensiveness of his mood over the forgotten soup, were touched and moved by the deep sorrow with which he looked on the dead woman, and admired the light, happy smile with which he surveyed the girl at play." See V. Pudovkin, *Film Technique and Film Acting*, trans. I. Montagu (London: Vision, 1968), 168. [Ivan Mosjoukine was a well-known Russian actor. The Soviet director Lev Kuleshov was one of the founders of the Film School in Moscow. He ran a workshop in the 1920s where cinematic techniques and theories were tried out. The "Kuleshov effect" refers to this phenomenon whereby shots acquire their meaning only in relation to other shots.—Trans.]

6. For some good ideas on spectacle, see G. Anaya, "Teoria del espectáculo dramatico," in *Arbor* 77 (Madrid, 1952).

7. [The French title of F. W. Murnau's *Der Letzte Mann* was

Le dernier des hommes. The film is known in English as *The Last Laugh*.—Trans.]

8. Pudovkin, *Film Technique and Film Acting*, 193.

9. Étienne Souriau et al., *L'univers filmique* (Paris: Bibliothèque d'Esthétique, Flammarion, 1952), 15.

10. F. Berge and A. Berge, article in *Cahiers du Mois*, nos. 16–17 (1925): 225.

11. All things being equal and not taking into account *recalcitrants* at the cinema, whose revealing case we will examine in another study.

12. M. Levin, in *Garbo and the Night Watchman*, ed. A. Cooke (London: Secker & Warburg, 1971), 108; J.-F. Laglenne, "Cinéma et peinture," *Cahiers du Mois*, nos. 16–17 (1925): 106.

13. Paul F. Lazarsfeld, "Audience Research in the Movie Field," in *Annals of the American Academy of Political and Social Science* 254 (November 1947): 160–68.

14. To make things easier, sometimes we only say *identification*, sometimes *projection*, according to whichever term indicates the most apparent or most important aspect of the (always implied) projection-identification complex being considered.

15. [See *The Stars*, trans. R. Howard (New York: Grove, 1960). —Trans.]

16. Lazarsfeld, "Audience Research in the Movie Field," 166.

17. Jean Epstein, *Bonjour cinéma* (Paris: La Sirène, 1921), 14.

18. René Clair, "Rhythm," trans. Richard Abel, in *French Film Theory and Criticism*, vol. 1, *1907–1929*, ed. Richard Abel (Princeton, NJ: Princeton University Press, 1988), 369.

19. R. C. Oldfield, "La perception visuelle des images du cinéma, de la télévision et du radar," *Revue Internationale de Filmologie* 1, nos. 3–4 (October 1948): 278.

20. A. Levinson, "Pour une poétique du film," *Art Cinématographique* 4 (1927): 79.

21. Béla Balázs, *Theory of the Film: Character and Growth of a New Art*, trans. E. Bone (New York: Dover, 1970), 63. [A chapter from *Der sichtbare Mensch oder die Kultur des Films* (1924; *The Visible Man or the Culture of Film*) is included in the later book.—Trans.]

22. [*Un état d'âme* in French is a "mood," "feeling," or "frame of mind," literally a "state of soul." In my translation, I am keeping

the "soul" element, with its connection to what we (and Morin in French) speak of as "the soul."—Trans.]

23. [André Ombredane directed the Centre d'études et de recherches psychotechniques in Paris and later taught psychology at the Free University of Brussels. He was the author of books such as *L'exploration de la mentalité des noirs: Le Congo T.A.T.* (1954; repr., Paris: Presses Universitaires de France, 1969). In a note in chapter 7, Morin refers to conferences held at the Institute of Filmology and UNESCO in February 1954, where Ombredane discussed responses to the projection of *La chasse sous-marine* and *Le Bon Samaritain* .—Trans.]

24. Maurice Jaubert, "The Cinema: Music," trans. Richard Abel, in *French Film Theory and Criticism*, vol. 2, *1929–1939* (Princeton, NJ: University Press, 1988), 209. [See the complete article, "Le cinéma: La musique," in *Esprit* 43 (April 1, 1936): 114–19.—Trans.]

25. On this subject, see the inspired theory of Eisenstein, Pudovkin, and Alexandrov on music in the sound film, which *safeguards* micro-macrocosmic communication: "The Sound Film," *Close-Up* (London, October 1928). [Now available as "Statement on Sound," in *The Film Factory: Russian and Soviet Cinema in Documents*, ed. R. Taylor and I. Christie, trans. R. Taylor (Cambridge, MA: Harvard University Press, 1988), 234–35.—Trans.] The principles are also put forward in Pudovkin's *Film Technique and Film Acting*, and in S. Eisenstein's *The Film Sense* (London: Dennis Dobson, 1948), 69–112.

26. The opposition between the epic and the romantic must be taken in its Brechtian sense, and also in the sense in which Jean Planiol opposes the "world of the eternal return" to that of "the sorcerer's apprentice." Jean Planiol, "L'univers du roman policier" (thesis, École des sciences politiques, 1954).

5. Objective Presence

1. A. Michotte van den Berck, "Le caractère de 'réalité' des projections cinématographiques," *Revue Internationale de Filmologie* 1, nos. 3–4 (October 1948): 257–58.

2. When movement cannot be deployed in space, the effects produced are nullified or atrophied; thus we have these races viewed front on (especially with a telephoto lens) where the horses

seem at once agitated, boxed in, and immobile, precisely because their movement is not displaced onto the screen.

3. P. Quercy, *Les hallucinations* (Paris: PUF, 1936), 25.

4. R. C. Oldfield, "La perception visuelle des images du cinéma, de la télévision et du radar," *Revue Internationale de Filmologie* 1, nos. 3–4 (October 1948): 276.

5. René Zazzo, "Niveau mental et compréhension du cinéma," *Revue Internationale de Filmologie* 2, no. 5 (1949): 33.

6. P. Fraisse, "Sur la mémoire des films," *Revue Internationale de Filmologie* 9 (1952): 34–64.

7. [The "croissants" are in fact a donut.—Trans.]

8. Jean-Paul Sartre, *The Psychology of Imagination* (New York: Citadel, 1961), 9.

9. These accommodations are much less easy with seats a long way from the stage where faces are scarcely discernible. With seats that are too close, it is the whole scene that is difficult to grasp. This is why there is a huge difference in price according to seats at the theater, whereas the tendency at the cinema is toward the standardization of prices.

10. Thus the profound relationships picked up on the psychological plane would allow us to give an account of the more and more accentuated influences exerted between the two spectacles. From its origins, with the "art film," the cinema was subjected to processes of theatricalization that are pursued in effects that play on the depth of field, passing through different types of filmed theater, from the performances of the Comédie française to *Les parents terribles*, passing by way of Pagnol's trilogy, born from a theater piece, *Marius*, and ending up with the original film, *César*. Reciprocally, not only have authors such as Elmer Rice and Jules Romains tried their hand at theater pieces in a cinematic style, but above all, mise-en-scène, lighting, cutting, the performance of actors, have been directed in a cinematic way. At the moment, the diverse tendencies of Vilar, Barrault, Serreau, and Lupovici have as a common denominator a certain cinematic vision of the spectacle. J. M. Serreau very consciously relies on a new psychological field born of the cinema, although it may still be the field of psychological vision that the cinema allows us to be conscious of, and that comes back to the theater, not to deny it or go beyond it, but to deepen it.

This note does not even pretend to formulate the dialectic of theater-cinema relations. It would be necessary to compare the doubling quality of the image and the actor being doubled, the absence that is present here, the presence that is absent there. It would be necessary above all to examine how the machines and techniques of the cinema allow the mind's eye to cast off its moorings, to sail into the infinite in a time and space that is free. In and through the cinema, the image is unchained and the imaginary once again launched upon all the horizons of the imagination and the real, but in the same stroke, it is subjected to a pressure more fantastic and more realist than the theater, which is always compelled to a stylization, whether it be of realism or of the fantastic.

11. In Menninger-Lerchenthal, *Das Truggebilde der eigenen Gestalt*, 180, cited by M. Merleau-Ponty, *Phenomenology of Perception*, trans. C. Smith (London: Routledge & Kegan Paul, 1965), 205. [The emphasis is Morin's.—Trans.]

12. M. Caveing, "Dialectique du concept du cinéma," *Revue Internationale de Filmologie* 1, no. 1 (1947): 77; also in *Revue Internationale de Filmologie* 1, nos. 3–4 (October 1948): 343.

13. [*Truc machin* are Morin's words to express the notion of indeterminacy. This can be translated as "thingamajig" or "whatchamacallit." See Claude Lévi-Strauss's discussion of mana in *Introduction to the Work of Marcel Mauss*, trans. F. Baker (London: Routledge & Kegan Paul, 1987), esp. pt. 3, p. 55, on *truc* and *machin*.—Trans.]

14. P. Gilson, "G. Méliès inventeur," *Revue du Cinéma* (October 15, 1929): 16.

15. Béla Balázs, *Theory of the Film: Character and Growth of a New Art*, trans. E. Bone (New York: Dover, 1970), 280.

16. G. Van Parys cites an experience often had by musicians, when the film is projected before the sound track is laid down. "In cases when the film is not very satisfactory, the musician responsible for the sound track sees himself treated with unaccustomed consideration. 'My dear friend, I can only count on you to save the film.'" G. Van Parys, "Le musicien," in *Le cinéma par ceux qui le font*, ed. D. Marion (Paris: Fayard, 1949), 268.

17. M. Ponzo, "Le cinéma et les images collectives," in *Revue Internationale de Filmologie* 2, no. 6 (1950): 148.

18. Steve Passeur: "Notre ami cinéma était un imbécile," *Crapouillot* (September 1929): 27.

19. Balázs failed to recognize the sensory dialectic when he said, "The characters in the silent film spoke, but their speech was only visible, not audible." *Theory of the Film*, 71.

20. René Clair, *Reflections on the Cinema*, trans. V. Traill (London: William Kimber, 1953), 26. [In 1950, Clair was looking back on what he wrote in 1923 about Jackie Coogan in *The Kid* and the expressive power of the child giving evidence in the court scene compared to the useless words written in bad subtitles added to the film. Clair had suggested that Coogan's silent statement reminded him of a scene in *A Midnight Bell:* "Charles Ray, alone in a chapel rumored to be haunted, tries to be brave, whistles, attempts to read a book, jumps at the slightest noise." The "silent images" he returns to are Jackie making the statement and Charles Ray beginning "to WHISTLE," to start "at the slightest NOISE." The capitals are Clair's.—Trans.]

21. Pierre Scize, "Le film muet," in *Le cinéma par ceux qui le font* (see note 16), 46.

22. J. Rivette, "Opinions sur le CinémaScope," *Cahiers du Cinéma* 6, no. 31 (January 1954): 45.

23. G. Altman, article in *Art Cinématographique* 8:102.

24. In fact silence makes itself felt by a suspension between two paroxysmic noises, one heard and the other waited for (the creak of the door, then the silent advance of an armed man: the silence is waiting for the gunshot), or by specific stereotypical noises: "A branch that breaks in a silent forest, a bird that takes flight with a flap of its wings, a bee that goes buzzing by: these are situations that make us conscious of a profound silence," says Werner Schmalenbach in "Dialogue et bruitage dans le film," in *Cinéma d'aujourd'hui* (Congrès international du cinéma à Bâle) (Geneva: Trois Collines, 1946), 109. Silence is a clock in the distance, a squeaking of a shoe sole, a chirping of a bird. In fact only noise can be a metaphor of silence. Cinema shows us that noise is revealing of silence, as, what is more, silence is reciprocally revealing of noise. Silent cinema, having neither this metaphorical instrument at its disposal nor noises whose suspension makes silence weigh upon us, was in this sense more noisy than sound film, and it is in this sense that Brasillach was correct.

25. According to investigations conducted on fifteen thousand subjects by the U.S. Navy's Center for Research from 1947

(Instructional Film Research Programs, Pennsylvania State College), no superiority in relation to color film was able to be established as far as pedagogical effectiveness was concerned, even in cases where it seemed that color played an important role with an anticipated effect in mind. The research of the Visual Aid Department of the University of Melbourne corroborates these conclusions. "Research Report of the Visual Aid Department of the University of Melbourne" (paper presented at the International Congress of Filmology, Paris, February 1955).

26. As the costumer Bilinsky said, "White hides the creases of a fabric and creates a halo on film. . . . This halo [can serve] for the creation of *unreal costumes. . . .* Black velvet . . . can be useful for certain effects in the domain of the *supernatural.*" B. Bilinsky, "Le costume," *Art Cinématographique* 6 (1929): 44.

27. Michotte, "Le caractère de 'réalité' des projections cinématographiques," 257.

28. C. Musatti, "Le cinéma et la psychanalyse," *Revue Internationale de Filmologie* 2, no. 6 (1950): 186. [In the bibliography, Morin shows this article as appearing in vol. 2, issue no. 1 of this journal.—Trans.]

29. Ponzo, "Le cinéma et les images collectives."

30. The stereophony that accompanies CinemaScope tries to remedy the faintness of the depth by means of sound.

31. Merleau-Ponty, *Phenomenology of Perception*, 235, 319.

32. On the secondary role of sound, see Fraisse, "Sur la mémoire des films," 64ff.

33. In 1911, Ponzo had noted the syncretism that comes from the cinema's visual image in "Di alcune osservazioni psicologiche fatte durante rappresentazioni cinematografiche," *Atti Accademia delle Scienze di Torino.* [Morin's "rameau de Salzbourg" and "crystallization" refer to Stendhal's description and metaphor in *Love*, where at the salt mines of Hallein, a miner would throw a bare bough into an abandoned mine, salty water would subsequently soak it, and, when the water receded, the bough would be covered with "an infinity of little crystals, scintillating and dazzling." A comparable "crystallization" process seems to occur, in Stendhal's view, in the perception of a person's object of desire. See Stendhal, "The Salzburg Bough," in *Love*, trans. G. Sale and S. Sale (Harmondsworth: Penguin, 1984), 284–92.—Trans.]

34. [See James Monaco, *How to Read a Film: The Art, Technology, Language, History, and Theory of Film and Media* (New York: Oxford University Press, 1981), 56–57. See also Kevin Brownlow's reference to this historic "legend" in *The Parade's Gone By . . .* (London: Columbus, 1968), 566.—Trans.]

35. See J. M. Lo Duca, "Le son, la couleur, le relief (contribution des techniques françaises au cinéma, II)," *Revue du Cinéma*, (new series) 2, no. 10 (February 1948): 52; Georges Sadoul, *Histoire générale du cinéma*, vol. 2, *Les pionniers du cinéma (1897–1909)* (Paris: Denoël, 1947), chap. 6, pp. 100–116, 130ff.

36. So little did the sound cinema appear as the product of an internal necessity, it was received as an intrusion by cineastes and aesthetes; in the Soviet Union, where threats of crisis and collapse played no role, it had to wait a number of years to be accepted (the same phenomenon nowadays with CinemaScope).

6. The Complex of Dream and Reality

1. [The Jivaro Indians of the Amazon were known to cut off and shrink the heads and of their enemies.—Trans.]

2. Reports of the Colonial Film Unit, cited by S. Maddison, "Le cinéma et l'information mentale des peuples primitifs," *Revue Internationale de Filmologie* 1, nos. 3–4 (October 1948): 25.

3. [Roland Barthes refers to this experiment, in which Congolese participants did not focus on what was most obviously the subject in the frame but instead on a chicken in the "background," in relation to his own experience in *Camera Lucida: Reflections on Photography*, trans. R. Howard (London: Vintage, 1993), 49–51. Contrasting the culturally shaped *studium* and the *punctum* that "disturbs" it, that "pricks," "bruises," and is "poignant" to him, he says: "In Ombredane's experiment, the blacks see on his screen only the chicken crossing one corner of the village square. I too, in the photograph of two retarded children at an institution in New Jersey (taken in 1924 by Lewis H. Hine), hardly see the monstrous heads and pathetic profiles (which belong to the *studium*); what I see, like Ombredane's blacks, is the off-center detail, the little boy's huge Danton collar, the girl's finger bandage; I am a primitive, a child—or a maniac; I dismiss all knowledge, all culture, I refuse to inherit anything from another eye than my own."—Trans.]

4. "Magic? Don't know what it is," a famous demystifier tells

us between a ritual and a devotion. Thus those who fear that the spotlight of reason might fully illuminate the totemic mask that they have on their face drape themselves in pseudorationality.

5. Jean Epstein, *Cinéma du diable*, in *Écrits sur le cinéma*, vol. 1, *1921–1947* (Paris: Éditions Seghers, 1974), 390.

6. See Jean Epstein, "On Certain Characteristics of *Photogénie*," trans. T. Milne, in *French Film Theory and Criticism*, vol. 1, *1907–1927*, ed. Richard Abel (Princeton, NJ: Princeton University Press, 1988), 315.

7. A. Michotte van den Berck, "Le caractère de 'réalité' des projections cinématographiques," *Revue Internationale de Filmologie* 1, nos. 3–4 (October 1948): 250ff.

8. [According to Charles Musser, the Electric Theater is still a storefront theater, and its debut took place on April 16, 1902. See Charles Musser, *The Emergence of Cinema: The American Screen to 1907* (Berkeley: University of California Press, 1994), 299ff.—Trans.]

9. And the attempts at nonfigurative cinema, of which the most recent are those of Norman McLaren. Although often admirable, they do not manage to undermine the empire of the photographic image.

10. Georges Méliès, "Cinematographic Views," trans. Stuart Liebman, in *French Film Theory and Criticism*, vol. 1 (see note 6), 41.

11. "The costume of the least important girl in the Casino de Paris is certainly produced with a greater imaginative liberty than the most fantastic costume fit for the most liberal cinematic production," says B. Bilinsky in "Le costume," *Art Cinématographique* 6 (1929).

12. Ibid., 46.

13. Lotte Eisner, *The Haunted Screen: Expressionism in the German Cinema and the Influence of Max Reinhardt*, trans. R. Greaves (London: Secker & Warburg, 1983), 214.

14. *Étude du Marché du Cinéma Français* (CNC, 1954).

15. Charles Ford, "Le doublage," in *Cinéma d'aujourd'hui* (Congrès international du cinéma à Bâle) (Geneva: Trois Collines, 1946), 91.

16. Kathleen Woolf and Marjorie Fiske, "The Children Talk about Comics," in *Communications Research: 1948–1949*, ed. Paul F. Lazarsfeld and Frank N. Stanton (Oxford: Harper, 1949), 3–50.

17. J. P. Mayer, *Sociology of Film: Studies and Documents* (London:

Faber & Faber, 1946). Boys prefer cowboys, detectives, *ghosts*. Girls prefer love, *ghosts*, cartoons.

18. [In France these were compiled from three Pearl White serials: *The Exploits of Elaine*, *The New Exploits of Elaine*, and *The Romance of Elaine*. —Trans.]

19. François Ricci, "Le cinéma entre l'imagination et la réalité," *Revue Internationale de Filmologie* 1, no. 2 (1947): 162.

20. [See the author's preface to the 1978 edition.—Trans.]

7. Birth of a Reason, Blossoming of a Language

1. As Jean Feyte points out, "a good rhythm is more important . . . than continuities of detail." Jean Feyte, "Le montage," in *Le cinéma par ceux qui le font*, ed. D. Marion (Paris: Fayard, 1949), 249.

2. In the memory, past vision appears in superimposition on the totality or one part of the image; in the dream, the dreamer is divided in two through double exposure and leaves to live his dream while his body remains prone.

3. André Bazin, "William Wyler, or the Jansenist of Directing," in *Bazin at Work: Major Essays and Reviews from the Forties and Fifties*, trans. A. Piette and B. Cardullo, ed. B. Cardullo (New York: Routledge, 1997).

4. The least of our stories already betrays, at the same time as our egocentrism, our cosmocentrism, our viewing angle perpetually changing, a vision of things in a freedom beyond the physiological limits of the eye.

5. Gentilhomme, 21.

6. On the magic of radiophonic voices, see Roger Veillé, "La radio et les hommes," and Paul Deharme, "Pour un art radiophonique," both in the July 1928 special issue of *Le Rouge et le Noir*.

7. See R. Ivonnet, "L'ingénieur du son," in *Le cinéma par ceux qui le font* (see note 1), 235.

8. The insertion of sound in film would merit a genetico-structural study in which we would find, much more accelerated and tangled, the same processes that have created the cinema from the cinematograph. We would be able to distinguish (a) the "*charm of sound*" or *phonogénie*, analogous to the charm of the image or *photogénie;* (b) the metamorphoses of the sound track according to processes analogous to the metamorphosis of the visual track, but

that are effected much more from the thing recorded (the laboratory) than the recording itself (the shooting); and (c) new problems posed by the synthesis of sound and image, whose theoretical solution was *given* in advance by Eisenstein and Pudovkin while visual synthesis (or montage) had come to crown a quarter of a century of spontaneous evolution, thanks to this same Eisenstein and Pudovkin. [See V. Pudovkin, S. M. Eisenstein, and G. Alexandrov, "Statement on Sound," in *The Film Factory: Russian and Soviet Cinema in Documents*, ed. R. Taylor and I. Christie, trans. R. Taylor (Cambridge, MA: Harvard University Press, 1988), 234–35.—Trans.]

9. "Though we may feel ourselves to be very far removed from magic, we are still very much bound up with it. Our ideas of good and bad luck, of quintessence, which are still familiar to us, are very close to the idea of magic itself. Neither technology, science, nor the directing principles of our reason are quite free from the original taint. We are not being daring, I think, if we suggest that a good part of all those non-positive mystical and poetical elements in our notions of force, causation, effect and substance could be traced back to the old habits of mind in which magic was born and which the human mind is slow to throw off." Marcel Mauss, *A General Theory of Magic*, trans. R. Brain (London: Routledge, 1972), 178. [Mauss's *Théorie de la magie* was first published in collaboration with Henri Hubert in *Année Sociologique* in 1902. The translation cited here is based on the edition published in *Sociologie et anthropologie* (Paris: Presses Universitaires de France, 1950).—Trans.]

10. G. Cohen-Séat, *Essai sur les principes d'une philosophie du cinéma* (Paris: PUF, 1946), 152. Cohen-Séat again says that it would be possible to observe "how the notions of semantics and grammar, of dialectics, eloquence, and rhetoric, inasmuch as they are a matter of the constitution of our mind, can serve, with regard to film, to pose the problem" (142).

11. Brecht and Pabst's *The Threepenny Opera* is an excellent example of this type of film. Brecht wanted, moreover, to bring about an Eisensteinian revolution in the theater by introducing the epic dimension of the cinema, modifying the performance of actors who are narrators (or *subjects* of projection-identifications that go beyond them and no longer individual heroes), substituting

for a restricted participation a generalized participation, finally provoking a distancing effect that allows a participation free from that which encloses and fixes it in the soul state and immediate affectivity, to arrive spontaneously at *the idea*.

12. R. Pagès, "Le langage, mode de communication," *Bulletin de Psychologie* 7, no. 9 (May 1954).

13. Cited in L. Lévy-Bruhl, *The Notebooks on Primitive Mentality*, trans. P. Rivière (Oxford: Basil Blackwell, 1975), 18.

14. Let us exaggerate nothing.

15. See Juan Antonio Bardem's *Death of a Cyclist* (1955).

16. Cited in A. F. Liotard, Samivel, and J. Thévenot, *Cinéma d'exploration cinéma au long cours* (Paris: Chavane, 1950), 87.

17. Béla Balázs, *Theory of the Film: Character and Growth of a New Art*, trans. E. Bone (New York: Dover, 1970), 63.

18. Pudovkin, Eisenstein, and Alexandrov, "Statement on Sound."

19. Cohen-Séat, *Essai sur les principes d'une philosophie du cinéma*, 96.

20. Music itself does not escape convention. C. Lalo has shown that fast and high-pitched rhythms signified mourning in ancient Greece, whereas they signify gaiety for us; slow and low-pitched rhythms, which signified joy, nowadays signify mourning. See Charles Lalo, *Eléments d'une esthétique musicale scientifique* (Paris: Vrin, 1939).

21. S. Maddison, "Le cinéma et l'information mentale des peuples primitifs," *Revue Internationale de Filmologie* 1, nos. 3–4 (October 1948): 310.

22. Conferences held at the Institute of Filmology and at UNESCO in February 1954; experiments carried out on the projection of Cousteau's *Chasse sous-marine* and an evangelical film, *Le Bon Samaritain*.

23. Bianca Zazzo and René Zazzo, "Une expérience sur la compréhension du film," *Revue Internationale de Filmologie* 2, no. 6 (1950): 159–70.

24. The particular scene could be forgotten by a certain number of children because of the fact that it was followed by a fight.

25. Zazzo and Zazzo, "Une expérience sur la compréhension du film," 169.

26. A. Marzi, "Cinema e minorati psychici," *Corso de Filmologia* (Rome, February 1949).

27. And yet: Irène, six years old, understands that the metamorphosis of the girl into a broom signifies the passage from dream to waking in Chaplin's *The Bank*. Yet it is the first metamorphosis she sees at the cinema.

28. See also H. Mendras, "Études de sociologie rurale," in *Cahiers de la Fondation Nationale de Sciences Politiques* (Paris: Armand Colin, 1954), 73.

29. [Balázs, *Theory of the Film*, 35.—Trans.]

30. The case of the educational film on malaria already cited, which definitively reassured its audience about the harmlessness of the minuscule fly, the true culprit being a gigantic insect unknown in the regions. "Health Education by Film in Africa," *Colonial Cinema* 7, no. 1 (March 1949), 18. It can be asked why we show archaic peoples these "educational" films full of didactic and awkward close-ups, and also why these boring films called "pedagogical" are shown to children.

31. See Edgar Morin, "Recherches sur le public cinématographique," *Revue Internationale de Filmologie* 12 (January–April 1953).

32. Sixty films per year.

33. On the games of children in Rhodesia, in the towns and villages on the Gold Coast, see *Colonial Cinema* 8 (December 1950).

34. Béla Balázs, *Der sichtbare Mensch, oder die Kultur des Films* (Vienna: Deutsch-osterreichische Verlag, 1924). [As noted in chapter 4, a section of this book is included in *Theory of the Film*, 39–45.—Trans.]

35. B. Fondane, "Grandeur et décadence du cinéma," in M. L'Herbier, *Intelligence du cinématographe* (Paris: Corrêa, 1946).

8. The Semi-imaginary Reality of Man

1. Jean Epstein, "The Senses 1(b)," trans. T. Milne, in *French Film Theory and Criticism*, vol. 1, *1907–1929*, ed. Richard Abel (Princeton, NJ: Princeton University Press, 1988), 244; and René Clair, "Rhythms," trans. Richard Abel, in the same volume, 368.

2. Henri Wallon, "De quelques problèmes psycho-physiologiques que pose le cinéma," *Revue Internationale de Filmologie* 1, no. 1 (1947): 17.

3. François Ricci, "Le cinéma entre l'imagination et la réalité," *Revue Internationale de Filmologie* 1, no. 2 (1947): 162.

4. Jean Epstein, "Le regard de verre," *Cahiers du Mois*, nos. 16–17 (1925): 11 [This became part of *Le cinématographe vu de l'Etna*, in *Écrits sur le cinéma*, vol. 1, *1921–1947* (Paris: Éditions Seghers, 1974), 136–37)—Trans.]; and Béla Balázs, *Theory of the Film: Character and Growth of a New Art*, trans. E. Bone (New York: Dover, 1970), 166.

5. ["The Donation of Constantine" was a document that purported to be a deed of gift from the Emperor Constantine to Pope Sylvester. Appearing in the eighth century, it was only discredited as a forgery in the fifteenth.—Trans.]

6. See Dr. Comandon, "Le cinématograph et les sciences de la nature," in *Le cinéma des origines à nos jours*, ed. H. Fescourt (Paris: Éditions du Cygne, 1932), cited by M. L'Herbier in *Intelligence du cinématographe* (Paris: Corrêa, 1946), 405; and Jean Painlevé, 'Le cinéma au service de la science," *Revue des Vivants* (October 1931), also cited by L'Herbier, 403. See also the perspectives sketched by E.-J. Marey in *La photographie du mouvement* (Paris: G. Carré, 1892). [See also E.-J. Marey, *La chronophotographie* (Paris: Gauthiers-Villars, 1899). Some of Marey's work has appeared in English, for example, *Movement*, trans. E. Pritchard (London: Heinemann, 1895), and *The History of Chronophotography* (Washington, DC: Smithsonian Institution, 1902).—Trans.]

7. H. Laugier, preface to G. Cohen-Séat, *Essai sur les principes d'une philosophie du cinéma* (Paris: PUF, 1946).

8. The spectator is like God before his creation. It is immanent to him and confounds itself in him: effectively the spectator-God is the ride, the fight, the adventure. But at the same time, he transcends it, judges it: the ride, the adventure, the fight are only his own fantasies. So the all-powerful God is still impotent: to the extent that his creatures escape him, he is reduced to the role of supreme Voyeur, who participates in a clandestine fashion, in spirit, in the ecstasies and follies that unfold outside of him. To the extent that they are only his own fantasies, he cannot give them total reality, and thus himself accede to total reality. The spectator-God and the God-spectator cannot truly incarnate themselves and become embodied, and equally cannot give body outside of their mind to creation, which remains ectoplasm.

9. In Japan, from the time of silent cinema to the beginning of sound cinema, the film's *phonographic narrative* played an equivalent

role to that of the film as a whole. Films were accompanied by sound commentaries as important as vision itself. There were great star readers of great popularity. It is obvious that it is "the West" that is at the forefront of the civilization of the eye.

10. See Georges Friedmann, *Où va le travail humain?* (Paris: Gallimard, 1963).

11. Élie Faure, "Vocation du cinéma," in *Fonction du cinéma: De la cinéplastique à son destin social* (Paris: Éditions Gonthier, 1953), 73–74.

12. Jean Tédesco, "Cinéma expression," *Cahiers du Mois*, nos. 16–17 (1925): 25.

Author's Preface to the 1978 Edition

1. [The first English translation of *Les stars* appeared in 1960. See *The Stars*, trans. R. Howard (New York: Grove, 1960).—Trans.]

2. [*City Girl* was made in the United States by the German director F. W. Murnau.—Trans.]

3. [See the introduction concerning Morin's upbringing in the popular quarter of Belleville. For some historical context for the cinema and the film, see Richard Abel, ed., *French Film Theory and Criticism*, vol. 2, *1929–1939* (Princeton, NJ: Princeton University Press, 1988). According to Abel, the Bellevilloise cinema had been bought by the Communist Party in the early 1920s and still functioned as one of the principal sites for the Party's cultural events in the early 1930s. *The Path to Life* (also known as *The Road to Life*) was a Russian film made in 1931 by Nikolai Ekk. See Marcel Carné's review of the film and Abel's note, 102–6.—Trans.]

4. [Chomsky quoted in Paul Chauchard, *Le langage et la pensée* (Paris: PUF, 1976).—Trans.]

5. [See note 9 to the introduction for information on Morin's five books on method, one of which is available in English translation.—Trans.]

Bibliography

This bibliography is not limited to scientific or so-called scientific studies; rather, it includes all kinds of texts inspired by the cinema: a work reputed to be "insignificant" can be for us highly significant, to the extent that it is a part of this total reality that is the universe of the cinema. Our "total" bibliography thus cannot be total, that is, complete; we would need a volume to signal all the texts consulted and at least a lifetime to study the documents that could be consulted.

This bibliography is also not total because it is not concerned with all the problems of the cinema: we have set aside texts more specifically devoted to the analysis of films, their contents and their aesthetics, to the social role of the cinema (we will address them in a subsequent study). This book is only an introduction.

It cannot be total because it has no filmography. In the present work, a filmography could only repeat what appears in various histories of the cinema, particularly those of Georges Sadoul, and we refer the reader to them.

Finally, in line with what has been said so far, it also follows that our bibliography cannot be organized hierarchically: if it includes them, it does not make its selection according to the most important texts in our opinion and to our knowledge. It does not allow us to give an account of the essential contribution of film criticism, which can be grasped only in the continuity of reading throughout the years: here we think of the critical oeuvre of an André Bazin, which is at the highest level of theory on the cinema.

Furthermore, our bibliography cannot be logically classified according to the order of the chapters of our work. This order does not correspond to the classification, implicit or explicit, according to which problems are normally divided up. So we have adopted a compromise. The large sections of this bibliography correspond in a hybrid fashion, on the one hand, to the plan of this work and, on the other hand, to common classifications.

The classification, then, must be understood as that which, in our eyes, presents the minimum of disadvantages.

We have still not been able to avoid a certain arbitrariness in dividing up the references. The same titles can often be classed in several categories without exactly corresponding to any one.

Translator's note: Although I have edited and amended some of the following bibliographic entries to make them more accurate and accessible, I have not undertaken archival research to address all of the discrepancies and issues of missing data that appeared in Morin's original bibliography. Interested French-speaking readers will find enough information to pursue most of the works listed here. The Bibliothèque du film in Paris and the Film Reference Library in Toronto are good places to start.

Bibliographies

Aristarco, G. "Bibliographia." In *Storia delle teoriche del film*, 255–80. Turin: Einaudi, 1951. (See sources concerning R. Canudo, L. Delluc, G. Dulac, H. Richter, B. Balázs, V. Pudovkin, S. M. Eisenstein, R. Arnheim, P. Rotha, R. S. Spottiswoode, U. Barbaro, and L. Chiarini.)

Bibliographie générale du cinéma. Rome: Edizione dell'Ateneo, 1953.

Bouman, J. C. *Bibliographie sur la filmologie considérée dans ses rapports avec les sciences sociales* (Cahiers du centre de documentation, no. 9). Paris: UNESCO, 1954.

Lo Duca, J. M. "Eléments pour une bibliothèque internationale du cinéma." *Revue du Cinéma* (new series) (n.d.): 1496–48.

Malfreyt, J. "Inventaire méthodique, analytique et critique des écrits de langue française touchant au cinéma et à la filmologie." *Revue Internationale de Filmologie* 11, 12, 13, 14 (1952–55).

History of the Cinema

General Histories

Artis, P. *Histoire du cinéma américain de 1926 à 1947*. Paris: Colette d'Halluin, 1947.

Bardèche, M., and R. Brasillach. *Histoire du cinéma*. Paris: Denoël. Vol. 1, *Le cinéma muet*, 1953; vol. 2, *Le cinéma parlant*, 1954. [Earlier English version, *The History of Motion Pictures*, translated by I. Barry. New York: Museum of Modern Art, 1938.]

Charensol, G. *Panorama du cinéma*. Paris: J. Melot, 1947.

———. *Quarante ans de cinéma (1895–1935)*. Paris: Sagittaire, 1935.

Le cinéma des origines à nos jours. (preface by H. Fescourt; collaboration by G. H. Auriol, C. Burguet, G. M. Coissac, Dr. Comandon, J. L. Croze, G. Faim, G. Dulac, et al.). Paris: Éditions du Cygne, 1932.

Coissac, G. M. *Histoire du cinématographe de ses origines à nos jours*. Paris: Cinéopse et Gauthier Villars, 1925.

Hampton, B. E. *A History of the Movies*. New York: Covich-Friede, 1931.

Jacob, L. *The Rise of the American Film*. New York: Harcourt Brace, 1939.

Jeanne, R., and C. Ford. *Histoire encyclopédique du cinéma*. Paris: R. Lafont. Vol. 1, *Tout le cinéma français (1895–1929)*, 1947; vol. 2, *Le cinéma muet (Europe-Amérique)*, 1953.

Lo Duca, J. M. *Histoire du cinéma*. Paris: Presses Universitaires de France, 1951.

Manuel, J. "D. W. Griffith: Panorama d'une oeuvre (1914–1931)." *Revue du Cinéma* (new series) 1, no. 2 (November 1946): 14–36.

Moussinac, L. *L'âge ingrat du cinéma*. Paris: Sagittaire, 1946. [This includes: *Naissance du cinéma (1920–24); Cinéma expression sociale (1923); Le cinéma soviétique (1928); Panoramique du cinéma (1929); L'âge ingrat du cinéma (1930–1945)*.]

Quinze ans de cinématographie soviétique. Moscow: Direction générale de l'industrie cinématographique 1935.

Rotha, P. and R. Griffith. *The Film till Now*. London: Vision, 1949.

Rotha, P., and R. Manvell. *Movie Parade, 1888–1949*. London: Studio, 1950.

Sadoul, G. *Histoire d'un art: Le cinéma des origines à nos jours*. 3rd ed. Paris: Flammarion, 1953.

———. *Histoire générale du cinéma*. Paris: Denoël. Vol. 1, *L'invention du cinéma (1832–1897)*, 1946; vol. 2, *Les pionniers du cinéma (1897–1909)*, 1947; vol. 3, pt. 1, *Le cinéma devient un art (1909–1920)*, 1952; vol. 3, pt. 2, *La première guerre mondiale (1914–20)*, 1952; vol. 4, pt. 1, *L'époque contemporaine: Le cinéma pendant la guerre (1939–45)*, 1954.

Vincent, C. *Histoire de l'art cinématographique*. Brussels: Trident, 1939.

Wood, L. *The Miracle of the Movies*. London: Burke, 1947.

The Origins and Beginnings of the Cinematograph

Blin, R. "Les travaux, les ouvrages et les inventions de Marey." *Revue du Cinéma* (June 1930).

Coissac, G. M. *Histoire du cinématographe de ses origines à nos jours*. Paris: Cinéopse et Gauthier Villars, 1925.

Demenÿ, G. *Les origines du cinématographe*. Paris: H. Paulin, 1909.

Edison, T. A. *Mémoires et observations*. Paris: Flammarion, 1949. [*The Diary and the Sundry Observations of Thomas Alva Edison*. Edited by D. D. Runes. New York: Greenwood, 1968.]

Grimoin-Sanson, R. *Le film de ma vie*. Paris: Henry Parville, 1926.

Marey, E.-J. *La chronophotographie*. Paris: Gauthier-Villars, 1899.

———. *Nouveaux développements de la chronophotographie* (extrait de *La Revue des Travaux Scientifiques*). Paris: Imprimerie Nationale, 1987.

Mesguisch, F. *Tours de manivelle: Souvenirs d'un chasseur d'images*. Paris: Grasset, 1933.

Muybridge, E. *Animal Locomotion: An Electro-Photographic Investigation of Consecutive Phases of Animal Movements*. Philadelphia: University of Pennsylvania, 1891.

Promio, A. "Carnets de route." In C. M. Coissac, *Histoire du cinématographe de ses origines à nos jours*. Paris: Cinéopse et Gauthier Villars, 1925.

Quigley, M., Jr. *Magic Shadows: The Story of the Origin of Motion Pictures*. Washington, DC: Georgetown University Press, 1948.

Sadoul, G. "Les apprentis sorciers (d'Edison à Méliès)." *Revue du Cinéma* (new series) 1, no. 1 (October 1946): 34–44.

———. *Histoire générale du cinéma*. Paris: Denoël. Vol. 1, *L'invention* du cinéma (1832–1897), 1946; vol. 2, *Les pionniers du cinéma (1897–1909)*, 1947.

Méliès and Special Effects: The Passage from the Cinematograph to the Cinema

Bazin, A. "Vie et mort de la surimpression." *Écran Français*, nos. 8–9 (August 22 and August 29, 1945).

Bessy, M., and J. M. Lo Duca. *Georges Méliès, mage et "Mes mémoires," par Méliès*. Paris: Prisma, 1945.

Gilson, P. *Merveilleux*. Paris: Calmann-Lévy, 1945.

Kress, E. *Trucs et illusions, applications de l'optique et de la mécanique au cinématographe*. Paris: Comptoir d'éditions de "Cinéma-Revue," 1912.

Langlois, H. "Notes sur l'histoire du cinéma." *Revue du Cinéma*, nos. 4–5 (October 1929).

Méliès, G. *Les vues cinématographiques*. In *Annuaire général et international de la photographie*. Paris: Plon, 1907. Reprinted in *Revue du Cinéma*, nos. 4–5 (October 1929). ["Cinematographic Views," translated by S. Liebman, is a slightly cut version of the original text. In *French Film Theory and Criticism*, vol. 1, *1907–1929*, edited by R. Abel, 35–46. Princeton, NJ: Princeton University Press, 1988.]

Sadoul, G. "Georges Méliès et la première élaboration du langage cinématographique." *Revue Internationale de Filmologie* 1, no. 1 (July–August 1947): 22–30.

Veno, R. *Cours magica*. Paris: A. Mayette, 1954.

The Cinema and Its People

Arlaud, R. M. *Cinéma bouffe (le cinéma et ses gens)*. Paris: J. Melot, 1945.

Cendrars, B. *Hollywood, la mecque du cinéma*. Paris: Grasset, 1936.

Ehrenbourg, I. *Usine de rêves*. Paris: Gallimard, 1936.

Kessel, J. *Hollywood, ville mirage*. Paris: Gallimard, 1937.

Powdermaker, H. *Hollywood, the Dream Factory: An Anthropologist Looks at the Movie-Makers*. London: Secker & Warburg, 1951.

Technique and Vocabulary

Techniques

Agenda technique du cinéma. 2nd ed. Paris: La Technique Cinématographique, 1939.

Anderson, L. *Making a Film: The Story of "Secret People"; A Complete Report of the Extremely Diverse Operations Which Go to Make a Modern Film*. New York: Macmillan, 1952.

Aristarco, G. "Il montagio." *Bis* 2, no. 16 (June 29, 1949).

Bataille, R. *Grammaire cinématographique*. Lille: A. Taffin Lefort, 1947.

Bendick, J., and R. Bendick. *Making the Movies*. London: Paul Elek, 1946.

Berthomieu, A. *Essai de grammaire cinématographique*. Paris: Nouvelle Édition, 1946.

Buchanan, A. *Film Making: From Script to Screen*. London: Faber & Faber, 1937.

Chartier, J. P., and R. P. Desplanques. *Derrière l'écran: Initiation au cinéma*. Paris: Spes. Éd., 1950.

"Le cinéma." In *Encyclopédie par l'image*. Paris: Hachette, 1954.

Delannoy, J. "Le réalisateur." In *Le cinéma par ceux qui le font*, edited by D. Marion, 116–27. Paris: Fayard, 1949.

Feyder, J., and F. Rosay. *Le cinéma, notre metier*. Geneva: Skira, 1944.

Feyte, J. "Le montage." In *Le cinéma par ceux qui le font*, edited by D. Marion, 244–61. Paris: Fayard, 1949.

Field, A. E. *Hollywood, U.S.A.: From Script to Screen*. New York: Vantage, 1952.

Flacon, M. "Propos sur le travelling." *Raccords*, no. 6 (December 1950): 10–14.

Ford, C. *Bréviaire du cinéma*. Paris: J. Melot, 1945.

Leprohon, P. *Les mille et un métiers du cinéma*. Paris: J. Melot, 1947.

Lods, J. *La formation professionnelle des techniciens du film*. Paris: UNESCO, 1951. (Includes an important bibliography.)

Lo Duca, J. M. *Technique du cinéma*. 3rd ed. Paris: Presses Universitaires de France, 1953.

Marion, D., ed. *Le cinéma par ceux qui le font*. Paris: Fayard, 1949.

May, R. *Il linguaggio del film*. Milan: Poligono, 1947.

Pudovkin, V. *Film Technique and Film Acting*. New York: Lear, 1949.

———. "Le montage." In *Cinéma d'aujourd'hui et de demain*. Moscow: Sovexportfilm, 1946.

Reisz, K. *The Technique of Film Editing*. New York: Focal, 1958.

Revue Internationale du Cinéma, no. 12, *Développements récents de la technique cinématographique*. Brussels: Office Catholique Internationale du Cinéma, 1952.

Sadoul, G. *Le cinéma, son art, sa technique, son économie*. Paris: Bibliothèque Française, 1948.

Sadoul, G., and J. Mitry. "Autour d'une controverse: Eisenstein et le montage des attractions." *Ciné-Club*, no. 6 (April 1948).

Silence! on tourne (comment nous faisons les films, par vingt artistes et techniciens d'Hollywood. Études réunies par Nancy Naumberg). Paris: Payot, 1938.

Spottiswoode, R. *A Grammar of the Film: An Analysis of Film Techniques*. Berkeley: University of California Press, 1950.

La technique du film (par 16 artistes et spécialistes d'Hollywood, textes recueillis par S. Watts). Paris: Payot, 1939.

Toland, G. "L'opérateur de prises de vue." *Revue du Cinéma* (1947).

Ucello, P. *Dizionario della tecnica cinematografica e della fotografia*. Rome: Cinespettacolo, 1950.

Vivie, J. *Traité général de techniques du cinéma: Historique du développement de la technique cinématographique*. Paris: Bureau de Presse et d'Informations, 1946.

Vocabulary of the Cinema

Giraud, J. "Le cinéma comme fait de langage." Paper presented at the International Congress of Filmology, Paris, February 1955.

Piraux, H. *Lexique technique anglais-français du cinéma*. Paris: Nouvelle Édition, 1946.

Reinert, C. *Kleines filmlexicon*. Einsûsdein-Zurich: Verlagstanstalt Benziger, 1946.

Vorontzoff, A. V. *Vocabulaire français-anglais et anglais-français du cinéma* (extrait de l'Annuaire professionnel, *Le Tout-Cinéma*, éditions 1950 et 1952). Paris: Édition Guilhamon.

General Problems: Theory, Anthologies, Encyclopedias

Aristarco, G. *Storia delle teoriche del film*. Turin: Einaudi, 1951.

———. "Théories sur le cinéma." *Revue du Cinéma* (new series) 3, no. 18 (October 1949): 32–41.

Arnheim, R. "Cinema e psicologia." *Cinema*, no. 23 (October 1949).

———. *Film als Kunst*. Berlin: Rowohlt, 1932.

Arnoux, A. *Du muet au parlant*. Paris: Nouvelle Édition, 1946.

Art Cinématographique 1–4 (1926–27) (articles by A. Beucler, C. Dullin, R. Allendy, L. P. Quint, G. Dulac, P. Landry, A. Gance,

A. Maurois, E. Villermoz, J. C. Auriol, A. Lang, A. Berge, M. L'Herbier, L. Moussinac, A. Valentin).

Auriol, J. G. "Formes et manières." *Revue du Cinéma* (new series) 3, no. 18 (October 1948): 42–48.

Bachlin, P. *Histoire économique du cinéma*. Paris: Nouvelle Édition, 1947.

Balázs, B. *Der Geist des Films*. Halle: Wilhem Knapp, 1930.

———. *Der sichtbare Mensch, oder die Kultur des Films*. Vienna: Deutsch-osterreichische Verlag, 1924.

———. *Theory of the Film: Character and Growth of a New Art*, translated by E. Bone. New York: Dover, 1970.

Barbaro, U. *Film, soggeto e sceneggiatura*. Rome: Editions Bianco e Nero, 1939.

———. "Problemi della filmologia." *Cinema* (new series) 2, no. 23 (September 30, 1949).

Bazin, A. "La stylistique de Robert Bresson." *Cahiers du Cinéma* 1, no. 3 (June 1951): 7–21. ["*Le journal d'un curé de campagne* and the Stylistics of Robert Bresson." In *What Is Cinema?* vol. 1, translated by H. Gray. Berkeley: University of California Press, 1967.]

———. "William Wyler ou le jansénisme de la mise en scène." *Revue du Cinéma* (new series) 2, no. 10 (February 1948). ["William Wyler, or the Jansenist of Directing." In *Bazin at Work: Major Essays and Reviews of the Forties and Fifties*, edited by B. Cardullo, translated by A. Piette and B. Cardullo. New York: Routledge, 1997.]

Beracha, S. *Le mirage du cinéma*. Paris: SERP, 1947.

Canudo, R. *L'usine aux images* (articles recueillis par F. Divoire). Paris: E. Chiron, 1927.

Caveing, M. "Dialectique du concept de cinéma." *Revue Internationale de Filmologie* 1, no. 1 (1947): 71–78; nos. 3–4 (October 1948): 357–60.

Cendrars, B. *L'A.B.C. du cinéma*. Paris: Les Écrivains Réunis, 1926.

Chiarini, L. *Cinématografo*. Rome: Edizione Cremonese, 1931.

Chiarini, L., and U. Barbaro. *Problemi del film* (recueil de textes de Canudo, Balázs, etc.). Rome: Bianco & Nero, 1939.

Cinéma (special issue). *Cahiers du Mois*, nos. 16–17 (1925).

Cinéma (special issue). *Le Rouge et le Noir* (July 1928).

Cinéma d'aujourd'hui (Congrès international du cinéma à Bâle). Geneva: Trois Collines, 1946.

Clair, R. *Reflexion faite: Notes pour servir à l'histoire de l'art ciné-matographique de 1920 à 1950*. Paris: Gallimard, 1951. [*Reflections on the Cinema*, translated by V. Traill. London: W. Kimber, 1953.]

Cohen-Séat, G. *Essai sur les principes d'une philosophie du cinéma: Introduction générale, notions fondamentales et vocabulaire de filmologie*. Paris: PUF, 1946.

———. "Filmologie et cinéma." *Revue Internationale de Filmologie* 1, nos. 3–4 (October 1948): 237–47.

Crapouillot, special issues, 1919, 1922, 1923, 1927.

Dekeukeleire, C. *Le cinéma et la pensée*. Paris: Éditions Lumière, 1947.

Delluc, L. *Cinéma et cie*. Paris: Grasset, 1919.

———. *Photogénie*. Paris: De Brunhoff, 1920.

Dulac, G. "L'essence du cinéma, l'idée visuelle." *Cahiers du Mois*, nos. 16–17 (1925).

———. "Les esthétiques, les entraves, la cinégraphie intégrale." *Art Cinématographique* 2 (1927).

Eisenstein, S. M. "La dramaturgie du film." *Bifur*, no. 5 (1930).

———. *Film Form: Essays in Film Theory*. London: Dobson; New York: Harcourt, Brace, 1949.

———. *The Film Sense*. London: Dobson, 1948. (Includes bibliography of texts by Eisenstein.)

———. "Les principes du nouveau cinéma russe." *Revue du Cinéma* 2, no. 9 (April 1, 1930): 16–27.

Epstein, J. *Bonjour cinéma*. Paris: La Sirène, 1921. [Epstein's two volumes of collected writings can now be found in *Écrits sur le cinéma, 1921–53*. Paris: Éditions Seghers, 1974.]

———. *Cinéma du diable*. Paris: J. Melot, 1947.

———. *Le cinématographe vu de l'Etna*. Paris: Écrivains Réunies, 1926.

———. *L'esprit du cinéma*. Paris: Jeheber, 1955.

———. "Le film et le monde." *Les Temps Modernes*, no. 65 (April 1951): 1701–9.

———. *L'intelligence d'une machine*. Paris: J. Melot, 1946.

Faure, É. *Fonction du cinéma: De la cinéplastique à son destin social, 1921–37*. Paris: Plon, 1953.

Folliet, J. "Petite sociologie du cinéma." *Chronique Sociale* 62, nos. 4–5 (1954): 319–33.

Friedmann, G., and E. Morin. "De la méthode en sociologie du cinéma." Paper presented at the International Congress of Filmology, Paris, February 1955.

―――. "Sociologie du cinéma." *Revue Internationale de Filmologie* 3, no. 10 (April–June 1952): 95–112.

Heuyer, G., S. Lebovici, and M. Rebeillard, in collaboration with G. Cohen-Séat. "Recherches sur les réactions des enfants et des adolescents." Paper presented at the International Congress of Filmology, Paris, February 1955.

Lapierre, M. *Anthologie du cinéma*. Paris: Bernard Grasset, 1948.

L'Herbier, M. *Intelligence du cinématographe* (anthologie de textes sur les multiples aspects du cinéma). Paris: Corrêa, 1946.

Malraux, A. *Esquisse d'une psychologie du cinéma*. Paris: NRF, 1946.

Marion, D., ed. *Le cinéma par ceux qui le font*. Paris: Fayard, 1949.

Merleau-Ponty, M. *Sens et non-sens*. Paris: Nagel, 1948.

Mitry, J. "Sur le style d'Eisenstein." *Ciné-Club*, no. 5 (March 1948).

Pegge, C. D. "Les processus de la pensée et le film." Paper presented at the International Congress of Filmology, Paris, February 1955.

Ponzo, M. "Cinéma et psychologie." *Revue Internationale de Filmologie* 1, nos. 3–4 (October 1948): 295–97.

Prevost, J. *Polymnie ou les arts mimiques*. Paris: Émile Hazan, 1929.

Pudovkin, V. *Film Technique and Film Acting*, translated by I. Montagu. London: Vision, 1949.

―――. "Filmographie et bibliographie."*Cahiers du Cinéma* 5, no. 26: 8–17.

"Recherches sur les problèmes de cinéma dans quatre pays (Italie, Grande-Bretagne, France, États-Unis)." *Revue Internationale de Filmologie* 3, no. 2.

Revue des Vivants, special issue (October 1931).

Richter, H. *Film Kritische Aufsaetze*. Berlin: Richter, 1920.

―――. *Der Spiel Film: Ansaetze zu einer Dramaturgie das Films*. Berlin: Richter, 1923.

Le rôle intellectuel du cinéma (by R. Arnheim, A. Arnoux, É. Faure, U. Barbaro, A. Cavalcanti, W. Disney, et al.). Paris: Institut international de coopération intellectuel, 1937.

Schmidt, G., W. Schmalenbach, and P. Bachlin. *Le cinéma, économie, sociologie, esthétique*. Basel, Switzerland: Éditions Holbein, 1951.

Sichel, P. "L'homme du cinéma." *Revue Européene* (1928): 1250–59.

Souriau, É. "Nature et limite des contributions positives de l'esthétique à la filmologie." *Revue Internationale de Filmologie* 2, nos. 7–8.

———. "La structure de l'univers filmique et le vocabulaire de la filmologie." *Revue Internationale de Filmologie* 2, nos. 7–8.

Souriau, É., et al. *L'univers filmique*. Paris: Bibliothèque d'Esthétique, Flammarion, 1952.

The Charm of the Image
The Image and the Double

This section of the bibliography is extremely basic. We will find once again the problem of the image and the double in the formation of the personality when we examine the role of the cinema in a subsequent work.

Bazin, A. "Ontologie de l'image photographique." In *Les problèmes de la peinture*, edited by G. Diehl. Paris: Confluences, 1945. ["The Ontology of the Photographic Image." In *What Is Cinema?* vol. 1, translated by H. Gray. Berkeley: University of California Press, 1967.]

Bossavy, J. *Les photographies des prétendues effluves humains*. Le Mans: Imprimerie de l'institut de bibliographie, n.d.

Cahn, P. "Remarque sur les réactions de l'enfant à son image et à celle de ses frères." Paper presented at the International Congress of Filmology, Paris, February 1955.

Fauré-Fremié, P. "Philosophie du réalisme." *Revue du Cinéma* (new series) 3, no. 18 (October 1948): 32–41.

Fournier, H. "Photographie spirite." *Nature*, January 15, 1894.

Fretet, Dr. *La folie parmi nous*. Paris: Gallimard, 1952.

Lancelin, C. *Méthode de dédoublement personnel*. Paris: H. Durville, n.d.

Leroy, E. *Les visions du demi-sommeil*. Paris: Alcan, 1926.

L'Hermitte, Dr. *L'image de notre corps*. Paris: Nouvelle Revue Critique, 1939.

Mauriac, C. *L'amour du cinéma*. Paris: Albin Michel, 1954.

Mead, G. H. *Mind, Self, and Society*. 5th ed. Chicago: University of Chicago Press, 1946.

Meyerson, I. "Les images." In *Nouveau traité de psychologie*, vol. 2, edited by G. Dumas, 574–81. Paris: Alcan, 1932–36.

Morin, E. *L'homme et la mort dans l'histoire*. Paris: Corrêa, 1951.

Ponzo, M. "Le cinéma et les images collectives." *Revue Internationale de Filmologie* 2, no. 6 (1950): 141–52.

Quercy, P. *Les hallucinations*. Paris: PUF, 1936.

Rank, O. *Don Juan, une étude sur le double*. Paris: Denoël & Steele, 1932.

Ricci, F. "Le cinéma entre l'imagination et la réalité." *Revue Internationale de Filmologie* 1, no. 2 (1947): 161–63.

Sartre, J.-P. *L'imaginaire*. Paris: Gallimard, 1940. [*The Psychology of the Imagination*. New York: Citadel, 1961.]

The Myth of the Total Cinematograph (Science Fiction)

Barjavel, R. *Cinéma total: Essai sur les formes futures du cinéma*. Paris: Denoël, 1944.

Bazin, A. "Le mythe du cinéma total." *Critique* 1, no. 6 (1946): 552–57. ["The Myth of Total Cinema." In *What Is Cinema?* vol. 1, translated by H. Gray. Berkeley: University of California Press, 1967.]

Bioy Casares, A. *L'invention de Morel*. Paris: Laffont, 1952. [*The Invention of Morel and Other Stories (from La Trama Celeste)*, translated from Spanish by R. L. C. Simms. Austin: University of Texas Press, 1964.]

Bradbury, R. *L'homme illustré*. Paris: Denoël, 1954. ["The Veldt." In *The Vintage Bradbury*. New York: Vintage, 1990.]

Clair, R. *Adams*. Paris: Grasset, 1928. [*Star Turn*, translated by J. Marks. London: Chatto & Windus, 1936.]

Gomez de la Serna, R. *Cinéville*. Paris: Kra, 1928. [*Movieland*, trans. from Spanish by A. Flores. New York: Macaulay, 1930.]

Grimoin-Sanson, R. *Le film de ma vie*. Paris: Henri Parville, 1926.

Huxley, A. *Le meilleur des mondes*. Paris: Plon, 1950. [*Brave New World*. London: Voyager Classics, 2001.]

Rice, E. *Voyage à Purilia*. Paris: Gallimard, 1934. [*Voyage to Purilia*. New York: Cosmopolitan, 1930.]

Participation

Projection, Identification, Transfer, Animism, and Anthropo-Cosmomorphism: Magic, Dream, and Cinema

Agel, H. "Finalité poétique du cinéma." In É. Souriau et al., *L'univers filmique*, 193–201. Paris: Bibliothèque d'Esthétique, Flammarion, 1952.

Allendy, Dr. "La valeur psychologique de l'image." *Art Cinémato-graphique* 1 (1926).

Bouman, J. C., G. Heuyer, and S. Lebovici. "Une expérience d'étude des groupes: Le processus de l'identification et l'importance de la suggestibilité dans la situation cinématographique." *Revue Internationale de Filmologie* 4, no. 13: 111–41.

Brunius, J. B. "Le rêve, l'inconscient, le merveilleux." *L'Age du Cinéma*, nos. 4–5 (August–November 1951): 10–14.

Chartier, J. P. "Les 'films à la première personne' et l'impression de réalité au cinéma." *Revue du Cinéma* (new series) 1, no. 4 (1948): 32–41.

Crawston, M. "The Pre-fabricated Daydream." *Penguin Film Review* 9 (1949).

Cressey, P. G. "The Motion Picture Experience as Modified by Social Background and Personality." *American Sociological Review* 3, no. 4 (1938): 516–25.

Deprun, J. "Le cinéma et l'identification." *Revue Internationale de Filmologie* 1, no. 1 (1947): 36–38.

———. "Cinéma et transfert." *Revue Internationale de Filmologie* 1, no. 2 (1947): 205–7.

Desoille, R. "Le rêve éveillé et la filmologie." *Revue Internationale de Filmologie* 1, no. 2 (1947): 197–203.

Eisenstein, S. M. "Spectateur-créateur." *Études Soviétiques*, no. 1 (August 4, 1948).

Eisner, L. *L'écran démoniaque*. Paris: André Bonne, 1952. [*The Haunted Screen*, translated by R. Greaves. London: Secker & Warburg, 1973.]

Fulchignogni, E. "Examen d'un test filmique." *Revue Internationale de Filmologie* 2, no. 6 (1950): 173–84.

Gemelli, A. "Le film, procédé d'analyse projective." *Revue Internationale de Filmologie* 2, no. 6 (1950): 135–38.

———. "La psicologia al servicio della cinematografia." In *Vita e pensiero*. Milan, 1937.

Gilson, P. *Ciné-magic*. Paris: André Bonne, 1951.

Glasser, F. "Filmkunst und Erziehung." *Zeitschrift für pädagogische Psychologie und experimentelle Pädagogik*, no. 35 (1934): 139–51.

Guicharnaud, J. "L'univers magique et l'image cinématographique." *Revue Internationale de Filmologie* 1, no. 1 (1947): 39–41.

Holstrom, I. "Le 'moi de rêve' (ou quand le spectateur s'identifie avec l'auteur)." *Revue du Cinéma*, no. 8 (1947): 33–48.

Kirou, A. "Romantisme et cinéma." *L'Age du Cinéma*, no. 1 (March 1951): 3–6.

———. *Le surréalisme au cinéma*. Paris: Arcanes, 1953.

Landry, L. "Formation de la sensibilité." *Art Cinématographique* 2 (1927).

———. "La psychologie du cinéma." *Journal de Psychologie*, no. 24 (1927): 134–45.

Lazarsfeld, P. F. "Audience Research in the Movie Field." *Annals of the American Academy of Political and Social Science*. 254 (November 1947): 160–68.

Lebovici, S. "Psychanalyse et cinéma." *Revue Internationale de Filmologie* 2, no. 5 (1949): 49–56.

Leenhardt, M. *Do Kamo: La personne et le myth dans le monde mélanesien*. Paris: Gallimard, 1947. [*Do Kamo: Person and Myth in the Melanesian World*, translated by B. M. Gulati. Chicago: University of Chicago Press, 1979.]

Lemaître, H. "Fantastique et merveilleux." In É. Souriau et al., *L'univers filmique*, 179–92. Paris: Bibliothèque d'Esthétique, Flammarion, 1952.

Levinson, A. "Pour une poétique du film." *Art Cinématographique* 4 (1927): 51–83.

Lévy-Bruhl, L. *Carnets*. Paris: PUF, 1949. [*The Notebooks on Primitive Mentality*, translated by P. Rivière. Oxford: Basil Blackwell, 1975.]

Mead, G. H. *Mind, Self, and Society*. 5th ed. Chicago: University of Chicago Press, 1946. See esp. chap. 3.

Méliès, G. *Les vues cinématographiques*. In *Annuaire général et international de la photographie*. Paris: Plon, 1904. Reprinted in *Revue du Cinéma*, nos. 4–5 (October 1929): 21–31.

Michotte van den Berck, A. "La participation émotionelle du spectateur à l'action représentée à l'écran: Essai d'une théorie." *Revue Internationale de Filmologie* 4, no. 13: 87–96.

Montani, A., and G. Pietranera. "First Contribution to a Psychoanalysis and Aesthetic of the Motion Picture." *Psychoanalytical Review*, no. 33 (1946): 177–96.

Morgenstein, S. "La pensée magique chez l'enfant." *Revue Française de Psychanalyse* (1937): 112.

Musatti, C. "Le cinéma et la psychanalyse." *Revue Internationale de Filmologie* 2, no. 1: 185–94.

Norton Cru, J. *Du témoignage*. Paris: Gallimard, 1930.

Parker, T. *The Hollywood Hallucination*. New York: Creative Age, 1944.

———. *Magic and Myth at the Movies*. New York: Henry Holt, 1947.

Piaget, J. *La représentation du monde chez l'enfant*. Paris: PUF, 1947.

Poisson, J. "Cinéma et psychanalyse." *Cahiers du Mois*. nos. 16–17 (1925): 176.

Powdermaker, H. *Hollywood, the Dream Factory: An Anthropologist Looks at the Movie-Makers*. London: Secker & Warburg, 1951.

Pratt, J. "Notes on Commercial Movie Technique." *International Journal of Psychoanalysis*, no. 24 (1943): 185–88.

Redslob, E., and A. Brini. "Les méfaits de la 'Symphonie pastorale.'" *Annales d'Occulistique*, no. 106 (1947): 104–6.

Sherif, M., and H. Cantril. *The Psychology of Ego-Involvements*. New York: Wiley, 1947.

Sherif, M., and S. Sargent. "Ego-Involvement and the Mass-Media." *Journal of Social Issues* 3, no. 3 (1947): 8–16.

Valentin, A. "Introduction à la magie blanche et noire." *Art Cinématographique* 4 (1927): 89–116.

Zazzo, B. "Effets de la grosseur et de la mobilité des plans sur les réactions des spectateurs enfants." Paper presented at the International Congress of Filmology, Paris, February 1955.

Perception and Film

Bazin, A. "Pour en finir avec la profondeur de champ." *Cahiers du Cinéma* 1, no. 1 (April 1951): 17–23.

Beucher, J. "Espace filmique et conscience d'écran." Paper presented at the International Congress of Filmology, Paris, February 1955.

Bruce, D. J. "Remémoration du matériel filmique." *Revue Internationale de Filmologie* 3, no. 12:21–38.

Colle, J. "Note au sujet de la classification des effets psychophysiologiques de la projection des films." Paper presented at the International Congress of Filmology, Paris, February 1955.

Fèbvre, L. *Le problème de l'incroyance au XVIe siècle: La religion de Rabelais*. Paris: Albin Michel, 1945.

Fulchignoni, E. "Cinéma et psychologie." *Revue de Psychologie Appliquée* 1, no. 2 (January 1951): 61–72.

Galifret, V., and J. Segal. "Cinéma et physiologie des sensations." *Revue Internationale de Filmologie* 1, nos. 3–4 (October 1948): 289–93.

Goldberg, H. D. "The Role of 'Cutting' in the Perception of the Motion Pictures." *Journal of Applied Psychology*, no. 35 (1951).

Laffay, A. "L'évocation du monde au cinéma." *Les Temps Modernes* 1, no. 5 (February 1946): 925–38.

Leboutet, C. "Étude comparative de la perception du positif sur papier et de l'image fixe projetée sur écran: Premiers résultats." *Revue Internationale de Filmologie* 3, no. 12:39–52.

Merleau-Ponty, M. *Phénoménologie de la perception*. Paris: NRF, 1945. [*Phenomenology of Perception*, translated by C. Smith. London: Routledge & Kegan Paul, 1965.]

Michotte van den Berck, A. "Le caractère de 'réalité' des projections cinématographiques." *Revue Internationale de Filmologie* 1, nos. 3–4 (October 1948):249–61.

Oldfield, R. C. "La perception visuelle des images du cinéma, de la télévision et du radar." *Revue Internationale de Filmologie* 1, nos. 3–4 (October 1948): 263–79.

Peters, J. M. L. La perception du film et le rythme filmique. Paper presented at the International Congress of Filmology, Paris, February 1955.

Rinieri, J. J. "L'impression de réalité au cinéma: Les phénomènes de croyance." In É. Souriau et al., *L'univers filmique*, 33–45. Paris: Bibliothèque d'Esthétique, Flammarion, 1952.

Wallon, H. "L'acte perceptif et le cinéma." *Revue Internationale de Filmologie* 4, no. 13 (April–June 1953): 97–110.

———. "De quelques problèmes psycho-physiologiques que pose le cinéma." *Revue Internationale de Filmologie* 1, no. 1 (1947): 15–18.

The Universe of the Film

Time and Space

Caillois, R. "Le tragique à la scène et à l'écran." *Revue Internationale de Filmologie* 1, nos. 3–4 (October 1948): 325–29.

Epstein, J. "Le monde fluide de l'ècran." *Les Temps Modernes* 5, no. 56 (June 1950): 2212–28.

Francastel, G. "Espace et illusion." *Revue Internationale de Filmologie* 1, no. 5:65–74.

Ingarten, R. "Le temps, l'espace et le sentiment de réalité." *Revue Internationale de Filmologie* 1, no. 2 (1947): 127–41.

Jolivet, S. "Le temps au cinéma." *Revue Internationale de Filmologie* 1, nos. 3–4 (October 1948): 331–34.

Leirens, J. *Le cinéma et le temps*. Paris: Éditions du Cerf, 1954.

Rinieri, J. J. "La réversion du temps filmique." In É. Souriau et al., *L'univers filmique*, 75–84. Paris: Bibliothèque d'Esthétique, Flammarion, 1952.

Second, J. "Rythme inhérent au film." *Revue Internationale de Filmologie* 1, no. 2 (1947): 159–60.

Sherred, T. L. "E for Effort." In *The Astounding Science Fiction Anthology*. New York: Simon & Schuster, 1952.

Souriau, É. "Succession et simultanéité dans le film." In É. Souriau et al., *L'univers filmique*, 59–73. Paris: Bibliothèque d'Esthétique, Flammarion, 1952.

Decor, Objects, and Costumes

Adrian. "Les costumes." In *La technique du film*, 68–72. Paris: Payot, 1939.

Annenkov, G. *En habillant les vedettes*. Paris: Robert Marin, 1951.

Auriol, J. G., and M. Verdone. "La valeur expressive du costume dans le style des films." *Revue du Cinéma* (new series), nos. 19–20 (Autumn 1949): 87–113.

Autant-Lara, C. "Le costumier de cinéma doit habiller des caractères." *Revue du Cinéma* (new series), nos. 19–20 (Autumn 1949).

Bandini, B., and G. Viazzi. *Ragionamenti sulla scenografia*. Milan: Poligono, 1945.

Barsacq, L. "Le décor." In *Le cinéma par ceux qui le font*, edited by D. Marion, 191–207. Paris: Fayard, 1949.

Bilinsky, B. "Le costume." *Art Cinématographique* 6 (1929): 25–56.

Eisner, L. "Aperçus sur le costume dans les films allemands." *Revue du Cinéma* (new series), nos. 19–20 (Autumn 1949).

Gibbons, C. "Le décorateur." In *La technique du film*, 59–67. Paris: Payot, 1939.

Mallet-Stevens, R. "Le décor." *Art Cinématographique*, 6 (1929): 1–24.

Manuel, J. "Esquisse d'une histoire du costume de cinéma." *Revue du Cinéma* (new series), nos. 19–20 (Autumn 1949): 3–63.

Poncet, M. T. "L'imagination cosmique dans les rapports du décor et des costumes." In É. Souriau et al., *L'univers filmique*, 101–18. Paris: Bibliothèque d'Esthétique, Flammarion, 1952.

Sallet, G. "René Clair et la notion d'objet." *Revue Internationale de Filmologie* 2, no. 2:165–69.

Schutz, M. "Le maquillage." *Art Cinématographique* 6 (1929): 57–66.

Souriau, É. "Fonctions filmiques des costumes et des décors." In É. Souriau et al., *L'univers filmique*, 85–100. Paris: Bibliothèque d'Esthétique, Flammarion, 1952.

Sound, Music

Aschen, R., and M. Crouzard. *Manuel pratique d'enregistrement et de sonorisation*. Paris: Technique et Vulgarisation, 1948.

Bourgeois, J. "Musique dramatique et cinéma." *Revue du Cinéma*, no. 10 (February 1948).

Chiarini, L. "La musica nel film." *Bianco e Nero* 3, no. 6 (June 1939).

———. "La musica nell'unita del film." *Cinema*, 5, no. 108 (December 25, 1940).

Germain, J. "La musique et le film." In É. Souriau et al., *L'univers filmique*, 137–55. Paris: Bibliothèque d'Esthétique, Flammarion, 1952.

Guillot de Rode, F. "La dimension sonore." In É. Souriau et al., *L'univers filmique*, 119–35. Paris: Bibliothèque d'Esthétique, Flammarion, 1952.

Hansel, C. E. M. "Les effets de la vision d'un film sur l'interprétation de sa musique." Paper presented at the International Congress of Filmology, Paris, February 1955.

Ivonnet, R. "L'ingénieur du son." In *Le cinéma par ceux qui le font*, edited by D. Marion. Paris: Fayard, 1949.

Jaubert, M. "Le son au cinéma." *Esprit*, no. 43 (April 1, 1936): 114–19. [Richard Abel gives the title of this article as "Le cinéma: La musique." An extract appears in translation as "The Cinema: Music." In *French Film Theory and Criticism*, vol. 2, *1929–1939*, edited by R. Abel, 206–11. Princeton, NJ: Princeton University Press, 1988.]

Keim, J. A. *Un nouvel art: Le cinéma sonore*. Paris: Albin Michel, 1947.

Laffay, A. "Bruits et langage au cinéma." *Les Temps Modernes* 2, no. 14 (November 1946): 371–75.

Lo Duca, J. M. "Le son, la couleur, le relief (contribution des techniques françaises du cinéma, II)." *Revue du Cinéma* (new series) 2, no. 10 (February 1948): 49–63.

Page, L. "Le chef opérateur du son." In *Le cinéma par ceux qui le font*, edited by D. Marion, 208–24. Paris: Fayard, 1949.

Panigel, A. "Le contre-point 'son-image.'" *Ciné-Club*, no. 5 (March 1948).

Pudovkin, V. "Le montage et le son." *Le Magasin du Spectacle* 1, no. 1 (April 1946): 8–20.

———. "Sound and the Future of the Cinema." *New York Theater* (March 1934).

Pudovkin, V., S. M. Eisenstein, and G. Alexandrov. "Programme sur le cinéma sonore." *Le Monde*, September 1, 1928. ["Statement on Sound." In *The Film Factory: Russian and Soviet Cinema in Documents*, edited by R. Taylor and I. Christie, translated by R. Taylor. Cambridge, MA: Harvard University Press, 1988.]

Schaeffer, P. "L'élément non visuel au cinéma (I: Analyse de la bande du son; II: Conception de la musique; III: Psychologie du rapport vision-audition." *Revue du Cinéma*, nos. 1, 2, 3 (October, November, December 1946).

Schmalenbach, W. "Dialogue et bruitage dans le film." In *Cinéma d'aujourd'hui* (Congrès international du cinéma à Bâle). Geneva: Trois Collines, 1946.

Taddei, N. "Funzione estetica della musica del film." *Bianco e Nero* 10, no. 1 (January 1949): 5–11.

Talleney, J. L. "Un cinéma enfin parlant." *Cahiers du Cinéma* 2, no. 9 (February 1952): 30–36.

Van Parys, G. "Le musicien." In *Le cinéma par ceux qui le font*, edited by D. Marion, 262–82. Paris: Fayard, 1949.

Vlad, R. "Musica, serva padrona." *Anteprima*, no. 7. (August 1951): 53–54.

Colors

Apard, A. "La technique du film en couleurs." *Revue du Cinéma* 2, no. 8 (Autumn 1947): 79–80; 2, no. 9 (January 1948): 78–80.

Arnheim, R. "Le leggi del colore." *Cinema* 2, no. 29 (September 10, 1937).

———. "Perché sono brutti i film a colori?" *Scenario*, no. 3 (1936).

Brunius, J. B. "Couleur du tragique." *Revue du Cinéma* (new series) 1, no. 2 (November 1946): 3–13.

"La couleur." In *Sequenze* (*Cahiers du Cinéma*), no. 1 (textes réunis par G. Aristarco). Parme, 1949.

Dourgnon, J. *La reproduction des couleurs*. Paris: Presses Universitaires de France, 1951.

Enlargement of the Screen—CinemaScope

Bazin, A. "Le CinémaScope sauvera-t-il le cinéma?" *Esprit*, nos. 10–11 (October–November 1953): 672–83. ["Will Cinema-Scope Save the Film Industry?" In *Bazin at Work: Major Essays and Reviews from the Forties and Fifties*, edited by B. Cardullo, translated by A. Piette and B. Cardullo. New York: Routledge, 1997.]

Chrétien, H. "La cinématographie panoramique par le procédé Hypergonar." *Afitec* (1952).

Gance, A. "Les nouveaux chapitres de notre syntaxe." *Cahiers du Cinéma* 5, no. 27:25–33.

Scherer, M., G. G. Wunberg, J. Doniol-Valcroze, A. Bazin, M. Dorsday, and J. Rivette. "Opinions sur le CinémaScope." *Cahiers du Cinéma* 6, no. 31 (January 1954): 36–48.

Zazzo, R. "Espace, movement et CinémaScope." Paper presented at the International Congress of Filmology, Paris, February 1955.

Depth

Galifret, Y. "La troisième dimension et la projection cinématographique." Paper presented at the International Congress of Filmology, Paris, February 1955.

Hansel, C. E. M. "La facilité de la vision de films en trois dimensions et l'impression de profondeur dans les films en deux dimensions considérées dans leurs rapports avec les indices dus à l'aberration chromatique." Paper presented at the International Congress of Filmology, Paris, February 1955.

Roux, L. *L'avenir du cinéma en relief*. Panorama, 1953.

Language and Intelligibility of the Cinema

Language

Cohen, M. "Ecriture et cinéma." *Revue Internationale de Filmologie* 1, no. 2 (1947): 179–82.

Cohen-Séat, G. "Le discours filmique." *Revue Internationale de Filmologie* 2, no. 5 (1949): 37–48.

Echeverria Yanez, J. R. "Virtualités du cinéma." *Revue Internationale de Filmologie* 2, no. 6 (1950): 199–205.

Di Giammateo, F. "Significato e consequenza del lingaggio cinematografico." *Bianco e Nero*. 11, no. 3 (1950).

Holaday, P. W., and D. G. Stoddard. *Getting Ideas from the Movies*. New York: Macmillan, 1933.

Meredith, G. P. "Techniques de recherches sur les problèmes d'intelligibilité." Paper presented at the International Congress of Filmology, Paris, February 1955.

Quint, L. P. "Signification du cinéma." *Art Cinématographique* 2 (1927).

Schuhl, P. M. "Pour un cinéma abstrait." *Revue Internationale de Filmologie* 1, no. 2 (1947): 183–85.

Souriau, É. "Filmologie et esthétique comparées." *Revue Internationale de Filmologie* 3, no. 10 (April–June 1952): 113–42.

Intelligibility of the Film: Children

De Ruette, V. "The Cinema and Child Psychology." *International Review of Educational Cinematography* 6, no. 1 (January 1934): 38–49.

Ford, R. *Children and the Cinema*. London: Allen & Unwin, 1939.

Gratiot Alphandery, H. "Jeunes spectateurs." *Revue Internationale de Filmologie* 2, nos. 7–8 (1951): 257–64.

Lanoux, A. *L'enfant en proie aux images*. Paris: La Bergerie, 1951.

Leroy, E. "L'enfant et le cinéma d'aujourd'hui." *Revue Internationale de l'Enfant*, no. 8 (1929): 704–15.

Miliaret, G., and M. G. Méliès. "Expériences sur la compréhension du langage cinématographique par l'enfant." Paper presented at the International Congress of Filmology, Paris, February 1955.

Rebeillot, M. "Les recherches de filmologie dans la neuropsychiatrie de l'enfant." Thesis, Paris, 1955.

Siersted, E., and H. L. Hansen. "Réactions des petits enfants au cinéma." *Revue Internationale de Filmologie* 2, nos. 7–8 (1951): 241–45.

Wallon, H. "L'enfant et le film." *Revue Internationale de Filmologie* 2, no. 5 (1949): 21–28.

Zazzo, B. "Analyse des difficultés d'une séquence cinématographique par la conduite du récit chez l'enfant." *Revue Internationale de Filmologie* 3, no. 9:25–36.

Zazzo, B., and R. Zazzo. "Une expérience sur la compréhension du film." *Revue Internationale de Filmologie* 2, no. 6 (1950): 159–70.

Zazzo, R. "Niveau mental et compréhension du cinéma." *Revue Internationale de Filmologie* 2, no. 5 (1949): 29–36.

Intelligibility of the Film: Neurotics

Berman, H. H. "Audio-Visual Psychotherapeutics: Portable Moving Pictures with Sound as a Rehabilitation Measure." *Psychiatric Quarterly* 20 (supp.) (1946): 197–203.

Heuyer, G. S., S. Lebovici, and G. Amado. "Enfants et adolescents inadaptés." *Revue Internationale de Filmologie* 2, no. 5 (1949): 57–65.

Heuyer, G. S., S. Lebovici, and G. Bertagna. "Sur quelques réactions d'enfants inadaptés." *Revue Internationale de Filmologie* 3, no. 9:71–80.

Katz, E. "A Brief Survey of the Use of Motion Pictures for the Treatment of Neuropsychiatric Patients." *Psychiatric Quarterly* 20 (supp.) (1946): 204–16.

Moreno, J. L. "Psychodrama and Therapeutic Motion Pictures." *Sociometry*, no. 7 (1944): 230–44.

Rome, H. P. "Audio-Visual Aids in Psychiatry." *Hospital Corps Quarterly* 18, no. 9 (1945): 37–38.

Zazzo, R. "Niveau mental et compréhension du cinéma." *Revue Internationale de Filmologie* 2, no. 5 (1949): 29–36.

Intelligibility of the Film: Archaic Peoples

Les auxiliaires visuels et l'éducation de base (Collection "La presse, le film et la radio dans le monde d'aujourd'hui"). Paris: UNESCO, 1952.

"Cinéma pour les Africains." *Revue International de Filmologie* 2, nos. 7–8 (1951): 277–82.

MacLaren, N. *La santé au village* (éducation visuelle en Chine). Paris: UNESCO, 1954.

Maddison, S. "Le cinéma et l'information mentale des peuples primitifs." *Revue Internationale de Filmologie* 1, nos. 3–4 (October 1948): 305–10.

The Cinema and Other Means of Expression

Agel, H. "Équivalences cinématographiques de la composition et du langage littéraires." *Revue Internationale de Filmologie* 1, no. 1 (1947): 67–70.

Arnheim, R. "Psychological Notes on the Poetic Process." In *Poets at Work*. New York: Harcourt Brace, 1948.

Asheim, L. *From Book to Film*. Chicago: Graduate Library School, University of Chicago, 1949. (Partially reproduced in *Hollywood Quarterly* 5 (1951–52): 289–304, 334–39; in *Quarterly of Film, Radio and Television* 6 (1952): 54–68; and in *The Public and Communications*, 299–306. Glencoe, IL: Free Press, 1950.)

Auriol, J. G. "Les origines de la mise en scène." *Revue du Cinéma* (new series) 1, no. 1 (October 1946): 7–23.

Bazin, A. "La stylistique de Robert Bresson." *Cahiers du Cinéma* 1, no. 3 (June 1951): 7–21.

Berge, A. "Cinéma et Littérature." *Art Cinématographique* 3 (1927).

Bourgeois, J. "Le cinéma à la recherche du temps perdu." *Revue du Cinéma* (new series) 1, no. 3 (December 1946): 18–38.

Chiarini, L. *Il film nei problemi della arte*. Rome: Ateneo, 1949.

Eisenstein, S. M. *The Film Sense*. London: Dobson, 1948.

Fuzelier, E. "Expression filmique et expression radiophonique." Paper presented at the International Congress of Filmology, Paris, February 1955.

Kiehl, J. *Les ennemis du théâtre: Essai sur les rapports du théâtre avec le cinéma et la littérature (1914–1939)*. Neuchâtel, Switzerland: Baconnière, 1951.

Laffay, A. "Le récit, le monde et le film." *Les Temps Modernes* 2, nos. 20–21 (May–June 1947): 1361–75, 1579–1600.

Laglenne, J.-F. "Cinéma et peinture." *Cahiers du Mois*, nos. 16–17 (1925).

Lang, A. "Théâtre et cinéma." *Art Cinématographique* 3 (1927).

Leglise, P. "Contribution de l'analyse filmique à l'étude critique du premier chant de l'Enéide." Paper presented at the International Congress of Filmology, Paris, February 1955.

Lemaître, H. "L'animation des tableaux et les problèmes du film sur l'art." In É. Souriau et al., *L'univers filmique*, 157–77. Paris: Bibliothèque d'Esthétique, Flammarion, 1952.

Micha, R. "La vérité cinématographique." *Cahiers du Cinéma* 1, no. 29 (December 1953): 16–30.

Nicoll, A. *Film and Theatre*. London: George G. Harrap, 1936.

Scherer, M. "Vanité que la peinture." *Cahiers du Cinéma* 1, no. 3 (June 1951): 22–29.

Soriano, M. "Lire, assister." *Revue Internationale de Filmologie* 1, nos. 3–4 (October 1948): 299–304.

Tribut, J. "La peinture et le film." *Revue Internationale de Filmologie* 2, no. 10:149–67.

Vardac, A. N. *Stage to Screen*. Cambridge, MA: Harvard University Press, 1949.

Animation

Lo Duca, J. M. *Le dessin animé: Histoire, esthétique, technique*. Preface by W. Disney. Paris: Prisma, 1948.

Poncet, M. T. *L'esthétique du dessin animé*. Paris: Nizet, 1952.

Vano, I. *Le dessin animé* (texte russe, avec nombreuses illustrations, dessins, gravures et planches en couleurs). Risovany Film, 1950.

Practical Utilization of the Cinematograph

Schiltz, J. *Le cinéma au service de l'industrie*. Paris: SDAC, 1948.

Thevenard, L., and G. Tassel. *Le cinéma scientifique français*. Paris: La Jeune Parque, 1948.

Nonbibliographical Sources

Exposition de la cinémathèque française.

Naissance du cinéma (documentary film by R. Leenhardt). Paris: Films du Compas, 1946.

And, preferable to everything, without discrimination: *films*.

Index of Names Cited

Edgar Morin, emeritus director of research at the Centre national de recherche scientifique, is one of France's leading contemporary thinkers. A member of the French Resistance, he was a wartime Communist who broke with the Party in 1951 over his anti-Stalinist stance. He has written on scientific method, philosophical anthropology, social theory, popular culture, and contemporary life, and his oeuvre combines the humanities and the social sciences in an ongoing dialogue that attempts to grasp the complexity of the real. Among his most important works are his six volumes of *La méthode* (1977–2004) and *Chronique d'un été* (1960), a landmark documentary film made in collaboration with Jean Rouch. He is also the author of *The Stars* (1960; reprinted by Minnesota, 2005).

Lorraine Mortimer is senior lecturer in sociology and anthropology at La Trobe University in Melbourne, Australia.